# A VISUAL
# HISTORY
*of the*
# ENGLISH BIBLE

# A VISUAL HISTORY

*of the*

# ENGLISH BIBLE

The Tumultuous Tale
of the World's Bestselling Book

## DONALD L. BRAKE

**BakerBooks**

*a division of Baker Publishing Group*
Grand Rapids, Michigan

Published by Baker Books
a division of Baker Publishing Group
P.O. Box 6287, Grand Rapids, MI 49516-6287
www.bakerbooks.com

Printed in Singapore

Library of Congress Cataloging-in-Publication Data
Brake, Donald L., 1939–
    A visual history of the English Bible : the tumultuous tale of the world's best-selling book / Donald L. Brake.
        p.   cm.
    Includes bibliographical references (p.        ) and indexes.
    ISBN 978-0-8010-1316-4 (cloth)
    1. Bible. English—History. I. Title
BS455.B635  2008
220.5′2009—dc22                                               2008005492

Interior design by Brian Brunsting

To Dr. John and Jean Hellstern
Loyal Friends and Wonderful Colleagues
Their love for Bible collecting and exhibiting is second to none.

# Contents

# Illustrations

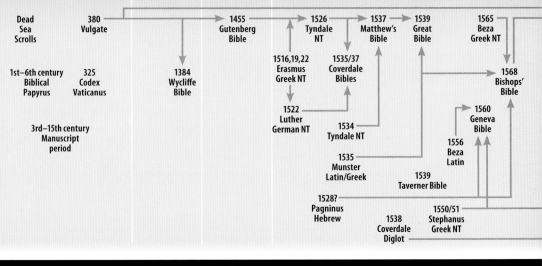

AD 1–6   7–13   1300   1400   1500

Dead Sea Scrolls

380 Vulgate

1455 Gutenberg Bible

1526 Tyndale NT

1537 Matthew's Bible

1539 Great Bible

1565 Beza Greek NT

1st–6th century Biblical Papyrus

325 Codex Vaticanus

1384 Wycliffe Bible

1516,19,22 Erasmus Greek NT

1535/37 Coverdale Bibles

1568 Bishops' Bible

3rd–15th century Manuscript period

1522 Luther German NT

1534 Tyndale NT

1560 Geneva Bible

1556 Beza Latin

1535 Munster Latin/Greek

1539 Taverner Bible

1528? Pagninus Hebrew

1538 Coverdale Diglot

1550/51 Stephanus Greek NT

# FROM ANCIENT MANUSCRIPTS

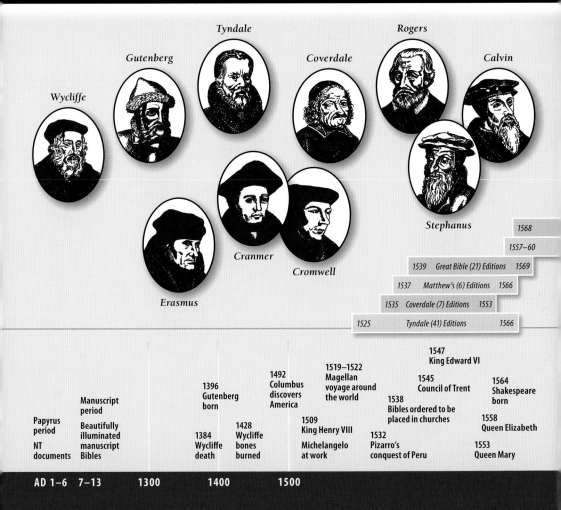

Wycliffe

Gutenberg

Tyndale

Coverdale

Rogers

Calvin

Erasmus

Cranmer

Cromwell

Stephanus

1568

1557–60

1539  Great Bible (21) Editions  1569

1537  Matthew's (6) Editions  1566

1535  Coverdale (7) Editions  1553

1525  Tyndale (41) Editions  1566

1547 King Edward VI

1519–1522 Magellan voyage around the world

1492 Columbus discovers America

1545 Council of Trent

1564 Shakespeare born

1396 Gutenberg born

Manuscript period

Beautifully illuminated manuscript Bibles

1538 Bibles ordered to be placed in churches

Papyrus period

NT documents

1384 Wycliffe death

1428 Wycliffe bones burned

1509 King Henry VIII

Michelangelo at work

1532 Pizarro's conquest of Peru

1558 Queen Elizabeth

1553 Queen Mary

AD 1–6   7–13   1300   1400   1500

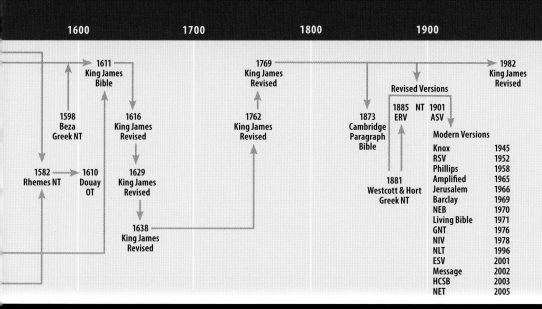

## TO MODERN TRANSLATIONS

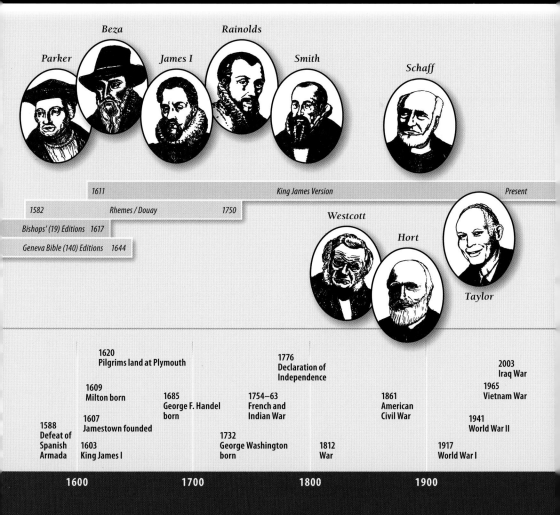

**Lindisfarne:** 698–721 Aldred's Anglo-Saxon Gospels and Stronghold of Vikings

**Sherborne:** 640–709 Aldhelm's Old English Psalter

**Wessex:** 950–1020 Aelfric's Old English Gospels

**Yorkshire:** 7th-century Caedmon's Anglo-Saxon songs and birthplace of Coverdale 1488–1568

**Wycliffe-on-Tees:** 1320/30 Birthplace of John Wycliffe

**Bristol:** 1388–92 Purvey's revision of Wycliffe

**Lutterworth:** 1428 Wycliffe's bones exhumed

**Stinchcombe:** 1492–1536 Birthplace of Tyndale

**Little Sodbury:** 1522 Tyndale with Walsh family

**Birmingham:** 1500–1555 Birthplace of John Rogers

**Hampton Court:** 16th- and 17th-century palace of Tudors and Stuarts

**Stratford-upon-Avon:** 1564–1616 Shakespeare's life

**Oxford:** Balliol College, Bodleian library, and center of Lollard activity

**London:** Center of English culture

**Canterbury:** Seat of Anglican archbishop

**Mainz:** 1450–56 Gutenberg Bible
**Eisenach:** 1497–1501 Luther's early education
**Eisleben:** Luther's place of birth (1483) and death (1546) (age 62)
**Erfurt:** 1501 Luther at university (age 17)
**Stotternheim:** 1505 Luther's promise to St. Anne (age 21)
**Wittenberg:**
    1512 Luther earns doctorate
    1513–15 Luther's lectures on Psalms
    1515–16 Luther's lectures on Romans
    1517 95 Theses nailed to Wittenberg church
    1524 Tyndale in Germany (meets Luther?)
**Augsburg:** 1518 Luther's debate with Cajetan over Pope's authority

**Leipzig:** 1519 Luther's debate with John Eck of Engolstadt
**Worms:**
    1521 Luther's famous quote: "Here I stand"
    1526 Tyndale's New Testament
**Wartburg Castle** (Eisenach): 1522 Luther's New Testament translation
**Cologne:** 1525 Tyndale's Cologne fragment
**Hamburg:** 1525 Tyndale's stay in Germany
**Vilvorde:** 1536 Tyndale's imprisonment and martyrdom
**Antwerp:** 1530–35 Tyndale's last years
**Rotterdam:** 1466–1536 Home of Erasmus
**Rhemes/Douay:** 1582/1610 Catholic Bible (France)

# Introduction

The twenty-first century is speeding forward on the Internet, cellular towers, and other channels of the future. Urgent and important messages circle the globe instantly and disappear just as quickly. Will the Bible with its ancient origins and multiple scribes maintain its relevancy in the postmodern world?

That question finds an answer neither in the Bible's age, nor in the beautiful art it has inspired, nor in its literary style, but rather in its intrinsic value as a guide for life. Seekers, from the ancients to today, have found the Bible to be their source for hope, direction, and consolation.

As any seminary student will tell you, the Bible is not just a dictation of facts or data. The book itself claims to be the very revelation of God, and the clear intention of the text is to help readers obtain knowledge and to touch them emotionally, to motivate the faithful to act upon God's commands. For centuries people of faith have believed the act of reading God's Word is the process whereby humans receive the thoughts of God. This is the revelation event. And this event began with God's inspiration of the prophets, the apostles, and others who wrote the Scriptures.

The very concept of an eternal, omnipotent God communicating to finite, mortal beings is problematic. For example, in what language should God reveal himself? Any language, after all, has inherent weaknesses. As it happened, the original languages of the biblical text were Hebrew, Aramaic, and Greek, which obviously creates problems for English speakers who want to understand the Bible's original meaning. And if the Bible holds the very thoughts of God, does it have any place in the vernacular of the masses? The first several centuries of Bible translation history were consumed with just this debate.

And the original manuscripts no longer survive. In fact, in many cases the copies of the copies of the copies have perished. To make matters even more difficult, our Western twenty-first-century lifestyle bears little resemblance to that of the times and places of the Scriptures. Biblical idioms, figures of speech, and words, even when translated into English, have unfamiliar meanings.

So who were these translators? How did they respond to the questions of authority, relevance, and meaning? What motivated them to take up quill and parchment to translate? The book you're holding tells their stories—stories of both anguish and great hope.

As we proceed, we will better understand the toil of the great translators of the Bible. Success in translation, then and now, depends not only on a thorough understanding of two languages but upon an acceptable interpretation of the source language. A new translation means new words, and new words often challenge old, established doctrines. Today, new translations that fail to receive wide acceptance may be labeled "heretical" or "uninformed," but at other times in history the consequences were much more severe: translators charged with heresy often faced excommunication or even death. Not surprisingly, resistance, persecution, Bible burning, and martyrdom have bloodied the path along which the history of Bible translation has passed.

The purpose of this book is to tell the story of how God's Word went from being strictly for those in the pulpit to being read, understood, and acted upon by laypeople. It is a story of tragedy and triumph: spilled blood and the preservation of a sacred treasure.

## A Bible Collector Is Born

Several years ago I began collecting Bibles that traced the history of the English Bible. A special emphasis in my collection is the development of the Greek New Testaments that supported the text used by various translators. The principles that guided my collecting were the preservation of these Bible documents; the story of how the English Bible came into the hands of every literate man and woman; and the tales of the people who suffered mightily for its production. History and its stories must not be forgotten in our age of multiple translations, easy availability of commentaries, accessible preachers, and willing teachers.

I am often asked, "How did you get involved in collecting rare Bibles? Isn't that a rich man's hobby?" Generally, that is true, but by barter and trading-up principles, I managed to creep closer to my goal.

One day early in my career as a professor at Multnomah Bible College and Biblical Seminary, I was perusing a catalog from a book dealer in London. Two rare Bibles caught my attention, a 1597 Geneva (also known as the Breeches' Bible) and a 1569 Bishops' Bible. The price was about three hundred dollars each. When I queried an esteemed mentor and colleague, the late Dr. Ed Goodrick, without hesitation he insisted, "You must." Dr. Goodrick was always encouraging me to buy something he thought I should have. He assured me they would make a wonderful "show and tell" for my students in Bible Introduction class and a great conversational piece in my home.

For the better part of two weeks I waited impatiently for the arrival of the magnificent pieces of biblical history. The moment they arrived, I hurriedly took my treasures to Ed's study to begin our examination. To our delight, the 1569 Bishops' Bible turned out to be a very rare 1569 Great Bible, the last one ever to be published. You would have thought it was Ed's Bible, the way he went on about its wonders. He never ceased to encourage me to collect more and more. We fed on each other's enthusiasm as we both continued to collect rare volumes as we had funds and opportunity.

# 1

# Ancient Bibles

*The Triumph of Beauty, the Tyranny of Power*

The first written communication from God came on Mount Sinai, chiseled on stone by the finger of God himself. These sacred words from the Ten Commandments have shaped the world and its ethical system for 3,500 years. Although God destroyed the stones because of the sin of the Israelites, he continued to communicate with human beings in written form using the language the receivers knew.

However, no portion of any original Old or New Testament book exists today. The original handwritten productions and most of the early copies of these manuscripts have perished. The materials upon which the original Scriptures were written could not stand up to the ravages of time. Constant use, damp climates, violence or war, and domestic fire are responsible for the destruction of untold tens of thousands of manuscripts. Yet some manuscripts did survive.

## Old Testament Manuscripts

The earliest known manuscripts of the Old Testament date from the Babylonian captivity in 586 BC. Written on leather in the form of a scroll, these documents were read at annual feasts and used in private study. The Syrians, just prior to the Maccabean revolt (the Jewish uprising against the ruling Syrians in 168 BC), destroyed most of the manuscripts of this period.

The final Jewish revolt against Rome in AD 135 signaled the beginning of the end of the Hebrew language. Most of the people forgot the language and what it sounded like. Sometime around AD 500 a group of Jewish scholars known as the Masoretes of Tiberius (a city in Galilee) began to preserve the Bible in the Hebrew language. The Masoretes flourished from AD 500 to 1000. They dedicated their lives to forming an intricate system to standardize and preserve the exact words of the biblical text. The oldest Hebrew Bible manuscripts we have today are the product of the faithful, meticulous copying of the Masoretes; we refer to these manuscripts as the Masoretic text.

Sometimes Christians worry that the text of the Masoretes is unreliable because it dates to more than five hundred years after the beginning of the Christian era. Before 1947 the oldest known manuscript of the Old Testament was *Codex Cairensis* (AD 895) and the oldest complete text was *Aleppo Codex* (tenth century AD). All that changed with the discovery of the Dead Sea Scrolls.

The importance of the Dead Sea Scrolls (dated from the first century BC to the first century AD) continues to grow and to be one of the most intriguing stories of modern times. Their value in the study of Scripture is unparalleled in archaeological history, indeed in His-story.

## The Dead Sea Scrolls and the Jewish State

Celebration sounds from honking horns, cheering youngsters, and families tuning radios to confirm details of what had been their prayer for nearly 1,900 years. Six thousand miles away the United Nations had voted to establish an independent Jewish State. Upstairs, in a room away from all the commotion, an ecstatic Hebrew scholar and professor of archaeology at the Hebrew University, Dr. Elazar Sukenik, was bursting inside from the discovery he had made that very evening. He ran into the street to celebrate with the exuberant crowd, not only for the vision of independence but for the joy of reading the greatest archaeological discovery of the twentieth century, the Dead Sea Scrolls. It was November 29, 1947. Israel's greatest twentieth-century archaeological discovery intersected with her greatest victory—a Jewish State.

A week earlier, an unexpected message from an Armenian antiquities dealer in Arab Bethlehem led Dr. Sukenik into a journey of high intrigue. The dealer wanted to show Dr. Sukenik an amazing piece of scrap leather. Travel was discouraged; Jerusalem was on high alert, anticipating war with its Arab neighbors, when the United Nations' vote for an independent Jewish State occurred in five days.

Barbed wire cut up Jerusalem for defense purposes, and meeting with the antiquities dealer meant talking through barbs. As Dr. Sukenik peered through the strands of wire, he soon recognized unusual Hebrew letters. The Armenian told him the story of a Bedouin who brought several parchment scrolls from a cave near the shores of the Dead Sea. Fearing they could be forgeries, he sought the expertise of Dr. Sukenik.

Masking his building excitement, Dr. Sukenik boldly asked for more specimens. On November 27 a phone call confirmed the rendezvous the next day. It meant meeting in a politically charged Arab sector in Bethlehem. In spite of a stern warning from his son, Yigael Yadin (the chief of operations of the Haganah in the Jewish underground self-defense movement in Palestine), of the dangers of war from the outcome of the United Nations' vote expected that day, Professor Sukenik boarded an Arab bus. He was bound for Bethlehem and the shop of Feidi Salahi, where the scrolls were housed. It was now November 28—the day the United Nations was scheduled to vote. But unexpectedly, the vote was delayed by one day and the road to Bethlehem was open to travel.

These precious pieces of leather were part of what we call the Dead Sea Scrolls: "The War of the Sons of Light against the Sons of Darkness," "The Thanksgiving Scroll," and the "Prophet Isaiah" (Isaiah 1QIsa[b]).[1]

In 1947 an Arab shepherd boy, pursuing a lost goat along the shores of the Dead Sea, tossed a stone into a cave and heard the sound of breaking pottery. Climbing into the cave, he discovered several leather scrolls stuffed into pottery jars. These fragments of the Old Testament became known as the Dead Sea Scrolls. Hailed at the time as the greatest discovery of modern times, nothing in the past sixty years has changed that assessment.

From 1947 through 1956, eleven caves were excavated, and hundreds of fragments and scrolls were rescued. Archaeologists found scrolls of every book of the Old Testament except Esther. In addition to biblical materials, theologians reveled in the discovery of writings from the Essenes, the group that lived in this area of Qumran and was responsible for hiding the scrolls. The new discoveries helped to fill in historical details about the life and times of the Essene community.

The significance of the biblical scrolls found at Qumran was not in the new information they provided, but in the general confirmation of the accuracy of the Masoretic text. The Qumran scrolls predate the previously known manuscripts, *Cairensis* and *Aleppo*, by over a thousand years. Many wondered whether the Qumran scrolls would disprove the authenticity of the texts we had been using up to that point. In fact, the text of the Dead Sea Scrolls confirmed much of the text used in our modern Hebrew Bible. It gives scholars and students complete confidence that the Scriptures we buy in the bookstore are the preserved text God gave to the original writers of the Bible.

## Papyrus Period

The most common writing material during the New Testament period was papyrus, a reed that grew in abundance along the Nile River. The ancient historian Pliny, writing about AD 112, describes the preparation of papyrus for a writing surface.[2] The reeds were cut into lengthwise strips and made into mat-like leaves. The strips were laid across at right angles to the first layer. The mud from the riverbed was used to adhere the strips to each other. The sheets were dried and then polished with stone, leaving a smooth

surface upon which the copyist could write the ancient script. Pulp strips taken from near the center were the best quality. The leaves were a little thicker than modern paper and when pasted together in rolls were often up to eight feet long. When necessary they could be even larger. Some writings were limited to the size of the rolls rather than the end of an author's thoughts.

Unidentified Greek papyrus fragments that date from the third to the sixth centuries AD, ancient pottery dating to the time of Abraham, and ancient coins. Papyrus was the main source of writing material in the early stages of writing the New Testament. It is made of plant material and is easily affected by dampness, fire, and excessive handling.    Photo: R. Maisel.

The word *paper* comes from the term *papyrus*. The Greek term for *books* (*biblia*) is believed to come from the city name Byblos, from which large quantities of papyrus were exported throughout the world. The word *Scripture* comes from the Greek term for *writing* and was the most common term in the New Testament to refer to the Holy Scriptures.

The library in Alexandria, Egypt, was famous for its extensive collection of ancient books, generally written on papyrus. A library in Pergamum, Asia Minor, became a rival to Egypt's literary dominance and began purchasing great quantities of papyrus from Egypt. In the spirit of commercial competition, Egypt cut off the supply of papyrus. Not to be outdone, Pergamum

An exact hand-written facsimile of the Gospel of Mark on papyrus, copied after the example of the ancient fourth-century books found at Nag Hammadi (an area in Upper Egypt). This was hand copied using the exact methods of ancient scribes by Vince Savarino. Early Christians preferred codices (book forms) for recording Scripture. Secular letters and other Christian writings were often in scroll form. Photo: B. Bahner.

businessmen developed a new writing material from the skins of animals, and it took its name "parchment" from the city of its origin.

Jews and Christians treasured the sacred books so much that they became holy objects. The high degree of accuracy demonstrated by the discoveries at Qumran displayed the care taken in writing and copying the Old Testament Scriptures many hundreds of years after their original production. Even 1,400 years after the original production of the New Testament, handwritten copies were still faithfully transmitting the Bible. Accurate copying of the sacred canon played an important role in providing a written text for Christianity.

Two basic styles of Greek letters existed during the handwritten period. The uncial hand formed large capital letters without spaces between words. Minuscule was a small cursive type of writing that developed gradually over several centuries. This style of writing, the speed of the scribal task, and the compact style reduced production costs. Each scribe developed his own distinct style, making the variety of handwriting infinite. Monks copied the earliest minuscule manuscript in Constantinople in AD 635.[3] All other manuscripts produced before this time were written in the uncial hand.

## Manuscript Period: Ninth to Fifteenth Centuries

No period in the history of the Bible is more exciting or represents a finer development in art form than the period that produced illuminated manuscripts. Not only was God's message revered, but Christians also treasured and beautified the pages of the sacred text. Monks carefully copied and ornately decorated each manuscript using bright colors and fine vellum or durable paper. Typically they painted portraits of biblical personalities on separate leaves and then carefully inserted them into the text. Today scholars call these "miniatures" because they were painted by hand with the color from a red leaf called *minium*.[4]

From the end of the first century to the fourth century, scribes copied and translated manuscripts in various languages such as Georgian, Coptic, Ethiopic, Gothic, Syriac, and Latin. It was widely recognized that the Bible must be translated into the languages of the people.

With the fourth century came a man who bridged the gap between the classical era and the Middle Ages. In the declining years of the Roman Empire, this man, Eusebius Hieronymus, known today as St. Jerome, was far ahead of his time. At a time in history when there was mass confusion surrounding the variety and number of biblical manuscripts, Jerome translated the Bible into Latin. Jerome, a master of biblical Hebrew and Greek, completed his project in twenty-two years. Not only did he standardize the text, his Bible became the official Latin version of the Roman Catholic Church. This edition would later be called the *versio vulgata* (or Vulgate), which simply means "the published translation."

Jerome's Vulgate added to the existing translations another version to compete for acceptance.[5] Since his version was a direct translation from the Hebrew and Greek manuscripts, some people questioned his judgments. Other critics challenged his abandonment of an earlier Latin version, known as the Old Latin version, which some considered divinely inspired. Many believed the ordained spiritual leadership should authorize a "once for all delivered version" for all believers. They thought that something akin to the divine should be vested in a particular version.

Like many new translations, much time passed before its final triumph. Not until AD 580, under Gregory the Great, did the Vulgate begin to challenge all other versions for superiority. Its success guaranteed a standardized text of the Latin for medieval Christianity.

The Vulgate emerged as the dominant translation and provided a text for transmission throughout history. The next several centuries not only witnessed the transmission of the text but also became a period for the establishment of a distinct art form. Some of the world's most beautiful art treasures are these medieval manuscripts with illuminations and miniatures.

These are early handwritten leaves on paper of the Gospel of Luke in the Coptic language. Paper took the place of parchment (skins of cows and mature sheep and goats) and vellum (skins of lambs and goats—often the fetus) in the fourteenth and fifteenth centuries. It was much cheaper and quite durable since it was made with a cloth base. Photo: M. Brake.

The Book of Kells is the oldest surviving fully illuminated book of the Middle Ages, usually dated by scholars between the eighth and ninth centuries. Many scholars believe this is the most beautiful manuscript in existence. The early eighth-century Lindisfarne Gospels, best known for its five carpet pages functioning as decorative frontispieces, no doubt is a close second.

The bindings of these treasures, often ornately decorated with precious jewels, ivory, and gold, helped beautify them. The Lindisfarne Gospels, housed in the British Library, is one such beautifully bound book. In the colophon the original binding is described:

Billfrith, the anchorite, forged the ornaments that are on it [referring to the binding] on the outside and adorned it with gold and with gems and also with gilded—over silver—pure metal.[6]

Little wonder many of these Bibles were chained to the pulpits in churches.

The process of illumination was time consuming and costly during the Middle Ages. The skins of calves, antelopes, or goats were carefully prepared and made smooth for handwriting. When paper became popular and practical in the fourteenth and fifteenth centuries, illumination became more available and less costly. Once the text was carefully inscribed on the writing material, spaces at the beginning of sections or chapters were left blank for illuminations or finely drawn pictures of saints or biblical characters. Gold was added for the most wealthy landowners or libraries. After the text was prepared, the leaves were bound in stiff leather covers and ready for use.

By the end of the thirteenth century, secular illumination shops often replaced the scriptoriums of the scribes, and the process led to producing art for profit. This explains the vast number of biblically related manuscripts produced in such expensive formats. They often became status symbols among the rich and powerful. Bibles in a format for the poor were soon to follow.

## Early Portions of Pre-English Bibles

No complete Bible in the language of the people of England existed before the fourteenth century. Even for the modestly educated clergy, the Bible was inaccessible—available only in the Latin language. Latin Bibles sitting

A chained Bible (1595 Geneva). Bibles were often chained to the pulpit to prevent theft. The wooden cover is adorned with a carving of an angel and the Ten Commandments and is accompanied by a twenty-inch chain.   Photo: B. Bahner.

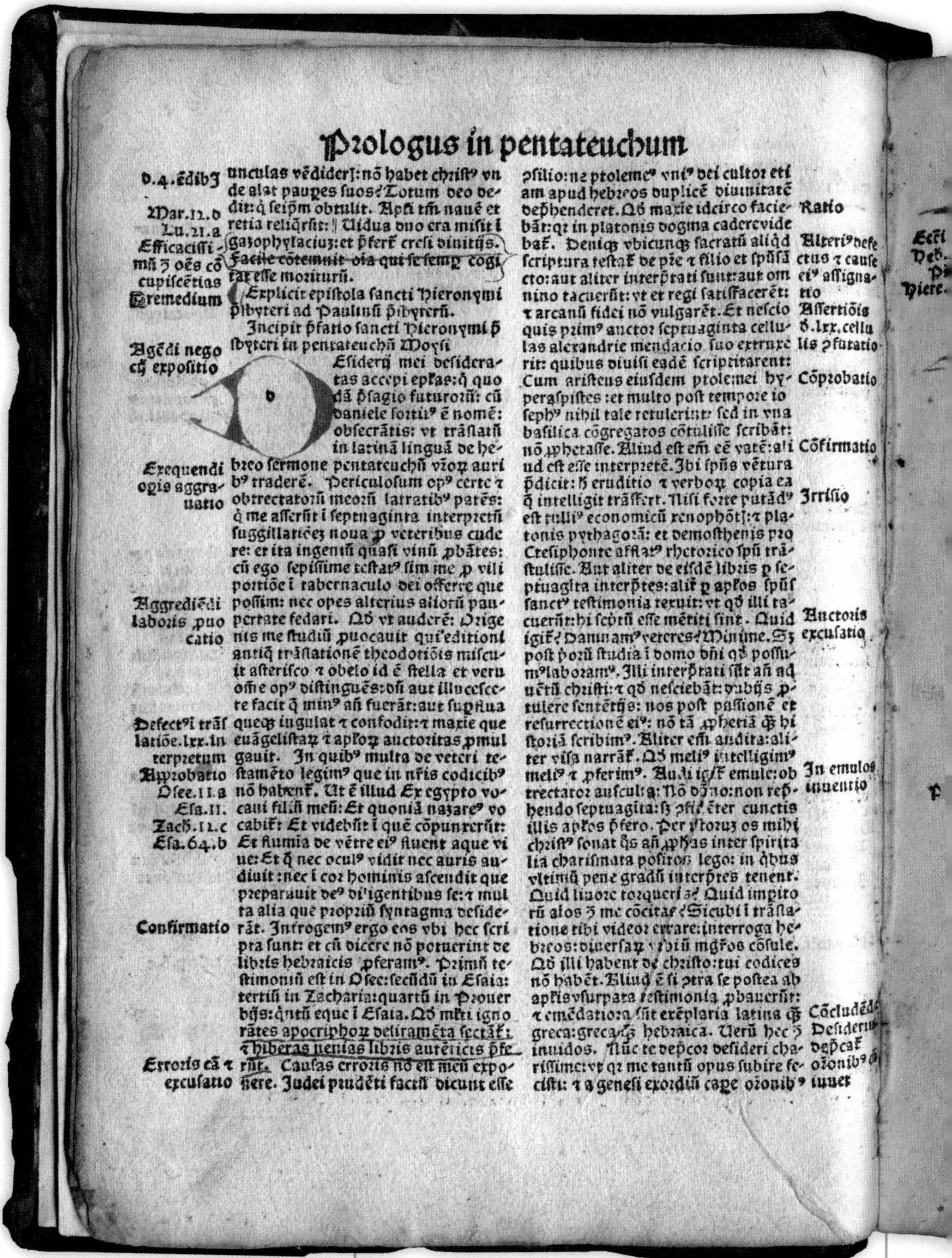

uenculas vendiderit: non habet christus vnde alat pauperes suos. Totum deo vendit: q seipsum obtulit. Apli tñ naue et retia reliqrũt: Uidua duo era misit i gazophylaciũ: et pferr cresi dinitijs. Facile cõtemnit oia qui se semp cogi tat esse morituru.

Explicit epistola sancti Hieronymi pibyteri ad Paulinũ pibyterũ.

Incipit pfatio sancti Hieronymi pibyteri in pentateuchũ Moysi.

Esiderij mei desideratas accepi eplas: q quodã pfagio futurorũ: cũ Daniele sottiũ e nomẽ: obsecratis: vt trãslatũ in latinã linguã de hebreo sermone pentateuchũ vroẽ auribus traderẽ. Periculosum opus certe z obtrectatorũ meorũ latratib᷒ patẽs: qui me asserũt i septuaginta interpretũ suggillatiõe᷑ noua p veteribus cudere: et ita ingeniũ quasi vinũ pbates: cũ ego sepissime testatus sim me p vili portiõe opus distinguẽs: vel aut illuescere facit q minus añ fuerat: aut supflua queq iugulat z confodit: z maxie que euãgelista᷑ z aplo᷑ auctoritas pmulgauit. In quib᷒ multa de veteri testamẽto legimus que in nris codicib᷒ nõ habent. Ut e illud Ex egypto vocaui filiũ meũ: Et quoniã nazare᷒ vocabit: Et videbis i que cõpunxerũt: Et flumia de vetre ei᷒ fluent aque viue: Et q nec oculus vidit nec auris audiuit: nec i cor hominis ascendit que preparauit de᷒ diligentibus se: z multa alia que propriũ syntagma desiderãt. Introeamus ergo eos vbi hec scripta sunt: et cũ dicere nõ potuerint de libris hebraicis pferam: Primũ testimoniũ est in Osee: secũdũ in Esaia: tertiũ in Zacharia: quartũ in Prouer bijs: qntũ eque i Esaia. Qõ multi ignorãtes apocripho᷑ delirametã sectãt: Thiberas nenias libris aureticis pfer rũt. Causas erroris nõ est mei exponere. Judei pudeti factu dicunt esse

psilio: ne ptoleme᷒ vni᷒ dei cultor eti am apud hebreos duplicẽ diuinitatẽ defhenderet. Qõ maxie idcirco faciebãt: qr in platonis dogma caderevide bat. Denicq vbicunq sacratũ aliqd scriptura testat de pie z filio et spũsancto: aut aliter interpti sunt: aut omnino tacuerũt: vt et regi satisfaceret: z arcanũ fidei nõ vulgaret. Et nescio quis primus auctor septuaginta cellulas alexandrie mendacio suo extruxerit: quibus diuisi eade scriptitarent: Cum aristeus eiusdem ptolemei hyperaspistes: et multo post tempore ioseph᷒ nihil tale retulerint: sed in vna basilica cõgregatos cõtulisse scribãt: nõ phetasse. Aliud est eim vatẽ: ali ud est esse interpretẽ. Ibi spũs vetura pdicit: h eruditio z verbo᷑ copia ea q intelligit trãsfert. Nisi forte putãd᷒ est tulli᷒ economicũ xenophõt: z platonis pythago᷑ã: et demosthenis pro Cresiphonte afflat᷒ rhetorico spu trãstulisse. Aut aliter de eisdẽ libris p septuagita interptes: alif p aplos spũsancti testimonia retulit: vt qõ illi ra cuerũt: hi scriptũ esse meriti sint. Quid igit? Damnamus᷒ veteres? Minime. Sz post poru studia i domo dñi qõ possumᵘ laboramus. Illi interprati sut añ aduetũ christi: z qõ nesciebat: dubijs᷒ ptulere sentetijs: nos post passione et resurrectione ei᷒: nõ tã phetia q̃ hi storiã scribimus. Aliter eim audita: aliter visa narrat. Qõ meli᷒ intelligimus meli᷒ z pferimus. Audi igit᷒ emule: ob trectator auscula: Nõ dãno: non reshendo septuagita: sz pfe᷑ eter cunctis illis aplos pfero. Per isto᷑uz os mihi christus sonat sz añ aplos inter spiritalia charismata positos lego: in qbus vltimũ pene gradũ interptes tenent. Quid liuore torqueri sz? Quid impito ru alos z me cõcitat? Sicubi i trãslatione tibi videor errare: interroga hebreos: diuersa᷑ vbii mg᷑fos cõsule. Qõ illi habent de christo: tui codices nõ habet. Aliud e si ptra se postea ab aplis᷒ vsurpata testimonia pbauerut: z emedatiora sut exẽplaria latina q̃ greca: greca᷑ q̃ hebraica. Veru hec z inuidos. Nuc te vep᷑cor desideri charissime: vt qz me tantũ opus subire fecisti: z a genesi exordiũ cape orouib᷒ iuues

### Marginal notes (left column)

D.4.ædibᴶ
Mar.11.d
Lu.21.a
Efficacissimũ z oẽs cõ
cupiscetias
Eremedium

Agedi nego
cũ expositio

Exequendi
ogis aggrauatio

Aggrediedi
laboris pro
catio

Defectᵘi trãslatiõe.lxx.in
terpretum

Approbatio
Osee.11.a
Esa.11.
Zach.11.c
Esa.64.b

Confirmatio

Erroris cã z
excusatio

### Marginal notes (right column)

Ratio

Alteriᵘ defectus z cause
ei᷒ assignatio

Assertiõis
d.lxx.cellu
lis pfutatio

Cõprobatio

Cõfirmatio

Irrisio

Auctoris
excusatio

In emulos
inuentio

Cõcludedo
Desideriũ
vep᷑cat
orouib᷒
iuuet

---

Poor Man's Latin Bible (1495). Most Bibles produced from about the ninth century were large, beautifully decorated, and produced for the wealthy or those studying in monasteries. This printed Bible, on the contrary, was small and affordable, with very little illumination so everyone could own one. Photo: M. Brake.

on medieval bookshelves were large folio copies bound in two or three volumes. The exorbitant price and the few extant copies made reading and studying impossible. The clergy could only hope to put their hands on portions of Scripture and, for the most part, relied heavily on the small portions of Scripture included in their prayer books. It was impossible to understand the flow, context, and meaning of the Scriptures.

These fragmented texts of the Scriptures, along with the circulation of apocryphal books, led the medieval church into strange and grotesque doctrines. English medieval language scholar Geoffrey Shepherd portrays the doctrine of hell: "The medieval hell has very little canonical authority. It was largely and horribly furnished from traditions established in the Apocalypses of Peter and Paul, and elaborated in the versions of men who had fed on such documents."[7] These distortions of biblical teaching were further spread by the artists who graphically displayed vile creatures eating the flesh and devouring sinners in the place of torment.

Without the availability of the Scriptures and the scarcity of literate clergy, one can easily imagine a church corrupted by false doctrine. The passing of the centuries awaited the reforms of John Wycliffe and Martin Luther. Even with the many controversies of the post-Reformation period, many believe the greatest problem was the inaccessibility of the Bible to common folk prior to the Reformation.

This period also produced a veneration of the words of the Bible that extended beyond the meaning of those words. Shepherd states:

> The Scriptures, however unclearly discerned, were not only the supreme documents of human achievement, they were divine oracles, texts numinous in themselves, whose full meaning was linked by divine arrangement with the language in which men received them. The very order of words was meaningful. . . . All words, not only biblical words, had an innate force and mystery for these people. . . . The very volumes of Scriptures possessed miraculous power.[8]

The picture is clear: the clergy and the church used the Bible not as daily guidance to spiritual maturity but as an object to be worshiped and venerated. One needs only to view these magnificently decorated manuscripts to understand the mentality, the superstition, and the highly mystical makeup of the medieval Christian. Shepherd sums it up: "To translate the Latin Bible would have been to transform the whole frame of knowledge human and divine."[9] That is exactly what happened, but not until the Reformation.

## Beginnings of an English Translation

English, as we know it today, is a relatively recent language. Over a few decades, the language of the Anglo-Saxons, a predecessor to modern English, radically changed. There were three distinct periods of English: Old English (the period to the Norman Conquest in AD 1066), Middle English (1100 to 1500), and Modern English (since 1500). Unlike the evolution of Greek or other ancient languages, English development saw massive changes from one period to the next.

When Julius Caesar landed in Britain a few years before the birth of Christ, English did not exist. By the sixth century, fewer people spoke English (or what would later become known as English) than currently speak Cherokee. One thousand years later, English was at its classical best. William Shakespeare's vocabulary included about 30,000 words, compared to the approximate average vocabulary of 15,000 words for an educated person today.[10]

### ÐÆT GODSPEL
#### ÆFTER MATHEUS GERECEDNYSSE.

I. HER is on cneorisse bóc Hælendes Cristes, Dauides suna, Abrahames suna. Soðlice Abraham gestrynde 2 Isáác; Isáác gestrynde Iacob; Iacob gestrynde Iudam and his gebroðra; Iudas gestrynde Phares and Zaram 3 of þam wife þe wæs genemned Thamar; Phares gestrynde Esrom; Esrom gestrynde Aram; Aram gestrynde 4 Aminadab; Aminadab gestrynde Nááson; Nááson gestrynde Salmon; Salmon gestrynde Booz of þam wife 5 Rááb; Booz gestrynde Obeth of þam wife Ruth; Obeth gestrynde Iesse; Iesse gestrynde þone cyning Dauid; 6 Dauid cyning gestrynde Salomon of þam wife þe wæs Urias wíf; Salomon gestrynde Roboam; Roboas gestrynde Abíam; Abía gestrynde Asa; Asah gestrynde 7 Iosaphath; Iosaphath gestrynde Ioram; Ioras gestrynde Ozíam; Ozías gestrynde Ioatham; Ioatham gestrynde 9 Achaz; Achas gestrynde Ezechíam; Ezechias gestrynde 10 Mannasen; Mannases gestrynde Amon; Amon gestrynde Iosíam; Iosías gestrynde Iechoníam and his ge- 11 broðru, on Babilonis geleorednesse: and æfter Babilonis geleorednesse, Iechonías gestrynde Salathiel; Sala- 12 thiel gestrynde Zorobabel; Zorobabel gestrynde Abiud; 13

B

An early Anglo-Saxon Gospel of Matthew (AD 995) edited by Benjamin Thorpe in 1842. The English language represented here is a relatively late form of the language that developed in the British Isles.

The Oxford English Dictionary, second edition, includes 600,000 words; with technical words, there are about 990,000 words in English. The Wikipedia Encyclopedia estimates 300 million to 400 million people speak English as their first language. Nearly one-third of the world's population (1.9 billion people) has a basic knowledge of English. Many think of English as the first genuinely global language.[11]

Because the Celtic island of Britain was a land rich in farmland and minerals, invasions were frequent and destructive. Its early history records successive invasions, beginning with Julius Caesar in 55 BC. The withdrawal of the Roman legions in AD 410 and the subsequent collapse of the empire allowed the Germanic people to invade the island. The Angles, Saxons, and Jutes came from Germany and Denmark beginning in the fifth century. The native Britons withdrew to the western areas of the island and dubbed it *wedlas*, from which the word *Welsh* came.[12]

> The love of the Anglo-Saxon for ambiguity, innuendo, and word play—shared with English in every age—characterizes its written literature.

The closely related language of the invaders formed the basis of an English that is known today as Old English or Anglo-Saxon. The love of the Anglo-Saxon for ambiguity, innuendo, and word play—shared with English in every age—characterizes its written literature.

In AD 597, Gregory the Great brought Christianity to England and with Christianity came the vast vocabulary of the Latin language. About thirty-five years later (AD 635), Aidan, a Celtic evangelist from the church in Ireland, independently began missionary work in the central part of England, along the border of what is now Scotland. The next two centuries witnessed the conversion of England to Christianity and the demand for Scripture in this new emerging language.

A Gothic translation of the Gospels called *Codex Argenteus* or "Silver Book," so called because it was copied in letters with a silvery hue, represents a pre-English language. Translated by the famous missionary Ulfilas in about AD 360 for the heathen Goths, it represents a pre–Old English version in the first vernacular translation ever produced. It is also a prototype of the Old English. Several phrases, when compared, reveal many similarities of the Germanic tongue to Old English.[13]

Gothic (360) / Anglo-Saxon (995) / Modern English

In bokom Psalmo / on tharn Sealme / In the book of Psalms
Ik in thata dour / Ic eom geat / I am the door
Kaurno whaiteis / Hwaetene corn / A grain of wheat
Wheitos swe snaiws / Swa hwite swa snaw / As white as snow

The earliest portions of Scripture in Anglo-Saxon were songs set to verse by a layman, Caedmon, at a Yorkshire monastery. A legend describes his habit of singing portions of Scripture in a highly complicated vernacular meter. The only surviving manuscript attributed to Caedmon is a hymn about creation:

Now we ought to praise the Guardian of the kingdom of heaven,
*Nu sculon herigean    heofonrices Weard,*

the might of the Creator and his understanding,
*Meotodes meahte    ond his modgethanc*

the works of the Father of glory, how he, the eternal Lord,
*weorc Wuldorfæder,    swa he wundra gehwæs*

established a beginning of each wonder.
*ece Drihten,    or onstealde.*

He, the holy Creator, first created
*He ærest sceop    eorthan bearnum*

heaven as a roof for the sons of the earth.
*heofon to hrofe,    halig Scyppend.*

Then the Guardian of humankind, the eternal Lord,
*tha middangeard    moncynnes Weard,*

the almighty Prince, afterwards created
*ece Drihten    æfter teode*

the world, the land for the people.
*firum foldan,    Frea ælmihtig.*[14]

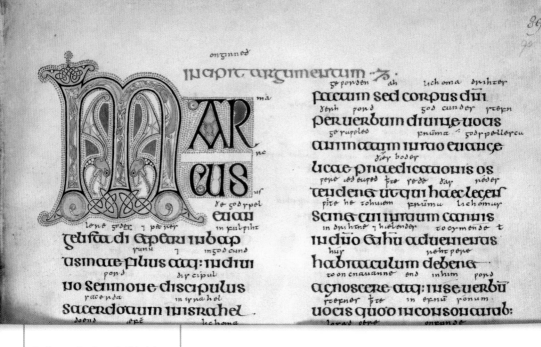

The first known translation of an actual biblical text in Old English was a work on the Psalter by Aldhelm, the first bishop of Sherborne in Dorset. It began sometime at the beginning of the eighth century.

The Venerable Bede, a great scholar of his day, continued the work of Aldhelm. Most commonly known for his ecclesiastical history, he also translated the Gospel of John. Tradition records his completion of the task at the very hour he lay dying. Unfortunately, his work has not survived.

The Old English period (to AD 1066) is characterized by its interlinear glosses in Latin manuscripts. Glossing, an Anglo-Saxon pedagogical method for introducing Latin to the reader, placed a word-for-word vernacular translation in direct juxtaposition to the Latin text. Undoubtedly the most famous example of this is seen in the eighth-century Lindisfarne manuscript, which contains a literal rendering of the text into an Anglo-Saxon dialect by the scribe named Aldred.[15] David Daniell, English Bible history scholar, points out, "The Old English gloss in the Lindisfarne Gospels is the first extensively written Old English that has survived."[16] Later scribes drew from these glosses to craft their translations.

The Vikings, people known by the Anglo-Saxons as "Danes," invaded the island from the north and gave rise to England's King of Wessex, Alfred the Great (AD 849–901). Alfred managed to raise a ragtag army and beat off the attacks of the Vikings at the Battle of Edington. The victory saved the last remaining English-speaking kingdom. Alfred contributed to developing English by insisting that schools teach in the vernacular. He went as far as to learn Latin at the age of forty in order to translate various texts into English.[17] In addition, Alfred translated the Ten Commandments, excerpts from Exodus and Acts, and a form of the Golden Rule from the Bible.[18]

> Perhaps the most important biblical expositor before Wycliffe was a prose writer from the Old English period named Aelfric.

Perhaps the most important biblical expositor before Wycliffe was a prose writer from the Old English period named Aelfric. While Aelfric cannot be dubbed a translator, his influence on the use of the vernacular set the stage for the translation of the Wessex Gospels. His partial translations (often called homilies) of the Pentateuch, Joshua, Judges, Kings, Job, Esther, and the Maccabees gained influence and set him apart as a key figure in the history of the English Bible.[19] Even though Aelfric did not translate the Scriptures into English, it was his aim to convey biblical and religious truth into plain and simple English for those who did not know Latin.

Were it not for certain events of the eleventh century, the complete Bible might well have been the progressive result of the work of Aelfric. The invasion of the Normans, however, delayed the development of the Anglo-Saxon language and any continual work on an English translation of the Bible.

The tenth-century translation of the four Gospels into Old English known as the Wessex Gospels is the first extended portion of the Bible translated into English. The Wessex Gospels is anonymous and does not bear a date. Several extant manuscripts, however, none of which are the original, bear witness to its early date. The earliest known manuscript dates to the twelfth century AD.[20]

By 1066, the Old English language, not yet well established as a written language, withstood the Norman-French influence that came with the

French invasion.[21] The French aristocracy ruling England repressed the Anglo-Saxon language and declared Norman French the official language of England, thus bringing to a close the Anglo-Saxon period and introducing Middle English. The strong French influence delayed the progress of an English Bible for two more centuries, as it would take this long for the Anglo-Saxons to assimilate the French influence into the Anglo-Norman language.

For nearly 150 years following the Norman invasion, English people were left with some Anglo-Saxon liturgy (religious instruction through the church calendar), lyric songs,[22] and poems as a substitute for the Bible. Popular medieval dramas depicted biblical themes. In fact, many of these dramas developed over the years and were repeated in every period of the English language.[23] Nevertheless, the common people continued to be deprived of the Bible as their rule of faith. They were forced to depend on plays, oral transmissions of Scripture stories, and Latin and French Bibles of the aristocracy and the priesthood for their understanding of God's Word.

> The clergy not only prevented the laity from reading the Scriptures; copies of the sacred text were simply not available.

Finally, in the thirteenth and fourteenth centuries, things started to change. William of Shoreham and Richard Rolle, both translating from the Latin Vulgate in a very literal form, each produced an Anglo-Norman translation of the Psalter. Rolle's elaborate commentary became a standard for more than a century. It not only influenced John Wycliffe's thinking but was also printed in the incunabulum period of printing (1456–1500).

From the mid-twelfth century a genuine English language began to replace the Anglo-Norman language. Various homilies and renderings of small passages of the Gospels began to emerge. In fact, simple phrases and short sentences of Anglo-Saxon would eventually find their way into the English translation of Tyndale's New Testament in the sixteenth century.[24] The laity, discontent with the claims of the Roman Church, refused to accept the church as supreme. France and England's attempts to unite over their support of popes Urban and Clement brought the respect of the church to an all-time low, and common people began to question its authority. England, in an age immortalized by Chaucer, was finally ready for the Scriptures in her own beloved tongue.

The pre-Wycliffe period epitomized the notion that only the clergy could own and read the Scriptures. The clergy not only prevented the laity from reading the Scriptures; copies of the sacred text were simply not available. They were either not in the laity's language, or they were too expensive to purchase. The use of the Bible by the poor was not possible until the end of the fourteenth century. Sarcastically called "poor men's" Bibles, these simply written books in the common language with very little adornment fed the hungry soul.

The Bible exclusively reserved for the clergy and wealthy was about to end. We now turn to the man who changed all of that for all time.

# 2

# He Dared to Act

*John Wycliffe and the Bible in English*

All day a soft rain had followed him across the English country-side, his walking stick tapping out a song of progress, encouraging his aching joints to keep the rhythm. The large hat he wore on this trip directed the water in trickles down his long wool tunic, allowing only his feet to catch the runoff.

Evening was closing in around him. How he longed to find a drier spot rather than huddle under a broad tree. Straightening his stance, he turned in a circle, straining to see a light or even a sniff of smoke from a cooking fire where he might find comfort that night. Nothing appeared except a silhouette on the horizon ahead to the left of the path. Could it be a cave or an abandoned hut?

As this somber, introspective man took refuge in the semi-dry hut, he quietly reflected over the past twenty years and pondered the future of his movement. For some months he had felt his mortality more than ever. Had he done all he could for his Savior? Would his work continue after his earthly exit? What if his message—so faithfully taught to his followers—ceased after he was gone?

What more could he do to insure the continuation of the principles he was willing to die for? The principles, that is, of justification by faith, a complete rejection of transubstantiation and the sale of indulgences, and the importance of giving every plowman, shopkeeper, and landowner access to the Bible.

His thoughts became as dismal as the weather outside.

The gloom settling over him was interrupted when a young man burst through the door. He too was seeking shelter from the cold, damp weather, but he wore a smile that warmed that place. His robust face and frame were a stark contrast to the old man's long, white beard and frail appearance. The young man presented himself well in their exchange about the weather.

After a brief silence, the young man leaned toward the old man and breathlessly asked, "Sir, have you heard of the Bible teaching as proclaimed by Dr. Wycliffe, the pastor at Lutterworth?"

The elderly gentleman smiled slightly. "Do tell me what you have heard."

The young man, so exuberant in sharing the Lollard teaching, could scarcely stay seated. He repeated the Lollard teaching point by point: God's Word should be in the language of the common man, and every layman was a priest before God. For nearly an hour, he earnestly shared what he knew of the teaching with the old man.

The young man gradually began to talk slower, as if savoring the words that proclaimed his faith in God. When he expressed his admiration of and desire to meet Dr. Wycliffe, the old man could contain himself no more, so he removed his hat and introduced himself as none other than Dr. Wycliffe!

The young man barely took a breath as he switched from an evangelist to a student. For the better part of another hour his questions were incessant. The patient Wycliffe, now with renewed energy, answered the young budding theologian with enthusiasm and joy.[1]

That young man was John Purvey, who continued Wycliffe's work long after his death.

Little did Wycliffe know the influence he would have on biblical and theological studies. His Bible was the first ever translated into English. Even though it was a translation from the Latin Vulgate instead of from the Greek and Hebrew, no matter how ardently people tried to destroy it, the English Bible survived.

The fourteenth-century movement Wycliffe began soon blossomed into a full reformation in the sixteenth century. For the next 130 years, the product of Wycliffe's faithful and daring translation into English became the Bible of every man.

The Wycliffe translation also gave rise to the established church's intense hatred for a vernacular Bible. First, the *De heretico comburendo* of 1401 promised death to heretics by means of burning the offender alive. In 1408 the infamous *Constitutions* were formulated in direct response to the overwhelming reception of Wycliffe's idea that every man should have a Bible in his own language. The *Constitutions* forbade the Sacred Latin Vulgate Bible to be translated into a common tongue without express supervision of the church.[2] It soon followed that translating Scriptures into English or reading the Bible in English were heretical acts. Scholars such as Thomas More needed permission before reading an illegal English translation to evaluate and condemn it.

> No matter how ardently people tried to destroy it, the English Bible survived.

Wycliffe's determination to make the Bible available to every layman in the vernacular was linked to the biblical teaching that everyone is answerable for his own deeds and responsible for personal faith in Christ.

The English Bible survived. No longer were the Scriptures to be worshiped as oracles; Scripture was to be obeyed. Wycliffe's deep opposition to the church's views of the Eucharist, the selling of indulgences, the church's authority, praying to the saints, and pilgrimages forced him to challenge the church and its doctrines. This inevitably led to the conclusion that everyone must have his own copy of the Bible in his own language. Wycliffe wrote:

Those Heretics who pretend that the laity need not know God's law but that the knowledge which priests have had imparted to them by word of mouth is sufficient, do not deserve to be listened to. For Holy Scriptures is the faith of the Church, and the more widely its true meaning becomes known the better it will be. Therefore since the laity should know the faith, it should be taught in whatever language is most easily comprehended. . . . Christ and His apostles taught the people in the language best known to them.[3]

## John Wycliffe, Scholar and Visionary

John Wycliffe was born in the early fourteenth century (some suggest as early as 1320 or the 1330s) in a small village called Wycliffe-on-Tees in Yorkshire.[4] As the son of a squire and owner of a small manor, he attended Balliol College in Oxford and in 1356 completed a Bachelor of Arts at Merton College. He received his Doctor of Theology in 1372 or 1373. By the time Wycliffe left Oxford he had been Master of Balliol College and Warden of Canterbury Hall. His studies, typical of medieval scholars, were rooted soundly in Latin.

Rejecting the metaphysics of the universities of his day, Wycliffe returned to the principles of the Bible for his authority. He found moral authority in the words of Scripture rather than in the cloaks of religious orders.

By the 1370s his views were interpreted as revolutionary at best and complete anarchy at worst. By now his peers in the priesthood and fellow university colleagues began to shun him, but a few loyal Oxford scholars gathered around him.

In 1382 the archbishop of Canterbury summoned a council at Blackfriars in London to condemn Wycliffe's teachings as heretical. After being found guilty, Wycliffe withdrew from his beloved Oxford to Lutterworth.

A portrait of John Wycliffe from an engraving by H. Cook. Wycliffe was the first to translate the Bible into English, although it was from the Latin. Greek was not widely studied until the fall of Constantinople in 1453, when the fleeing Christians brought the Greek language to Europe. Photo: H. W. Hoare, *The Evolution of the English Bible* (1901), frontispiece.

My wife, Carol, and I were speeding along the highway from a day's hunt for Bibles in Scotland heading for an appointment with a rare Bible dealer just north of London. The day was beautiful and the Yorkshire countryside a blur as we were anxious to get to our destination for an intense search of that rare treasure awaiting us on the dealer's shelves.

Carol suddenly burst out, "Wyclif, Wyclif, there is a Wyclif sign. Stop, stop." Sitting nestled along the highway on a very small sign was the name "Wyclif," and an arrow pointing toward a narrow, unpaved road. My mind firmly set toward my goal, yet mixed with disbelief, I suddenly got a grip on my thoughts as she repeated again, "Go back, go back."

I reluctantly slowed, did a quick U-turn, and started up the narrow winding lane. The short drive soon opened into a picturesque glen with a very old rock church and a quaint stone cottage. A gentle brook called the Tees meandered ever so slowly behind the church.

We approached the cottage next to the church and asked if we could look around. The caretaker briefly told us John Wycliffe was born in the lower portion of the current church. Our excitement must have been obvious. She pointed out the key hanging on the front gate and invited us to have a look. We quickly began an afternoon of joyful discovery. Stepping over the threshold of Wycliffe's birthplace transported us back into fourteenth-century England. Never was a detour so gratifying.

Two years later, on the last day of 1384, the great theologian, master translator, beloved leader, and saint "justified by faith" passed into the eternal presence of him whom he served faithfully. He was gone but by no means forgotten. For his contribution to the Great Reformation and modern Christianity, every Christian can be grateful that the "morning star of the Reformation" has given us the Bible in English.

Wycliffe's work created a hunger for a Bible in the tongue of the common man.[5] The aristocracy spoke French, Anglo-Norman, and Latin. The laity spoke Middle English, the common language used by Chaucer, and the dialect used in the Wycliffe Bible. The thirst created by this Middle English

*Wycliffe's work created a hunger for a Bible in the tongue of the common man.*

version led to an insatiable desire for Bible translations that came to fruition in the sixteenth century, just two centuries later.

One cannot overemphasize the importance that the English translation of the Bible had in the process and success of the Reformation. For the first time, every literate person could read and understand God's Word and thereby ascertain the principles for Christian living. Without it, the English Reformation would have languished in the dungeons of King Henry VIII.

## The Translators

The translators of the Wycliffe Bible sought to establish an authority opposing the church. Wycliffe and the Lollards appealed to "Goddis lawe" and "Christis lawe" (New Testament themes) as the source of authority. They didn't believe authority should come from the church, whose priests thought the greater the clerical robe, the more authority and power one could wield. The Lollards further asserted that these laws were open to all men. As Wycliffe explained, "It seems first that the knowledge of God's law should be taught in that tongue that is more known, for this knowledge is God's word."[6]

Later he would write,

> That the New Testament is of full Authority, and open to understanding of simple men, as to the points that have been most needful to salvation. . . . That men ought to desire only the truth and freedom of the holy Gospel, and to accept man's Law and ordinances only in as much as they have been grounded in holy Scriptures.[7]

Thus, the production of a translation in the vernacular brought into clear focus the contrast of authority between the church and the laity.

Most scholars today believe that John Wycliffe did not actually translate the entire Bible that bears his name.[8] Wycliffe's principles of translation can be extracted from his sermons. The Old Testament part of the translation,

A rare leaf from an original early fifteenth-century Wycliffe Bible (Romans 6). The language is similar to that used by Chaucer, author of *The Canterbury Tales*, and is often difficult for modern English readers.

notorious for its strict literalness, is unlike Wycliffe's free rendering in his sermons. This lends support to the possibility that someone else translated the Old Testament. By contrast, the Wycliffe New Testament is more in keeping with Wycliffe's style of translation. Wycliffe also gave more credence to the New Testament than the Old. Wycliffe's ability to translate the Bible is not questioned, but his failing health and lack of time were factors. It does seem reasonable to conclude, however, that Wycliffe participated at some level in the work itself.

Two early manuscripts of the early version may shine light on the discussion of authorship. Manuscript Bodley 959 at the Bodleian Library in Oxford is a large manuscript that was once believed to be the original autograph of the Wycliffe Old Testament. The manuscript followed the order of books found in the Paris Vulgate Bible wherein the book of Baruch (see sidebar "The Apocrypha Book of Baruch") is among the prophets. The manuscript ends abruptly at the end of the manuscript leaf in the middle of Baruch 3:20, *"ye place hem /risen /ye (the) yunge,"* with the following note: "Here ends the translation of Nicholas." The suggestion is obvious. Nicholas de Hereford, not John Wycliffe, did the translation of the Old Testament. The remainder of the Old Testament was most likely completed by some of Wycliffe's followers.[9]

A second manuscript, Douce 369, also the early version,

A leaf from an early fourteenth-century version of the New Testament Apocrypha on vellum: Account of Virgin Mary's Childhood. Many early Christian writers produced works often attributed to Mary or the apostles, and some claimed the right to be in the Christian canon. While they have value, they were not accepted by the church as part of God's Word.

## The Apocrypha Book of Baruch

Baruch is one of the twelve to fifteen Apocrypha books (meaning "hidden," but has come to mean "not accepted") not found in the Hebrew Bible but surviving in the Septuagint (LXX) Greek version of the Bible. These books were written two centuries before the birth of Christ. Jews looked upon them as a means of spiritual enrichment, but after the council of Jamnia in AD 90 (a council restructuring Judaism because of the destruction of the temple and sacrificial system in AD 70), they were considered "books that do not defile the hands." This was a Jewish way of saying they were not a part of revealed Scripture that defile the hands if improperly handled. The early Christian church did not see a need to expunge the Apocrypha from their Bibles but did not consider them on equal ground with Scripture. The church saw them as a bridge supplying information about Israel during the years between the Old Testament and the New Testament.

A controversy began as various church fathers (ca. AD 225–430) began to use the Apocrypha in their writings. Jerome, the famous Bible translator who translated the Bible into Latin, included the Apocrypha in his work even though it is questionable whether or not he accepted their authority. Origen, Cyprian, and others used them and may have considered them canonical. By the time of the Protestant Reformation, the Roman Catholic Church (following the Latin of Jerome) accepted the Apocrypha as canonical. The Reformers Luther, Tyndale, and others (following all the church councils) looked to Scripture as their sole source of authority and rejected the Apocrypha.

The English Bible translator Miles Coverdale collected the Apocrypha from among the Old Testament and placed them in between the Old Testament and New Testament in his 1535 translation of the Bible, declaring them to be valuable as spiritual guides but not on the level of "God's Word." The Roman Catholic Council of Trent in the sixteenth century declared the Apocrypha to be part of the canon and therefore carrying the same authority as other Scripture.

There were New Testament Apocrypha also, such as the Gospel of Judas Iscariot, Gospel of Thomas, and The Miracles of Mary. They never became part of the canon.

ends abruptly at the very same place in the text but only one quarter down the second column of the page. Added to the abrupt ending is *"Explicist translacom Nicholay de herford"* (Here ends the translation of Nicholas of Hereford).[10] Some have suggested that the early version began as glosses and then went through various dialects, and varying stages of translation theory, after which it was copied by at least five scribes.[11] The obvious implication is that Nicholas Hereford[12] translated this portion of the Old Testament and that there may have been other Lollards involved. It is certainly not unthinkable with five other handwritings and the vastness of the Old Testament.

A Cambridge manuscript, MS Ee.10, ends at exactly the same place in Baruch and records, *"Here endith the translacioun of N and now bigynneth the translacioun of J & of othere men."* It is obvious "N" refers to Nicholas Hereford, but the "J" is a question. Several suggestions have surfaced: John Purvey, John Wycliffe, and John Trevisa.[13] It is generally accepted that Wycliffe himself did not personally translate the entire Bible into English. While he most probably had a hand in the work, it can be attributed to some of his followers.

Scholars have always been mystified by the story of these three Wycliffe manuscripts. Christopher de Hamel, expert in medieval and illuminated manuscripts, has a very interesting view that provides a simple explanation:

Nicholas Hereford was indicted by the Blackfriars Synod in May 1382 and was excommunicated for heresy on 1 July. Instead of attempting to answer the charges in London, he appealed to the pope and set off for Rome, doubtless with a dossier or quickly assembled manuscripts in order to vindicate the orthodoxy of the Oxford Wycliffites. He must have taken Bodley 959 with him. He may even have had it copied rapidly that summer for that very purpose. It would be needed to demonstrate to Urban VI that the primitive translation was extremely literal and exact, precisely from the Vulgate. Perhaps he even deliberately stopped in the opening pages of Baruch. Consider this: the order of selection of the biblical books in Bodley 959 corresponded exactly with that of the thirteenth-century Paris Bible, sanctioned by the Dominicans, papal champions in the war on heresy. Bodley 959 furnishes all proof Nicholas Hereford would have needed. Once his Bible located Chronicles in the right place after Kings (and it does), and once the major prophets were put in the new Paris sequence

Nicholas Hereford's note: "Here endith the translacioun of N and now bigynneth the translacioun of J & of othere men." The note suggests Hereford translated up to this point in the Old Testament and then began the work of "J" (perhaps John Purvey) and others (including, perhaps John Wycliffe, John Trevisa, or others).

following the books of Solomon (and they are), and once these prophets can be shown to include the much-disputed Baruch immediately after Jeremiah (where it appears), then the whole of the rest of the Bible automatically falls into order.[14]

If de Hamel's argument is true, then transcribing the Old Testament up to the beginning of Baruch would serve to prove that the text was the one sanctioned by the Dominicans in Paris and therefore the Wycliffe translation was acceptable. Anything after Baruch was not necessary. However, it was all for naught, because Hereford was found guilty and imprisoned.

Despite the controversy surrounding the translators of the Old Testament, Wycliffe's name became synonymous with the work of translation.[15] The earliest mention of Wycliffe's association with the Bible translation is Henry Knighton's reference in his *Chronicon*. Writing in the 1390s, he refers back to 1382 as the time John Wycliffe translated the Gospels.

In those days flourished master John Wycliffe, rector of the church of Lutterworth . . . the most eminent doctor of theology of those times. . . . This master John Wycliffe translated into English, the gospel which Christ gave to the clerks and doctors of the Church, in order that they might sweetly minister it to laymen and weaker men, according to their need. . . . [The gospel] is become more common and open to laymen, and women who are able to read. . . . Thus the pearl of the gospel is scattered abroad and trodden under foot of swine, and what is wont to be the treasure both of clerks and laymen is now become the jest of both.[16]

While the original Old Testament translation bears no compelling evidence of Wycliffe's work, the New Testament (and perhaps the Gospels in particular) is more likely to have had some of his direct influence. Regardless of Wycliffe's direct participation in actual translation, it does not detract from the influence he had on its production.

> Despite the controversy surrounding the translators of the Old Testament, Wycliffe's name became synonymous with the work of translation.

Wycliffe scholar Michael Wilks argues that too much attention has centered on Wycliffe's participation in the Old Testament and then comments, "Genuine evidence exists for thinking that the New Testament was in fact available before the Old Testament, and that Wycliffe might have approved of this order of procedure."[17] His point is that Wycliffe viewed the Old Testament as a prelude—and sometimes a misleading one—to the law code of Christ in the New Testament.

Archbishop Arundel, an avid opponent of Wycliffe, penned the following to Pope John XXIII in 1411:

This pestilent and wretched John Wyclif, of cursed memory, that sone of the old serpant . . . endeavored by doctrine of Holy Church, devising—to fill up the measure of his malice—the expedient of a new translation of the Scriptures into the mother tongue.[18]

John Huss of Prague also attributed the translation to Wycliffe, saying, "By the English it is said that Wyclif translated the whole Bible from Latin into English."[19]

Some scholars attribute the New Testament directly to the work of Wycliffe. Conrad Lindberg, a recognized scholar of the Wycliffe Bible, writes:

> I think it is reasonable to assume that Wycliffe undertook to translate the New Testament himself (with or without helpers) and left the Old Testament to one or more of his disciples. This assumption would account for the inferior quality of EV1 [Early Version], as we have seen it exemplified, while it preserves the possibility that Wycliffe himself had a share in the actual translation of the Bible.[20]

Long-respected scholars Josiah Forshall and Frederic Madden supported Lindberg's observations when they wrote, "This translation might probably be the work of Wycliffe himself; at least the similarity of style between the Gospels and the other parts favors the supposition."[21]

## The Translation

Forshall and Madden, in their scholarly, printed edition of the Wycliffe Bible in 1850, distinguished two editions of the Wycliffe Bible.[22] The first named appropriately "The Wycliffe Version" (Early Version or EV) was especially literal. Latin word order was maintained at the expense of clear meaning and natural English word order. It made the Old Testament awkward and even inaccurate in places. The masses more readily accepted the second edition called "Purvey's revision" (Later Version or LV) because it abandoned much of the wooden literalness of the Wycliffe version.

The first complete Bible in English was a strict, literal translation from the Latin Vulgate. In fact, some of the translation is so literal that one cannot understand it without knowing Latin. Although there were a few Greek scholars in medieval England, it was only natural to translate from their Latin Bible.[23] It was not until the fall of Constantinople in AD 1453 that Greeks fleeing for their lives brought the Greek language into England and Europe. In the decades that followed, Greek became available in the universities for the study of Scripture in the original language.

Political expediency was another reason Wycliffe translated from the Latin. Because of doctrinal disputes Wycliffe and his followers were already

An engraving of John Wycliffe leaving the English Parliament's convocation in 1377. Wycliffe was called before the tribunal to face charges (the exact nature is unknown but they were certainly theological). Wycliffe's leaving St. Paul's Church with his powerful protectors at his side prevented the authorities from achieving their sinister plans.　Photo: W. L. Watkinson, *John Wycliffe* (1884), 75.

at odds with the established church. Attempting a translation from the original languages would have further alienated them from the church.

Translating the Bible from Latin to English was a formidable task. Beside glosses and some biblical books translated by English hermit and mystic Richard Rolle of Hanpole (1295–1349), Wycliffe did not have an example to follow. He and his colaborers were left to their own devices. Their original plan may have included a word-for-word translation with a quick revision intended for a later date. Bodley 959, for example, includes many handwritten corrections throughout, which suggests an immediate revision of its text, perhaps a common practice.

Rolle, one of the first religious authors to write in the English vernacular, translated books very literally and word-for-word following the Latin versions. His theological writings played an important role in the doctrinal position of the Lollards.[24] The style, influence, and popularity of Rolle's Psalms set a precedent in translation principles for Wycliffe and his followers to emulate. Not unexpectedly, a Bible of similar style resulted.

## The Revised Wycliffe Translation (1388/95)

Among Wycliffe's stalwart friends worked the devoted associate and scholar John Purvey. Unlike Nicholas Hereford and Philip Repingdon, two vocal scholars who fearlessly defended the Lollard doctrines, John Purvey was quiet though highly esteemed. Educated at Oxford, ordained a priest in 1377, and probably a doctor of theology, Purvey was an acknowledged scholar by his contemporaries. He became Wycliffe's secretary at Lutterworth, where Wycliffe was pastor. Many scholars use the phrase "Lollard's librarian" to refer to Purvey, testifying to his scholarship and access to the studies necessary for translation and writing.[25]

Purvey was imprisoned for his Lollard activities in 1400 and was released in 1401 after recanting under pressure. Two years later he again returned to preaching the Lollard doctrine.[26] From Forshall and Madden's work in 1850, scholars accepted the later version of the Wycliffe Bible to be the work of John Purvey. In recent days, and especially in the writings of Anne Hudson, doubt has been cast on the contribution of Purvey.[27]

But perhaps one should not abandon the idea of Purvey's contribution so quickly. Writing in 2001, Christopher de Hamel writes, "The revision [1388/95] is commonly and creditably attributed to Wycliffe's personal assistant, John Purvey (ca. 1353–ca. 1428), though there is no real evidence of his authorship other than reasonable conjecture."[28] Michael Wilks, although he denies Wycliffe's responsibility for translating the Old Testament, writes concerning the revision, "Eventually Purvey, seeking to achieve a clearer and more readable translation, must be accredited with a second revision of the whole Bible in the middle years of the 1390s."[29]

Shortly after Wycliffe died, Purvey took refuge in Bristol, where he began a thorough revision of the complete Bible. His emphasis on English idiom and word order enabled the revision to attain remarkable popularity. The "people of the plow"[30] finally had a translation they could understand.

Forshall and Madden propose that this revision came at the suggestion of Wycliffe himself. They write:

> The part translated by Hereford differed in style from the rest; it was extremely literal, occasionally obscure, and sometimes incorrect; and there were other blemishes throughout incident to a first essay of this magnitude, undertaken under very unfavorable circumstances, by different persons and at different times, upon no agreed or well defined principle. These defects could not have escaped the attention of Wycliffe, and it is by no means improbable that he suggested, if he did not himself commence, a second or revised version of the whole Bible.[31]

Early scholars of Wycliffe's version thought Purvey's revision was a product completed before Wycliffe's time. This would have meant that Wycliffe's version was not the first English translation. The error has been traced to the words of Thomas More (1478–1535) who, in his *Dialogues*, claimed to have seen copies prior to those of Wycliffe.

> The whole Bible was long before his [Wycliffe's] days by virtuous and well-learned men translated into the English tongue, and by good and godly people with devotion and soberness, well and reverently read. . . . Myself have seen and can show you Bibles, fair and old, in English, which have been known and seen by the Bishop, the diocese, and left in laymen's hands and women's.[32]

Forshall and Madden point out that the nineteenth-century Wycliffe biographer, Thomas James, after examining several Wycliffe manuscripts, also mistakenly asserted there was an English translation long before the Wycliffe Bible. Archbishop Ussher arbitrarily assigned the date of the early non-Wycliffe edition to be somewhere about 1290. According to Forshall and Madden, Henry Wharton correctly held the date of the early translation to be 1382.[33] He became the first to assign Wycliffe's early version to 1382 and the version More and James thought to be an earlier edition to 1388/95, well after the death of Wycliffe.[34]

John Lewis, the eighteenth-century Wycliffe author, acknowledges some English translations prior to Wycliffe, but only parts of the Old and New Testaments.[35]

Wycliffe undoubtedly would have referred to a previous translation as a justification for his own undertaking if one had been done. Wycliffe's silence implies no translation of the Bible existed prior to his own.

## The General Prologue

A long, general prologue accompanies the revision of the Wycliffe version (LV). It contains fifteen chapters encouraging all men, princes, lords, justices, and common men to read the law of God. The first nine chapters give an outline of Old Testament history, and chapters 12–14 discuss the rules for interpretation.[36] Chapter 15, the most important for our purposes, records the method used by the translator in his revision.

The principles used to revise the cumbersome Wycliffe version (EV) can be summarized as follows:

- The first principle suggested use of the most accurate text. Because all Bibles were in handwritten form, variants were inevitable. A careful comparison of the variants, including the use of commentaries, would enable one to determine the correct Latin text.
- Second, the writer believed a translator must be a competent interpreter of the Word. One cannot

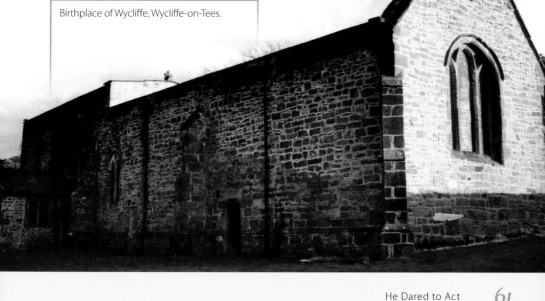

Birthplace of Wycliffe, Wycliffe-on-Tees.

translate a passage he does not understand. For interpretation, the writer relied heavily on Nicholas of Lyra.

- The third principle called for the consultation of grammars, dictionaries, and other reference works that enabled the translator to understand difficult words. He described his approach to translation according to meaning rather than a literal, word-for-word translation.
- Finally, it had to be carefully checked by holy and scholarly men.[37]

The extremely literal translation of the early Wycliffe version read as if it were an interlinear edition (glossing). This practice focused on writing the English text directly beneath the Latin equivalent. You can imagine the confusion in reading the English, where word order was ignored. The revised edition used common English word order. Christopher de Hamel writes, "This revised English Bible was directed at a very much wider and less learned public than the professional or even royal audiences of the earlier text."[38]

The identity of the author of the prologue is not entirely certain. Some scholars are convinced the author was the reviser of the EV and that the prologue was finished by 1395. Internal references indicate a revision of the "English Bible late translated" and the principles listed are followed by the revision. Wycliffe biographer Margaret Deanesly concludes her defense of Purvey as the author when she writes, "It is thus clear that but one person wrote the *General Prologue*, and that he edited also the second version of the Wycliffite Bible. This person was Wycliffe's secretary and literary executor, the leader of the remnant of his sect, the 'eximius doctor' John Purvey."[39]

Some manuscript evidence suggests Purvey is associated with the prologue and revised version. In the library at Trinity University in Dublin is manuscript T.C.D. MS 75, which contains the New Testament in the early

Two monograms that suggest Purvey's name is associated with Wycliffe's general prologue.
Photo: Josiah Forshall and Frederic Madden, *The Holy Bible* (1850), vol. 1, ix, lxi.

version and the prologue. The volume belonged to Purvey. While the New Testament was in the early version, the introductions to certain books of the Bible and parts supplied by a second scribe were in the revised version. Forshall and Madden discovered that these parts were in the handwriting of Purvey.[40]

At the end of Revelation a monogram resembles a kite with a tail. Inside the right loop in very small but clear letters is "ervie." The left loop forms a "J," and the right loop clearly spells "Pervie." Another leaf, also in Purvey's handwriting, contains the phrase "Christus homo factus, J. P. prosperet actus" with the "J. P." looking identical to the monogram at the end of Revelation but without the spelling in the loop of the "P." Then follows a brief harmony of the Gospels (in the same hand), followed by a Table of Lessons, the Epistles, and Gospels in calendar form. Prologues to Mark, Luke, John, and Revelation are in Purvey's handwriting and in the later version.[41]

Forshall and Madden dated the prologue to 1388. However, a statement in the prologue would suggest a date closer to 1395.

*The Thirty Seven Conclusions of the Lollards* is considered a work of Purvey or at least prepared under his editorship. Margaret Deanesly points out that long sections "are so verbally similar [to the prologue] as to render it certain that they are quotations from the one book to the other."[42]

## Popularity of the Wycliffe Bible

Not everyone embraced the arrival of a Bible in the English tongue. The English Catholic Church's opposition to a vernacular translation was predictable.[43] The authority of the priests rested solely in the church. The church's powerful hold on the laity depended on biblical ignorance. Any free use of the Bible in worship and thought signaled a deep threat to the church's authority.

The Oxford Council summoned in 1407–8 by Thomas Arundel, archbishop of Canterbury, restated the restriction of English translations. The church historian John Foxe quotes the seventh enactment:

## Contribution of a Bible Collector

Several years ago I sought to find a project that would contribute to the history and academic nature of the story of the Bible and the men who inspired it.

After extensive searching, I realized no one had ever produced an exact facsimile of the Wycliffe New Testament. Several reprints have been published since John Lewis in 1731. Lewis reprinted Purvey's version and in 1810 Henry Baber reprinted Lewis's work. In 1848, Charles Whittingham reprinted the earlier edition of Wycliffe. Otherwise, only a few New Testament portions have appeared in polyglots and in special editions. The publishing of an actual photocopy of a Wycliffe New Testament seemed to be a worthy contribution to the field of study.

The Bodleian Library at Oxford University, England, has the most extant copies of the Wycliffe translation, so I contacted them about the project. After several letters and a personal trip to Oxford to convince them of my academic qualifications, my passion for Wycliffe, my knowledge of the issues, and my motives in doing such a project, they agreed to open their priceless rare manuscript library. They even went the extra mile by assuring me they would not let another Wycliffe be produced in the future.

Instead of selecting a beautifully illuminated manuscript, I chose a small pocket-size copy. I wanted to reproduce a New Testament that was used by the man in the pew—Wycliffe's great passion in translating. I was given free access to the entire library and handled nearly all of their approximately eighty handwritten manuscripts of Wycliffe. I chose the manuscript named Rawlinson 259 (Purvey's revision, 1388) because it was a small, more readable edition suitable for the common man to tuck into his robe or his pocket.

My exact facsimile of a Wycliffe was in commemoration of the six-hundredth anniversary of Purvey's revision, an appropriate date for my contribution to collecting. In keeping with early tradition, I sold subscriptions and published the

We therefore decree and ordain, that no man, hereafter, by his own authority translate any text of the Scripture into English or any other tongue, by way of a book, libel, or treatise, now lately set forth in the time of John Wickliff, or since, or hereafter to be set forth, in part or in whole, privily or apertly, upon pain of greater excommunication, until the said translation be allowed by the ordinary of

names of the subscribers in the introduction. I contacted Kingston Photographic Services Ltd., who had photographed the 1526 Tyndale New Testament. They went to the Bodleian Library, photographed the manuscript, printed it, and had it published by International Bible Publications in Portland, Oregon.

The author's edition of a facsimile of Purvey's revision of Wycliffe's translation of the New Testament (ca. 1388). These small and popular translations were meant for the masses.

A collector's limited edition of 100 copies was produced in full-grain leather on acid-free paper and 899 in maroon buckram. To provide a low-cost edition for libraries, 1,000 copies were printed on plain white paper using a cloth binding.

A leaf from the author's facsimile of Purvey's revision of the Wycliffe New Testament (ca. 1388). While some of the Wycliffe manuscripts have illuminations, most were rather simplistic compared to Latin manuscripts of the period. **Photo: M. Brake.**

Today it is hard to imagine that men and women actually risked their lives to own and read this small Wycliffe New Testament. What a treasure it is now to have the entire Bible readily available in so many good English translations.

the place, or, if the case so require, by the council provincial. He that shall do contrary to this, shall likewise be punished as a favourer of error and heresy.[44]

Certain priests and rich men received license to own an English Bible, but anyone else possessing a Wycliffe Bible was tried as a heretic. Anytime a charge was leveled at a defendant, the first question asked by the inquisitors was, "Do you have a Bible in English, or have you memorized any portion of an English translation?" Any answer in the affirmative was a confession to an act of treason.

In spite of bitter opposition, the reading of the English Bible continued. There are today—six hundred years later—about 250 recorded copies of the Wycliffe Bible. The large number, in spite of intense Bible destructions and confiscations, testifies to the widespread distribution of the Bible during those early years.

While answers to many of the questions of the Wycliffe Bible are yet to be firmly established, several conclusions can be drawn with a degree of confidence:[45]

- The Wycliffe Bible was written by 1382 by several Lollards under the direction of John Wycliffe.
- Nicholas de Hereford clearly participated in the translation of the Old Testament.
- It seems probable that Wycliffe translated parts or most of the New Testament.
- It is possible that John Trevisa also had a hand in some of the work.
- John Purvey took up the mantle of translation at the death of Wycliffe and revised the Bible, perhaps with the help of other devotees, completing the task no earlier than 1388 and no later than 1395.

The Wycliffe Bible opened the door for the future multiplication of English translations. The Bible was now in the hands of the people.

# 3

# The Man of the Millennium

*The Triumph of the Press over the Quill*

The turn of a third millennium provided an unusual opportunity for the news media. Television, magazines, and documentaries highlighted twentieth-century milestones and romanticized the most important events of the millennium. We all stood in awe at the progress of civilization and advancement of technology in the last thousand years. Religion dominated the first millennium, but the early part of the second millennium confronted us with the beginning of scientific discovery.

Scholasticism—a Christian theology developed by scholars early in the medieval period of European history based on Scriptures and the writings of patristic fathers—started about AD 1050 and continued slowly over the next three hundred years. It found a home in cathedrals and monastic schools, which later formed the curriculum in universities. Religious influences naturally led to learning in theology rather than scientific studies. The "Doctorate" was the gold standard of education and a mark of authority and knowledge. It was not until the Renaissance that education began to shape studies in science. The foundation was laid for the technological explosion to follow.

## Religious Power Challenged

Power and authority were addictive. Fourteenth-century men who sat in seats of authority refused to share it. Clergy enjoyed their elevated positions as learned and pious leaders of the people even though they often were ignorant of biblical teachings, and their control often came from forbidding the laity to read "unauthorized" Bibles. They considered themselves the only authorities who could interpret the "will" of Scripture. Thus the Bible for many was a "forbidden book."

John Wycliffe, however, dared to challenge their authority. Wycliffe's belief in God's call to translate the forbidden book into the language of the common man set him against traditional church teachings. He reasoned,

> Wycliffe's belief in God's call to translate the forbidden book into the language of the common man set him against traditional church teachings.

Those Heretics who pretend that the laity need not know God's law but that the knowledge which priests have had imparted to them by word of mouth is sufficient, do not deserve to be listened to. For Holy Scripture is the faith of the Church.[1]

Wycliffe's overriding message was that the laity must know and obey God's Word, and he knew this could only happen by reading the Bible in the vernacular.

Even still, how could a Bible in the language of the people become available to the masses? How could this be achieved in light of its standing as a "forbidden book"?

The time was right and society was ready for what was about to happen. New ideas, the desire for spiritual revival, and the new power base of the masses could not wait for the tedious, laborious work of the copyist's quill. The Bible, now available in the vernacular for all to read, was ready for a machine that would enable widespread distribution. One hundred years after Wycliffe, a German goldsmith invented the vehicle by which Wycliffe's dream would be fulfilled. The invention of moveable type used in the printing press made possible an inexpensive Bible that could be mass produced.

A facsimile page from the *Biblia Pauperum*. The earliest printing was formed by carving the letters and images into blocks of wood. The wood was rolled with ink and pressure applied to the block as if it were a large stamp.

## From the Quill to the Press

The story of the printing press does not begin with Gutenberg and the invention of a Western printing press. The seeds of automated printing belong to the Chinese, who first invented printing in the ninth century, an art that was later imported by Europe. Wood-block illustrations and playing cards appeared in France by 1250.[2]

The earliest form of block printing surfaced at the beginning of the fourteenth century in the form of the block style as typified by the *Biblia Pauperum* (Poor Man's Bible). In a typological motif, these "Picture Bibles" supplied the unlearned preacher with pictures and a short biblical text from which he could gain material for sermons. Each *Biblia Pauperum* contained thirty-four to forty-eight scenes of New Testament incidents sandwiched between Old Testament prefigures of these New Testament events. A short explanation rested at the foot of the page.[3]

By the middle of the fifteenth century, early woodblocks and the inclusion of brief titles provided a natural transition to moveable type. When printers needed letters from a woodblock title, they were chiseled out individually and used in other blocks. Moveable type was born.

## The Man behind the Book: Johann Gutenberg

Johann Gutenberg has long been recognized as the printer of the first Bible—no later than 1456 and probably 1454–55. (Gutenberg's Bible was called "Mazarin Bible" or "42 Line Bible.") This towering monument to the craft of printing is now the most sought after printed book in the world. The romance and mystery of its production has the fascination of all bibliophiles.

Johann Gutenberg was born at the turn of the fifteenth century into a middle-class German family in Mainz. Very little is known of his early life, but apparently the family moved to Strasburg during his childhood. He was trained as a gem polisher and goldsmith, but in the mid-1430s he began some experiments in conjunction with "artificial writing." By 1437 he became involved with Ennel von der Iserin Thuere, whom he is thought to have married after being sued by her for breach of contract. Gutenberg's modest resources dwindled as he secretly worked on his invention, and by 1442 he was in debt. As one author describes the situation, "Gutenberg's inheritance was swallowed up, not by drinking, dandyism, or debauchery, but by his research work."[4] No patent laws existed to protect inventors, so most of his early work on moveable type was done in secret by trial and error.

A leaf from the Gutenberg Bible dated 1454–56. Gutenberg is credited with inventing moveable type and printing the first book in Europe—a Bible. **Photo: A. Sanchez.**

Lawsuits followed as creditors sought to collect for monies spent on presses, metal punches, molds, and lead. Gutenberg's refusal to divulge his use of money to the courts resulted in their attributing his spending to "unbridled whims."[5] In order to recoup some of his expenses, Gutenberg printed twenty-four different editions of Donatus's Latin grammar, four calendars, a German translation of a papal bull, and a missal.[6] His reputation as a printer grew, but the accompanying funds were not enough to retire his growing debt.

Gutenberg's associate Johann Fust, later a printer himself, loaned Gutenberg 800 guilders (a master craftsman earned 20 to 30 guilders per year), an amount enabling him to begin printing the Bible. By 1452 when the operation was ready for production, the 800 guilders were spent and another 800 had to be borrowed. Fust, now a partner in the printing business, demanded payment in 1455 after the Bible was printed (at least partially) but before it was sold. The total debt including interest reached 2,026 guilders. Fust, seeing a business opportunity, repossessed the press, Bibles, and shop.

Peter Schoeffer, a disciple of Gutenberg and son-in-law of Fust, joined Fust in printing from Gutenberg's press the famed *Mainz Psalter* of 1457. This volume, magnificently printed in three colors on vellum, solidified their place in printing history. After 1457 no printed document can be attributed to Gutenberg.[7] Fust and Schoeffer, however, both gained immediate international fame as printers, but eventually Gutenberg, by virtue of his association with the famous Gutenberg Bible, would be remembered as the greatest printer of all time.

## Gutenberg's Legacy

Gutenberg, destitute and forgotten, died February 3, 1468, in his native Mainz. By 1500, a mere thirty-two years after his death, Bibles from printing presses were found in seventeen European countries. Towns with presses grew to 260, and there were 1,120 printing offices. Almost forty thousand different works in various editions totaling more than ten million copies had flooded the market.[8] Clearly Gutenberg had an impact.

The Gutenberg Bible is the most beautiful piece of printing art ever produced and the most valuable printed book in the world. Hand-bound in two volumes, there were 648 pages in the first volume and 634 in the second. An illuminator handwrote the first letter of each chapter and the headings. Each copy, individually illuminated, makes every copy a unique piece of art. Gutenberg's Bible is truly a living legacy to a great man, not in his own time but in God's.

> The Gutenberg Bible is the most beautiful piece of printing art ever produced and the most valuable printed book in the world.

Because no date or printer can be found in a Gutenberg Bible, there has been some debate as to whether it was indeed Gutenberg who printed the first Bible. However, the evidence supports the traditional view that the first complete book—a Bible— was by the hands of Johann Gutenberg.

The Pierpont Morgan Library has a copy of the *Constance Missal* that they attribute to Gutenberg and believe predates the Gutenberg Bible by five years. Only three copies of the *Missal* are known to exist. Its more primitively designed letters are suggested as evidence of its earlier production. The quality of the Gutenberg Bible was such a superb example of beautiful typography, it was thought by critics to have been produced later. As a matter of fact, it is considered today to be the finest example of printing ever done. Later scholars, however, have placed the date of the *Missal* at about 1480, more than a decade after Gutenberg's death.

A 1451 Donatus's Latin grammar, *De octo partibus orationis* (*Concerning the Eight Parts of Speech*), laid modest claim to being a book printed earlier than the Gutenberg Bible. While it is quite possible some of these minor pamphlets could have been printed before the Bible, and while even Gutenberg probably printed minor works as a trial run, the Gutenberg Bible must be considered the first major book. In 1471, shortly after the death of Gutenberg, the rector of the University of Paris, Guillaume Fichet, heaped great praise upon Johann Gutenberg and credited him with the invention of printing.

The impact of printing and the rise of renowned printers of the fifteenth century resulted in society forgetting the name of Gutenberg. It took many

years before he was finally honored as the inventor of moveable type and printer of the first Bible. A German writer, Ulrich Zell, in his *Cologne Chronicle* of 1499, called attention to Gutenberg and Fust for being the first to print the Bible.[9] The first known depiction of Johann Gutenberg shows him holding a die full of letters of the alphabet in 1584. Generally speaking, Gutenberg was overlooked until the eighteenth century, but gradually he was recognized for his accomplishments. A 1750 engraving printed by Uruck U. Verlag and F. Silber celebrated his work. It depicted Gutenberg in his shop, proofing a page just off the press. This laid to rest the question of Gutenberg's accomplishment.

Printed more than five hundred years ago, the Gutenberg Bible recently began to speak for itself. In October 1982, science weighed in with its support of Johann as the printer of the first Bible.[10] A copy of the Gutenberg Bible from the collection of Doheny Memorial Library in Camarillo, California, was submitted for a scientific experiment. Physicist Tom Cahill applied a cyclotron proton accelerator to a leaf of the Gutenberg Bible. By focusing a low-intensity beam on the document and analyzing the spray of X-rays emitted after protons collide with atoms in the target, he could define the compositions of the ink and paper. Using a controlled sample of a single leaf from the University of California Riverside library, the scientists were surprised to find the composition of the ink was not the expected carbon-based type. Gutenberg had used ink with high levels of copper and lead. By developing his own formula for ink, he left a unique chemical "fingerprint."

Armed with the knowledge of the ink formula used in the Gutenberg Bible, the researchers continued their use of the cyclotron. The results of the testing far exceeded the researchers' expectations. Not only did the Bible have the same ink formula as the controlled sample, the results also supported the thesis that the ink on various pages was mixed in small amounts as the pages were printed. The ink showed slight variations in consistency. A picture emerged of the printing operation in the fifteenth-century print shop. The shop had two printing presses and six production crews, with an additional two presses added later. Pages were printed in sequence, typesetters reset plates when each page's run was completed, and after about sixty pages the soft moveable type needed to be recast.

Gutenberg's forced bankruptcy and loss of the press may support the findings of the scientific tests. The last pages of the Gutenberg Bible were printed with a carbon-based ink, not the copper and lead-based ink of Gutenberg's signature formula. The clear implication is that Gutenberg printed the first portion, and when he lost the printing press he did not provide his ink formula.

Today the forty-seven extant copies of the Gutenberg Bible are evidence of its enduring quality. Twelve are printed on vellum and the rest on paper. It is believed that there were originally about two hundred copies printed, twenty of which were on vellum. The most famous copy of the Gutenberg is called "The Mazarin" copy. The rubricator's[11] note established the latest possible date for its publication. The note reads, "This book was illuminated, bound and completed by Henry Cremer, vicar of the collegiate church of St. Stephens of Maguntum (Mainz) in the year of our Lord one thousand, four hundred and fifty-six, on the feast of the Ascension of the Glorious Virgin Mary. Thank the Lord. Alleluia."[12] May that same benediction be etched over Gutenberg's legacy of the Bible and a press to multiply it. "Thank the Lord. Alleluia."

Johann Gutenberg's careful attention to detail and technical achievement, and his desire to print an accurate and complete text, guaranteed his success. Gutenberg's contribution to printing made him *Time* magazine's "Man of the Millennium." The message of God's Word in Latin—and within a few years in other languages too—and the format for its printing now made the Bible's availability possible for all.

## Bible Printing in Transition ("The Cradle of Printing")

Between the printing of the first Bible around 1454–56 and 1500, Bibles and books were printed in several different languages. Books and Bibles printed during this time are known as "incunabula," which refers to printing in its infant stage.

The style of handwriting used by scribes in the manuscript period became the basis for the design of the printed fonts. After 1500 the letters took on a form that simplified printing and reading. It was similar to our change in the letter "a" from handwritten form "*a*" to printed form "a." Books in printed form were often looked upon with disdain

A 1985 facsimile of the Gutenberg Bible produced in France. Not only was the Gutenberg Bible the first printed book, but it is acknowledged by modern printers as one of the most beautiful books ever printed.    Photo: M. Brake.

while handwritten copies were considered superior. The incunabula helped to bridge the gap from a handwritten book to a printed book. Some have suggested that Gutenberg's obsession with printing a magnificent copy was to win over the skeptics who were devoted to the beautiful manuscript form of writing.

All printed books were formatted like the handwritten manuscripts. The detailed abbreviations used by the scribes appear in the incunabula period, a special sign language developed with marks to indicate omission of vowels, case endings, and conjunctions. These produced clean margins that framed the printed page.

> The earliest printed books did not contain title pages with title, date, or publisher.

Unlike the book you are holding in your hands, the earliest printed books did not contain title pages with title, date, or publisher. When printers began to date and sign their publications, it was placed at the end of the book in the form of a "colophon." The first colophon appeared at the end of the *Mainz Psalter* of 1457. It translates from the Latin as follows:

> The present book of Psalms, adorned with beauty of capitals, and sufficiently marked out with rubrics, has been thus fashioned by an ingenious invention of printing and stamping, and to the worship of God diligently brought to completion by Johann Fust, a citizen of Mainz, and Peter Schoeffer of Gernsheim, in the year of our Lord 1457, on the vigil of the Feast of Assumption.[13]

The fully developed title page was introduced in 1462.

Woodcuts, a means of illustrating biblical stories, had been in practice for many years. The first printed book to be illustrated with woodcuts was the Edelstein Bible that appeared at Bamberg in 1461. Although some unsuccessful attempts were made by Gutenberg to print in colored ink, it did not become common until about 1490.

The printed book emerged in its modern form with a title page bearing the author's name, title, place of printing, and date by the end of the incunabula period (1500). Each page was numbered, engraved initial chapter letters were inserted, and occasionally illuminated letters beautified its pages.

## Famed Incunabula Bibles

**The Bamberg Bible (1460)** was believed for a long time to be the first printed Bible. A fragment discovered in an old abbey in Bamberg was dated March 21, 1460.[14] This clue produced enough evidence to conclude that the Bamberg Bible was the second printed Bible. Although printed second, its rarity exceeds that of the more famous Gutenberg Bible.

**The Fust and Schoeffer Bible (1462)** was the first Bible to be presented with a date, name of printer, and place of printing. It is a large folio 11 × 15½ inches containing 481 leaves with forty-eight lines to a page, usually bound in two volumes.

Fust and Schoeffer clearly used Gutenberg's Bible for their text but used a smaller book-type more suitable for common use. Gutenberg's liturgical Gothic letter style was replaced by a type style very close to the handwriting of its designer, Peter Schoeffer. As a result of its easy-to-read style, it was the script imitated throughout Germany and Italy. The colophon with the printer's device in red was the first used by a printer and reads in English translation, "This present work was completed, and that to the honor of God, in the industrious city of Megence by John Fust, citizen, and Peter Schoeffer of Gernsheim, clerk of the same diocese, in the year of the incarnation of our Lord MCCCCLXII. On the Vigil of the assumption of the glorious Virgin Mary."[15] Some leaves of the Fust and Schoeffer Bible suggest the beginnings of experimental color printing.

Fust and Schoeffer did not escape the printing business without some of Gutenberg's financial difficulties. A few years after the successful printing of this Bible, Fust was selling a large number of printed Bibles as handwritten manuscripts in Paris. Fust's wizardry in printing led to accusations of being a magician. The red ink was seen as the blood of the devil. He was arrested, found guilty of witchcraft, and cast into prison. Later released, he became a victim of the plague in 1466.

**The Koberger Bible (1475).** The famous printer Anton Koberger produced fifteen Latin Bible editions before 1500. This 1475 edition was a folio of 481 leaves printed in double columns with forty-eight lines per page printed in beautiful deep black ink Gothic style. Koberger's emphasis on printing Bibles made him very successful. Today any of these Bibles are highly desired by collectors simply because of their beauty and the extensive use of woodcut illustrations.

It may be surprising to learn that more books were printed in the last half of the fifteenth century than were produced in all previous human history.[16] The vehicle of the printing press made possible the Reformation, the Enlightenment, and the triumph of vernacular Bibles. This new method of transmitting ideas enabled books, pamphlets, and Bibles to be printed inexpensively in great quantities.

A special incunabulum must be mentioned before we leave this period. The Golden Legend (1483) was the first attempt to print parts of the Bible in the English language. It is surprising to find that not a single Bible was printed in English in the incunabula period (1456–1500). This is very strange in light of the vast number of Wycliffe Bibles available for printing. In fact, no complete English New Testament was finished until Tyndale's work in 1525—but that story is for later. The possible heretical association with the Wycliffe

Incunabula Bibles. From left to right:
1475 The first Latin Bible printed in Venice with the original binding.
1486 The first Bible with a title page.
1491 An illuminated Froben Bible.
1497 An illustrated Bible.
1495 The Poor Man's Bible (standing right rear).
Incunabula Bibles were Bibles printed prior to the sixteenth century (1455–1500). Because Gutenberg was under pressure to print a Bible as beautiful as the handwritten manuscripts, he formed the moveable-type letters to look exactly like the handwritten ones. After 1500 the letters took on a new shape that was easier to form and place in typeset molds.    Photo: R. Maisel.

Bible among the clergy and the probations of the *Constitutions* of 1408 undoubtedly prevented printers from entering the highly charged controversy.

William Caxton imported the art of printing into England in 1475 and translated Jacobus de Voragine's *Golden Legend* into English. Instead of printing the "forbidden book," he chose the safe route by printing a surrogate of the biblical text. The popular medieval work consisted of the lives of saints from texts in Genesis, Exodus, and passages from the New Testament. It also included valuable information about the lives of many early church saints.

As popular as it was in the late fifteenth century, the English *Golden Legend* could not survive when the English New Testament came on the scene. Caxton's successor, Wynken de Worde, also issued editions of the *Golden Legend* in 1493, 1498, and several in the early sixteenth century. The last *Legend*, published in 1527, became "a quaint and long-lived relic," whose partial biblical text in English avoided the early prohibitions of Bible publishing in England.[17] Its demise was due to the availability of the complete Bible in English just one year before the last edition of 1527. However, it was the primary source of biblical teaching in print for the English-speaking world for more than forty years.

A well-developed and successful printing business at the end of the fifteenth century set the stage for the beginning of the Reformation age and its battle for the Bible. The 1492 and 1495 small quarto editions of Koberger were known as "Poor Man's Bibles." These unadorned, simply printed, and inexpensively produced volumes were for use by the layperson. Although not completely successful, the "Poor Man's Bibles" served as a transition to a Bible that would soon be available for the masses.

This period of the assembly line Bibles (1455–1500) ends the era of the beautifully

An embroidered Bible binding. Bibles became symbols that needed to be revered and beautified; therefore, bindings were also an important part of the decoration to honor God. This 1634 binding picturing King David, embroidered in silver thread, is an example of the extent to which publishers would go to make them attractive.   Photo: M. Brake.

che to gyue thankynges & praysinges to god & to this holy cofessour saynt Edwarde for these myracles & for his delyueraunce fro the thre sekenesses / Wherfore god be praysed in his seruaut wout ende. Amen.

¶Here foloweth the lyfe of saynt Luke the euangelyst. And fyrst of his name.

Luke is as moche to say as reisynge or enhausyng hymselfe / or Luke is said of lyght. He was reysynge hymself fro the loue of the worlde /& enhausynge in to the loue of god And he was also the lyght of the worlde. For he enlumyned the vnyuersall worlde by holy predicacion. And hereof sayth saynt Mathewe. Math.v. ye ben the lyght of the worlde /the lyght of the world is the sonne /& the lyght hath heyght in his sete or spege / & hereof sayth Ecclesiastes the xxvi.chapytre. The sonne rysynge in the worlde is the ryght hye thynges of god / he hath delyte in beholdynge. And as it is sayd Ecclesiastes.xi. The lyght of the sonne is swete /and it is delectable to the eyen to se the sonne. He had swyftnes in his mouynge /as it is sayd in the seconde boke of Esdre the fourth chapytre. The erthe is grete / and the heuen is hygh /and the course of the sonne is swyfte /and hath profyte in effecte. For after the phylosopher man engendreth man and the sonne. And thus Luke had hyghnesse by the loue of thynges celestyall / delectable by swete couersacyon /swyfte by feruent predycacyon / and vtylyte and profyte by conscrypcyon and wrytynge of his doctryne.

Luke was of the nacyon of Syrye and Anthyochyen by art of medycyne /& after some he was one of the lxxij dyscyples of our lorde. Saynt Jherome sayth that he was dyscyple of the apostles & not of our lorde. And the glose vpon the xxv.chapytre of the boke of Exodi sygnefyeth that he ioyned not to our lorde whan he preched /but he came to the fayth after his resurreccyon. But it is more to be holden that he was none of the lxxij.disciples /though some holde oppynyon that he was one. But he was of ryght grete perfeccyon of lyfe /& moche wel ordeyned as toward god /& as touchynge his neyghbour /as touchyng hymselfe /& as touchynge his offyce. And in sygne of these foure maner of ordynaunces he was descriued to haue four faces /that is to wyte /the face of a man /the face of a lion /the face of an oxe /& the face of an egle /& eche of these beestes had foure faces & four wynges /as it is sayd in Ezechiel the first chapytre /& bycause it may the better be seen /let vs ymagyne some beest that hath his heed foure square /& in euery square a face /so that the face of a man be tofore /& on the ryght syde the face of the lyon /& on the lyft syde the face of the oxe /& behynde the face of the egle. And bycause the face of the egle appered aboue the other for the length of the necke /therfore it is sayd that this face was aboue /& eche of these foure had foure pennes. For whan euery beest was quadrate as we may ymagyn In a quadrate ben foure corners /& euery corner was a pene. By these four beestes after the sayntes saye ben sygnefied the foure euagelystes /of whome eche of them had foure faces in wrytynge /that is to wyte /of the humanite /of the passion /of the resurreccyon & of the dyuynite /how be it these thynges be syngulerly to synguler. For after saint Jherom Mathew is sygnefyed in the man For he was syngulerly moued to speke of the humanite of our lorde. Luke was fygured in the oxe /for he deuysed about the preesthode of our lord Jesu chryst. Marke was

kk.ij.

The Golden Legend (1521) by Wynkyn de Worde. In this copy the pages containing the life of fallen Saint Thomas à Beckett were expunged. This was a common practice for those who fell out of favor with church authorities. The Golden Legend was devoted to preserving the history of saints from Old Testament and New Testament characters to church saints of the fifteenth century. This book recorded the first printed biblical texts of the Scriptures in the English language.

## Honor among Bibliophiles

A trip to the used bookstore was more than a habit among various faculty at Multnomah. Drs. Ed Goodrick, Al Baylis, Dan Scalberg, and I often took excursions to seek those treasures overlooked by other bibliophiles. It became common practice to view the shelves together, peering intently over shelf after shelf, hoping to spy the treasure first.

The person who found the treasure first got the first right of refusal to purchase it. It was not unusual for one person behind the others to suddenly spy an interesting book and aggressively reach over the others to get his hands on it in friendly competition.

It was an ordinary Friday afternoon, classes completed, and the weekend near. Several of us headed for Powell's used bookstore. In those days Powell's had a special room for rare books. We entered those "sacred" doors to a room only the most avid bibliophile could truly appreciate. High above the door was a two-volume boxed book that stood out plainly to all. Dr. Scalberg spotted it first and pointed it out. He was not a Bible collector, so he was unsure of its identity.

I calmly identified it as a 1961 Coopersquare Gutenberg facsimile. On the front cover, the price of $100 was clearly marked. We carefully examined it without much conversation. It was returned to the shelf and we continued to explore for another hour. When we were ready to leave, I casually brought to Dr. Scalberg's attention the possibility of his purchasing the Gutenberg he had spotted first. He thought for a moment, calculated its price, and refused. I quickly told the clerk I would take it. Dr. Scalberg had his chance; there is after all "honor" among bibliophiles!

hand-copied and elaborately illuminated Bibles. Beginning in the sixteenth century, Bibles were printed for the purpose of reading; they were no longer seen as sacred objects for worship. What was lost in art was gained in access. Soon the printing press would begin rolling out Bibles for everyone to read and drink from its deep well of spiritual truth. The soil was soft and tilled—ready for the seed of the Reformation.

The Reformation in England had its roots in Germany, where a young Augustinian monk had challenged the pope and his authority over the church. We will now focus on the story of this incredible Reformer.

# 4

# He Dared to Take a Stand

*The Monk Becomes a Knight*

Piercing the darkness high above the castle's wall, a flickering candle barely illuminated a small window. An inquisitive traveler was told it was the temporary residence of "Knight George." In this dimly lit room, an impatient reformer battled attacks of depression and anxiety while working diligently on his writing project. Pacing restlessly in his ten-by-fifteen-foot room, he pondered his predicament: "I know my supporters meant well when they abducted me and brought me here to the Wartburg Castle. Now living under a pseudonym, I feel I am a prisoner to my own safety. What will happen to my ministry at the church and the university in Wittenberg while I am cooped up here? I will not give in to my enemy. I will make it my purpose to fight Satan with 'ink.'"

## The New Testament in German

During his ten-month confinement at Wartburg, Martin Luther, with pen in hand, translated the New Testament into the German language of the common people from Erasmus's Greek New Testament. In Luther's mind, this spelled a major defeat for Satan.

A portrait of Martin Luther by Lucas Cranach. Contrary to popular ideas, Luther was a man of small stature. Photo: Arthur C. McGiffart, *Martin Luther: the Man and His Work*, (1911), 366.

Medieval Europe felt the perpetual nearness of death. The church stressed the fear of hell and the awfulness of a God of judgment watching over the torment of the damned. Art depicted death as a place filled with skeletons, while horrible beasts feasted on the flesh of men and women; funeral manuals detailed how to prepare for death and judgment. Christ was most commonly depicted as a victim of the horrible death by crucifixion. The church emphasized the need for penitents to show sorrow for their sins and accept the blame for Christ's death. Into this world came Martin Luther, who sensed more than most the need to show sorrow and to confess his sins.

Martin Luther was born Martin Luder to Hans (a copper miner) and Margarethe Luder, in Eisleben, Germany, in 1483. Martin's upbringing was stern and strict, not uncommon for the time. Hans saw the academic potential in Martin and set about to educate him for a lucrative law vocation.

Hans recognized the limitations of the educational system in Eisleben, so at the age of thirteen, Martin was sent forty miles away to Magdeburg. For some unknown reason Martin was later sent to Eisenach. Martin's father was not satisfied entirely with the school at Eisenach. In 1501, he decided to send Martin to an important law school at Erfurt, which was already a very famous university.

A rain storm was the catalyst to mold the life of the young Luther. During his trip from the university in Eisenach back to his home in Mansfield,

## A Monk's Vow—A Hard Life

The order of Augustinian monks was founded in Italy in the thirteenth century by hermits living in solitude. It was an order that lived in monasteries under very strict rules. The order in Erfurt, while enforcing a strict lifestyle, did enable the monks to study at the university. Only two meager meals were served daily in the monastery. This left the monks to beg on the streets for additional food. Living quarters were plain and only one room in the monastery was heated. Deprived of common comforts of everyday life, monks spent time in prayer and confession.

Salvation was never a surety. Living as a monk in a monastery was a man's attempt to be restored to the original state of grace in purity. Daily life consisted of reciting psalms, early morning prayers, daily masses, and added masses on special occasions. The long, cold winters, the boredom of daily routine, and fear of God's punishments made for a very difficult life. Luther was constantly fearful he did not merit God's mercy, and his confessions centered on his fear of God's justice. His life as a monk was exactly what he wanted, and his studies at the university provided the background for his ultimate reforming convictions.[1]

Luther encountered a lightning storm near the city of Stotternheim. A bolt of lightning struck near him and he fell to the ground. In a moment of terror he promised the patron Saint Anne, the popular saint of miners, he would become a monk. Upon his return to the university his friends encouraged him to disregard the promise, but Luther was compelled to abide by it.

Luther's entrance into a monastery (against his father's strong objection)[2] would make a drastic change in his life, from carefree student to the monastic life of deprivation in the order of an Augustinian monk.

Luther's life at the monastery in Erfurt was one of devotion and study, and the beginning of a lifetime struggle with the guilt of sin and fear of damnation. His exaggerated litany of confession and penitence became legendary. Through it all, a man of the church was developing into a servant of Christ who would change the face of Christianity not only in Europe but around the world.

It was not long before the gifted Luther would turn to teaching. Ordained in 1507, Luther put his mind to the task of learning and preaching. His lectures on medieval theologian Peter Lombard's *Sentences* and various commentaries on this central textbook began to set him apart as a teacher and lecturer. By this time Luther's soon-to-be mentor, Johann Von Staupitz, and the powerful elector, Frederick the Wise, were establishing a new university in Wittenberg. In 1508, Luther was invited to teach for a year at the new university. After one term, he returned to Erfurt for two years to fill a teaching post. He eventually returned to Wittenberg, and in 1512 he completed his doctorate and began teaching three days later. Luther's study began to take a turn from nominalism to a humanistic view.[3]

Luther's deeply spiritual struggles influenced much of his life as a devoted priest. Luther's study from 1512 to 1515 intensified his struggle with depression and the demands of God for purity. He felt under intense attack by Satan. When a medieval Christian sinned, he was compelled to confess it before a priest. If the offender was genuinely contrite, the priest would pronounce absolution and prescribe acts of satisfaction such as prayers, a pilgrimage, or other duties. With the next sin, the cycle began all over again. Luther's "war within" focused on his fear that he was not contrite enough or didn't really mean what he said when he confessed. This led Luther to hours of confession, often much to the chagrin of the priests hearing his confession.

Luther's early lectures at Wittenberg centered on his intense studies of the book of Psalms while at Erfurt. These studies led to his new appreciation of the cross of Christ. Instead of seeing Christ's death as a satisfaction of the justice of God, Luther began to see the acknowledgement of sin, suffering, and temptation as Christ's work to humble the sinner and to save him. Human works, religious activity, and wisdom had no part in the salvation process. This was the beginning of Luther's emphasis on *sola Christus* (Christ alone).

Luther's writings began to shape his Reformation theology. Sometime during this period of Luther's life he began preaching on the book of Romans. Erasmus's Greek New Testament (published in 1516) was a turning point for Luther. Prior to the Reformers, it was universally believed that "the

## A Nightmare Turns into a Fulfilled Dream

I rubbed the sleep from my eyes, vigorously blinking myself awake at 4:00 a.m. I was about to bid on a number of rare Bibles by telephone. This particular auction in New York had about fifteen Bibles listed for sale. I wanted most of them but was working under the handicap of a budget. I plotted, planned, and prioritized my wants. The plan had to be comprehensive to cover all possible scenarios. The plan took at least two days to formulate.

The day began with the first few books going to very aggressive bidders. Plan A went out the window and plan B was now in play. The next few minutes went by in a blur. Why were so many bidding so high on the Bibles that I thought were destined for my shelves? I was shocked.

The distant voice of the telephone representative bidding for me said the Bibles were finished. I was stunned; my heart sank as he wished me "better luck next time." I didn't fully appreciate his attempt at encouragement. His next question was, "Can I do anything else for you?" Pushing down my disappointment, I remembered there was an unidentified work attributed to Martin Luther listed later in the catalog. I gave him my tiny bid and sadly put the phone down.

Two weeks later I received a bill for the unidentified Luther fragment. I paused for a moment trying to recall what it was. The total was quite reasonable, so I sent off a check. When it arrived, I went to several sources from my collection to confirm its identity but couldn't find anything. Finally, in an extensive multiple-volume listing of printed books I found a single entry of two lines.

You can imagine my disbelief and rapid heartbeat when I discovered and positively identified it as a first edition of Martin Luther's translation of Psalm 119. A more perfect fit to my collection it could not be: A psalm that meditates on the excellencies of God's Word. My nightmare became a fulfilled dream—what a treasure!

righteousness of God" in Romans 1:16 meant the "justice of God."[4] God's demand for perfection required that his justice be satisfied; that meant the sinner had to pay for his sin. This led to the doctrine of purgatory and the need for penance. Luther's study from the Greek New Testament helped him come to the conclusion that God's righteousness was a gift to sinners.

The sinner possessed the righteousness that God demanded the moment he believed. The Christian does not do good works to become righteous, but because he is righteous he does good works. This was Luther's famous doctrine called *sola fide* (faith alone) in Latin.

The direct cause of the Reformation was the reaction to the sale of indulgences. Indulgences were designed to demonstrate that the penitent acknowledged his offense before God. It was a part of medieval culture and practice. When Johann Tetzel began selling indulgences outside Wittenberg, he was abusing the normal practice. Cardinal Albrecht of Brandenberg was one of the most ambitious churchmen of his time. After being elected archbishop of Magdeburg, Albrecht began to accumulate various powerful offices. He found a way to amass multiple offices (an illegal practice even then) by paying Pope Leo X fees per office.[5]

Luther's first edition of a German translation of Psalm 119 (1521). Luther's early lectures at Wittenberg centered on the book of Psalms, which directly influenced his view of Christ alone (*sola Christus*) as opposed to human works and religious activity.

A Visual History of the English Bible

In order to pay the pope, Albrecht permitted Tetzel to sell indulgences and share in the income.

The practice of the sale of papal indulgences was very inflammatory. Thinking laymen asked inquisitively, "If the pope can forgive sins, why doesn't he just forgive all sins? Why ask for any payment?" In some cases one could buy an indulgence as a prepayment for fulfilling the sinful appetite. Since Albrecht's territory did not include Wittenberg, which was the territory of Frederick the Wise, he was selling outside of Luther's town. Upon hearing of the growing abuse of the sale of indulgences, Luther set forth ninety-five articles questioning the validity of the sale of "papal indulgences." He posted the ninety-five theses on the door of the Wittenberg Church on October 31, 1517.[6] This became the signal "Reformation" cry, yet Luther had no intention to break with Rome at this point in his life.

The ninety-five theses did not create an immediate controversy, but as word spread and copies of them were printed and distributed (in Leipzig, Nuremberg, and Basel), the storm gathered.[7] Luther soon heard of the potential crisis coming and began expanding on the theses, insisting that the pope cannot forgive sins. If he could, why not just forgive all sinners without collecting the fees? The gathering storm was about to form into a tornado.

By 1521, Luther had been summoned to Augsburg, Leipzig, and Worms, not to defend the abuse of indulgences but to answer to the charge of failing to acknowledge the authority of the pope. In his debate at the Diet of Worms, he was asked to denounce all of his writings. Luther refused and he made his now-famous speech, ending with:

> Unless I am convinced by the testimony of the scriptures, or by clear reason (for I do not trust in either the pope or in councils alone, since it is well known that they have often erred and contradicted themselves), I am bound by the scriptures I have quoted and my conscience is captive to the word of God. I cannot and I will not retract anything, since it is neither safe nor right to go against conscience.[8]

Luther's responses will come as no surprise. He was a man of action. His unyielding conviction that God's authority was in the Scriptures alone (*sola*

Luther's castle home at Wartburg where he penned his translation of the New Testament.
Photo: D. Lockwood.

A rare 1883 German facsimile of Luther's September New Testament (1522).

Scriptura) would soon lead to his most important writing, the translation of the Greek New Testament into the common language of the German people. The common thread among the Reformers was their intense belief that the authority of God was expressed in God's Word, not through church canon or papal dictates, and every man, woman, and child must be able to read it in their own language.

The length of Luther's life was now in question. Luther left Worms with the promise of papal protection but under an edict of condemnation as a heretic. His life was now subject to anyone who would do the pope a favor by executing him. In the middle of the night, as Luther was on his way back to Wittenberg, he was kidnapped by a band of followers and taken to Wartburg Castle just outside Eisenach. A prisoner for his own protection, in the following ten months this condemned heretic translated the New Testament. The common German, armed with a Bible he could read and understand, was now ready for the greatest spiritual battle of the sixteenth century.

# 5

# The Fire of Devotion

*The Plowman Reads the Bible*

The fifteenth century slept. It was as if the church in Europe was waiting for Prince Charming to revive her from a century of hibernation and impotency. The Renaissance was in the midst of giving birth to the modern world. The church was still suffering from the Great Schism that had divided the seat of authority of the pope and the church. Monarchs challenged her power, the Lollards (followers of Wycliffe) defied her claims, and the faithful questioned her ability to reform.

The medieval church, unwilling to accept the reforms of Wycliffe and the Bohemian reformer John Huss, resisted the emergence of a middle class, and when aided by the failure of land reform, a sixteenth-century reformation was inevitable.

## The Legacy of the Sixteenth Century

After all this, there was no common language Bible for the person in the pew. Prior to the Renaissance, the Bible of Western Europe was Jerome's fourth-century Latin Vulgate. It was a book the priests could have, but to the people, it was a still a "forbidden book." The authority of the church depended on laity ignorance of biblical teaching. Out of the corruption of scriptural teaching and the personal decadence of fifteenth-century Christianity came the birth of the new movement that was to change the form of the Christian faith forever. The printing press was the instrument that made possible the wide distribution of affordable copies of Scripture. Once the Bible was available, the flames of Reformation were unquenchable.

The Renaissance accentuated the study of the Scriptures in the original languages. The Protestant Reformation emphasized the authority of Scripture, personal piety, and scholarship. Reformers firmly believed that without the knowledge of the Word of God, it was impossible to live a pious and faithful life. The theological temperament and academic climate was ready for the fruit to be gleaned from the work of the intrepid and scholarly translator, William Tyndale.

It may seem strange that for more than fifty years after the invention of moveable type, no Greek New Testament had been printed. The absence of the forbidden English Bible is understandable, but there was no printed Greek New Testament either. That was about to change. Greek learning remained the domain of the Eastern Church until the fall of Constantinople (1453). When the Turks took control of this center of learning, scholars fled to the West and with them came the resurgence of the Greek language.

Both the emphasis on the interpretation of Scriptures,[1] now available to all, and the rebirth of Greek language studies brought great promise for a resurgence of a

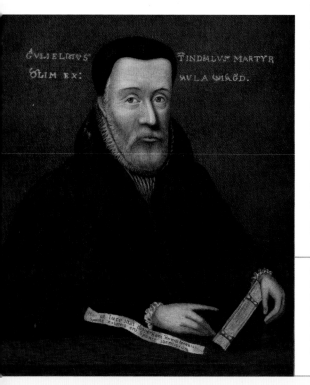

An anonymous portrait of William Tyndale. Tyndale translated the first Bible into English from the Greek New Testament. Wycliffe translated the first Bible into English from the Latin. Whereas Wycliffe's translation was handwritten, Tyndale's was from the printing press. Photo: George Offor, *The New Testament* (Editors Extra Illustrated Copy) (1836), 98.

reformed Christianity. The recipients of this new academic climate were the pre-reformer and able humanist Erasmus of Rotterdam and a Roman Catholic priest and scholar, Ximenes of Alcala, Spain.

Cardinal Ximenes edited the first printed Greek New Testament in his massive six-volume multilingual Bible in 1514. His carefully edited Greek New Testament was not published until 1520. It could have been the standard for years to come except for the work of Johann Froben, an enterprising publisher who wanted to be the first to publish a New Testament in Greek.

A modern businessperson will not be surprised that an entrepreneur would emerge to fill the economic gap. Johann Froben, an opportunist, employed Desiderius Erasmus to edit a Greek New Testament after receiving word or rumor of Ximenes's project. In 1515, Erasmus began searching for manuscripts of sufficient quality to be typeset. Since the project required the utmost haste, Erasmus did not take the time to find a complete manuscript of the Greek New Testament. After all, these manuscripts were hand copied centuries before and were quite rare even in the sixteenth century. With approximately five manuscripts in hand, he began the task of editing. When

parts of the text were indecipherable, Erasmus used the Latin text and translated it back into Greek. Oddly, several of his renderings do not appear in any known Greek manuscript, and yet are still used in some modern translations.

Although Erasmus's text appeared to be inferior in quality to the one produced by Ximenes, it gained early dominance because it was published in 1516, four years before Ximenes's *Complutensian* (1520). With the Greek text available to the English

A portrait of Erasmus of Rotterdam by G. Penn. Erasmus was the first to print a Greek New Testament in 1516, just ten years before Tyndale translated the first New Testament from Greek into English.   Photo: W. J. Heaton, *The Bible of the Reformation* (1913), 5.

A picture of Tyndale imprisoned in Vilvorde in 1536. Henry Phillips befriended Tyndale with the express purpose of betraying him to the authorities. Tyndale was arrested and imprisoned. While in prison he asked for his Hebrew Bible and dictionary, so it is believed he translated some of his unpublished Old Testament. **By permission: J. Hellstern.**

scholar, it was the moment for the greatest English biblical scholar of the Reformation. So we turn next to his amazing story—a story of tireless work and ultimate sacrifice.

### William Tyndale: "The Fire That Could Not Consume"

Time passed slowly for the condemned "heretic." He waited with measured anxiety for the hour the sticks would be laid at his feet and the flames would consume his garments and devour his flesh. This forty-year-old man tried not to ponder his plight. He had witnessed threats, torture, and even death for anyone who dared read his translation of God's Holy Word. Was it not God's grace that would soon call on him to stand for what others had triumphantly endured?

William Tyndale's thoughts were rudely interrupted by a growling, vulgar prison guard. "Why do you waste your 'bleep, bleep' time with those books and that writing project? The 'bleeping' gallows await you. Prepare to meet your Maker," he said in a condescending tone. Tyndale was ever ready to give reason for the hope that was in him and calmly laid out the gospel message to this angry and lost soul. It was not long until the young, violent jailer calmed down and came to the realization that this avid Bible reading and pious prisoner was no ordinary criminal. Tyndale looked calmly into the eyes of the troubled jailer and then, as if an angel stood in his presence, continued to explain to his captor the values of eternity. Finally, in the wee hours of the morning, exhausted but fulfilled, Tyndale fell asleep.

These were times that threatened the survival of the Reformation and the "forbidden" Bible. Tyndale, though locked away in prison for nearly a year, knew that the Bible in the language of the people was the only way faith could survive such perilous times. Foxe writes, "I [Tyndale] defy the pope, and all his laws; and further added, that if God spared him life, ere many years he would cause a boy that driveth the plough, to know more of the Scripture than he [the pope] did."[2]

The story of William Tyndale has long been neglected in the church and in modern historical studies. Shakespeare gets much attention, but Tyndale's contribution to literature and the Bible in particular remains unappreciated in many circles. Sometime between 1493 and 1495, William Tyndale[3] was born to a simple Welsh family in Stinchcombe, Gloucestershire. He matriculated at Oxford University in 1510 and completed his master of arts in 1515. He continued his studies at Cambridge for another six to seven years where the influence of Erasmus's Greek studies prevailed.

Tyndale himself rejected most biblical and theological studies taught at the universities. The revival of Hebrew and Greek stirred English scholarship to a new appreciation for the study of the Bible—but still it languished in dark oppression to the "sacred" Latin Bible. Many of the religious teachers were considered "apostles of ignorance." Tyndale's words are biting:

> And in the Universities they have ordained that no man shall look at the scripture, until he be noselled in heathen learning eight or nine years, and armed with false principles; with which he is clean shut out of the understanding of the scripture. . . . And when he taketh first degree, he is sworn that he shall hold none opinions condemned by the Church; but what such opinions be, that he shall not know. And then, when they be admitted to study divinity, because the scripture is locked up with such false expositions, and with false principles of natural philosophy, that they cannot enter in, they go about the outside, and dispute all their lives about words and vain opinions, pertaining as much unto the healing of a man's heel, as health of his soul.[4]

He became a scholar of the original Bible languages, an effective speaker, and a man determined to advocate the rights of common people to explore Scripture in their own language.

## The Birth of the English Vernacular Bible

The story begins a few years before Tyndale's work was introduced to the world. John Colet, humanist and theologian, came to England about 1496 and began lecturing in Latin on Paul's epistles.[5] His literal method of interpretation and direct appeal to the words of Paul brought a new vigor to the universities and to the young scholars. His position as dean of St. Paul's Cathedral in London gave him a bully pulpit upon which he gladly began a new movement. The older scholars looked on with skepticism and often accused him of heresy. However, his teachings began to stir the intellectual youth and soon found fertile soil in Thomas More and Erasmus of Rotterdam.

Scholars began to study Scriptures for what their authors said. Church corruption and the belief that church custom and practice could not measure up to the higher standards of a New Testament soon became a threat to the dominance of the "Sacred Vulgate." English Bible readers refused to blindly accept the statements of former interpreters as the traditional scholastic method demanded. Once again the Bible was viewed as the Word of God.

The English Reformation was under way. Tyndale was convinced of his mission in life and had boldly abandoned the traditional theology without a whimper. Every truth was analyzed in light of Scripture—not in light of past customs or scholars' opinions. Even at this early stage, one can anticipate the end that must meet such an uncompromising and principled man as William Tyndale; it could only be in the hangman's hand.

The story of England's failure to support an English Bible continues with

Tyndale. England's religious turmoil and the enemies of reform abounded. Tyndale realized it would be impossible to translate the Bible in England. It had been more than a century since the enactment of the *Constitutions* at Oxford in 1408 forbade the reading of any non-approved English Bible. Neither Bishop Tunstall nor Cardinal Wolsey[6] made any attempt to authorize the reading or translating of any Bible other than the Latin. The bishops were

Engraving by H. Holl of Cardinal Wolsey.  Photo: George Offer, *The New Testament* (1836), 47.

unrelenting in their attempts to enforce the *Constitutions*. Yet no religious authority stepped forward to improve on Wycliffe's revision of 1388/95.

Tyndale had two choices. He could remain in London and wait for better days or leave his beloved England and translate elsewhere. His enthusiasm and burden to see even the plowboy have the Scriptures in his language dictated against postponement. The only option was to set sail for Germany. After all, Germany was a hotbed of reformation and there he could find sympathizers and proceed unhindered in his work.

Tyndale arrived in Hamburg, Germany, in the midst of Luther's Reformation in May 1524.[7] Indulgences, or certificates of forgiveness, were no longer sold in public, disgruntled priests deserted their religious orders, and mass gave way to the Lord's Supper. People were even reading the Bible in the German language followed by theological discussion of the current issues of the day. What a contrast to Tyndale's England! No wonder Tyndale abandoned his beloved but troubled London. His place in history was now assured.

> People were even reading the Bible in the German language followed by theological discussion of the current issues of the day.

Some zealous scholars, fearful that Tyndale may have leaned too heavily on Luther, deny that Tyndale ever met him. However, little question remains among most scholars that Tyndale did visit Luther in Wittenberg. Foxe insists that Tyndale went to Germany and met not only with Luther but also with "other learned men."[8] It was while living in Wittenberg, where the university provided all the necessary scholarly tools, that Tyndale translated all or most of the New Testament. Tyndale certainly consulted the New Testament Luther had translated into German. It does not follow, however, that Tyndale's New Testament was an English translation of Luther's German New Testament. Tyndale was probably more competent in Greek and Hebrew than Luther, and his German was limited. No doubt the fear of reducing Tyndale's work to a mere translation of Luther has led some people to deny Tyndale's association with Luther.[9]

No fear or physical threats could sidetrack this determined man of God. Tyndale returned to Hamburg in April 1525 after spending a year in Wittenberg. Sometime in August, he made his way to Cologne, where Peter

Quentel began printing his New Testament. After Quentel had completed about ten sheets (eighty quarto pages), the city senate, upon learning of its production, forbade the work to continue.[10] Tyndale, having been warned of possible harm, fled to Worms with the sheets that contained portions of Matthew. The sheets and the manuscript of the rest of the New Testament were taken to Peter Schoeffer, son of the fifteenth-century printer, to be printed.

Scholars believe an enemy of reform, John Cochleaus, who at the same time was living in Cologne using Quentel to print some of his own works, discovered Tyndale's project. The secret was soon out and Tyndale had to flee Cologne. William Roye may have been the culprit with loose lips. Roye was Tyndale's secretary while translating the New Testament. He was known for occasional indiscretions and was later rebuked by Tyndale.

The earlier Tyndale edition of eighty pages in quarto (1525) was abandoned for the octavo edition, perhaps due to the inability to match the type set of the previous edition or the absence of notes in the Cologne printing. The eighty pages of the Cologne edition contained the book of Matthew through chapter 22, verse 12a only. While some spelling differences separate the editions, the translation is the same. The quarto had extensive notes, some of which are nearly identical to Luther's work. The notes were omitted

The title page to the Gospel of Matthew from Tyndale's partially printed 1525 New Testament. This is a reprint edited by Edward Arber in 1871. This translation was printed with many notes in Cologne, Germany, by Peter Quentel. Known as the Grenville fragment, this incomplete New Testament contains eighty quarto leaves. Being warned by friends of an impending raid and destruction of his work, he fled to Worms where it was completed without the notes in 1526.

in the Worms printing, possibly to cut costs or maybe because Tyndale decided not to encourage readers to rely on the notes but rather to focus on the text itself. Or, it could have been from fear that controversy over the content of the notes might detract from the Testament's acceptance; the notes were thoroughly Lutheran.

In Tyndale's Cologne printing, he chose to follow a practice begun by Luther (1522) in separating Hebrews, James, Jude, and Revelation from the rest of the New Testament books. This practice did not survive in modern translations. Luther's New Testament reflected his view that these four books did not have the same canonical authority as the rest of the New Testament. This does not suggest that Tyndale held to the same canonical view, but simply that he followed this practice begun by Luther. This provides further evidence that he had a copy of Luther's German translation before him. The Great Bible of Coverdale (1539) standardized the order of books as we have them today.

England must bear the responsibility once again for failing to be the home of an English Bible translation. The first printed New Testament in the English language was completed in Worms in 1526 in a small octavo edition. The completion of the entire New Testament signaled a new problem for the English church hierarchy. Bishop Cuthbert Tunstall of London feared Tyndale's translation. In October 1526, Bishop Tunstall, the champion defender of the *Constitutions*, began confiscating the New Testaments as they were smuggled into England. Public burnings of the copies and punishment of all offenders blackened the spirits of the masses.

A popular story tells how Tunstall began using merchants to purchase copies on the Continent to slow down the supply. Augustine Packington, a London businessman, was one such merchant. Packington met with Tyndale to inform him of the plot, believing that the bishop had overstepped his prerogative. To his surprise, Tyndale met the news with enthusiasm. He encouraged Packington to do as Tunstall commanded. Tyndale felt the burning of "God's Word" would gain popular condemnation, and the profits from the sale could enable him to relieve his debt and provide for future revisions.[11]

Tunstall's plot for destruction utterly failed. New Testaments continued to pour into England, and the demand increased at an alarming rate. In fact, pirated copies were circulating and selling in England with very little fear of consequences. Tyndale had a "London Times" bestseller on his hands!

## The New Testament in English

Would a Tyndale translation suffer from the strict grammatical literalness that afflicted the Wycliffe New Testament? Tyndale was gifted in the use of the English language both in expression of the simple Anglo-Saxon

An anonymous portrait of the bishop of London, Cuthbert Tunstall. The *Constitutions* of 1408 forbade the translation of the Bible into English without proper authority. Tyndale approached Tunstall for permission but was denied.
Photo: George Offor, *The New Testament* (1836), 25.

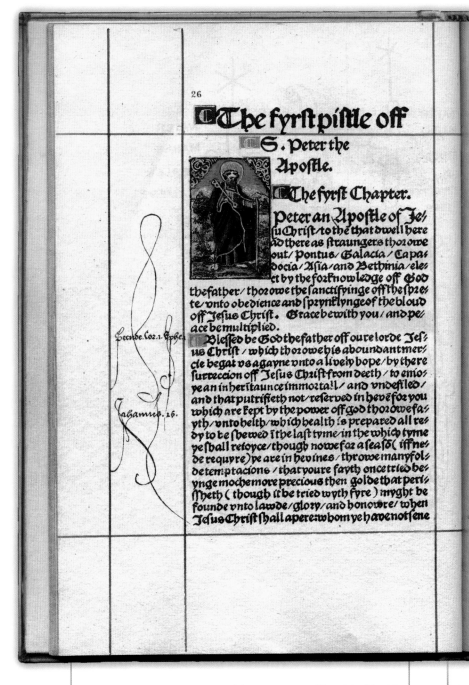

26

# The fyrst pistle off
### S. Peter the Apostle.

### The fyrst Chapter.

Peter an Apostle of Jesu Christ/to the that dwell here and there as straungers thorowe out/ Pontus/ Galacia/ Capadocia/ Asia/ and Bethinia/ elect by the forknowledge off God the father/ thorowe the sanctifyinge off the sprete/ vnto obedience and sprynklynge of the bloud off Jesus Christ. Grace be with you/ and peace be multiplied.

Secunde Cor. 1. Ephe.

Blessed be God the father off oure lorde Jesus Christ/ which thorowe his aboundant mercie begat vs agayne vnto a lively hope/ by there surreccion off Jesus Christ from deeth/ to enioye an inheritaunce immortall/ and vndefiled/ and that putrifieth not/ reserved in heve for you which are kept by the power off god thorowe fayth/ vnto helth/ which health is prepared all redy to be shewed i the last tyme in the which tyme ye shall reioyce/ though nowe for a seaso ( iffnede requyre) ye are in hevines/ throwe manyfolde temptacions / that youre fayth once tried beynge moche more precious then golde that perissheth ( though it be tried wyth fyre ) myght be founde vnto lawde/ glory/ and honoure/ when Jesus Christ shall apere: whom ye have not sene

Abamus. 16.

An exact facsimile of the original Tyndale New Testament. The original Tyndale New Testament was printed in Worms, Germany, in 1526 and is the first edition of the complete New Testament. These forbidden handheld-size New Testaments were smuggled into England in bales of cloth, confiscated upon entry, and publicly burned.   Photo: Francis Fry, *The first New Testament Printed in the English Language* (1862), 26.

vocabulary and his use of syntax. David Daniell lists several expressions that have become a part of the modern English language: "Blessed are the poor in Spirit," "I am the good shepherd," and "Fight the good fight of faith." Daniell continues,

> He had a complete understanding of the complex art of rhetoric. His twin achievements as a translator, still admired, were accuracy and clarity, the latter allowing him variety of expression. Feeling himself free not to use the same English word every time for the same word in the Hebrew or Greek (a method labeled in the late twentieth century "formal correspondence"), he made his own meaning-for-meaning translations (lately labeled "functional equivalence").[12]

It was not a forgone conclusion that an English Bible would result in royal sanction. By 1530, Tyndale had translated the Psalms and the Pentateuch, and George Joye had translated Isaiah, Jonah, and other Old Testament books. With the financial and circulation successes of the 1526 edition, Tyndale was encouraged to revise the New Testament in 1534. The political climate in England was changing. Henry VIII had a severe falling out with the pope, Thomas More had resigned as chancellor on ethical and moral grounds, and Thomas Cromwell was well on his way to finding favor in Henry's eyes. Cromwell advocated the reading of the Bible in English. This good fortune would ultimately bring about the triumph of the English Bible and its official licensing by the king. A new day was dawning.

It will come as no surprise that Tyndale, the perfectionist, was not satisfied with his first attempts at translation. Revisions were inevitable, and his 1534 edition was his finest work. It was a small octavo edition of about four hundred pages with Tyndale's name appearing on it for the first time. Two prefaces occupy a fairly large section of the work. The first is a treatise emphasizing faith, while the second is a rather scathing rebuke to George Joye, who had taken on himself a revision of Tyndale's work.

A colleague of Tyndale, George Joye took the liberty of revising Tyndale's New Testament and penning his own name to the work. Joye's revision was totally unacceptable to Tyndale, who spoke in no uncertain terms of his displeasure. Tyndale was upset with Joye for distributing his version and taking

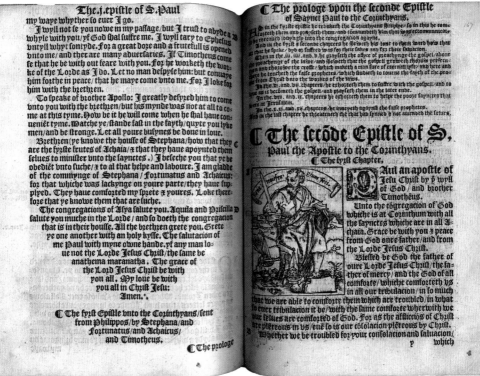

The last edition of Tyndale's New Testament published before his death in 1536. It is known as the Blankstone copy (for a woodcut depicting St. Paul standing on a stone with no lettering, hence "blankstone").

personal credit for it. Tyndale suggested Joye should do his own translation and not tinker with his work. His statement is short and terse, "[I do not want others to] take my translations and labors, and change and alter, and correct and corrupt at their pleasures, and call it their own translations, and put to their own names, and not to play boo peep after George Joye's manner."[13] The revision also contained prefaces to the various books of the New Testament.

Only one fragment of the 1525 Cologne printing survives today. Two copies of the 1526 Worms printing are accounted for: one resides at St. Paul's Cathedral Library, missing seventy-one leaves, and the other is a complete copy missing only the title leaf. It was recently purchased from the Bristol Baptist College by the British Library for a reported one million pounds. An American group is said to have attempted to purchase it at a greater price but was denied an export license. The irony of ironies is that in 1526 it was denied entry into England, and in 1993 it was denied an exit permit! (Recently a third complete copy was found in a German library.)

Tyndale's last revision in his lifetime was in 1535.[14] This edition became the basis of the primary edition of the English Bible known as the Matthew's version of 1537. In 1536, the same year of Tyndale's death, several New Testaments were printed in Antwerp and at least one in England.

## "Lord, open the King of England's eyes"

Tyndale must have suspected his life on earth was to be cut short. He lived in Antwerp for the closing years of his life. His enemies were denied access to him while he lived outside of England. Antwerp, however, was under the jurisdiction of Charles V, a staunch Roman Catholic. An accusation of heresy would be more acceptable to Catholic Charles than any other charge. Tyndale found safe haven while staying with Thomas Poyntz in Antwerp. Poyntz was a relative of the Walsh family, Tyndale's home-away-from-home in Little Sodbury where Tyndale may have begun his original translation of the New Testament. The room preserved today, as it was in the sixteenth century, is in the hands of a private homeowner.

With so many enemies it was inevitable that they would eventually get the upper hand. On May 21, 1535, betrayed by trusted friend Henry Phillips, Tyndale was kidnapped by the king's officers and imprisoned in Vilvorde near Brussels.[15] By now Thomas Cromwell and Henry VIII held some sympathy for an English translation and had made token attempts earlier to intervene on his behalf.[16] But Charles V, the nephew of Henry's recently divorced wife, Catherine of Aragon, was in no mood to accommodate Henry.[17]

One of England's most important personalities was about to finish the race. In August 1536 Tyndale was found guilty of heresy. On October 6, 1536, Tyndale, the most important reformer of the English church, was tied to a stake, strangled, and burned. Tyndale's final words at the stake were, "Lord, open the King of England's eyes." Little did he know that not only did his prayer open the king's eyes, but all of England was soon to have open eyes.

Tyndale's prayer from the flames of martyrdom sealed Henry's change of mind for sanctioning a Bible in the English Language. With Henry's recent support of an authorized translation of the English Bible and permission for the Bible to be printed in England, the flames of desire for Bible reading would never be quenched. England's eyes were finally opened, and though they would blink occasionally, be glassy-eyed perhaps, and be even impaired at times, they would never again be blinded by the lack of an English Bible to read. In addition to a royally sanctioned and authorized Bible, Tyndale's New Testaments were nearly always printed in inexpensive small quartos, octavos, duodecimos, and sextodecimos,[18] which were easily transported (or hidden), meaning that the Tyndale New Testament officially passed from the pulpit to the people.

Imagine for a moment the sixteenth-century world and the way Tyndale related to it. He began as a commoner who gradually became a major voice ringing throughout the courts, the manors, and the huts of the lower classes. A hero to those wanting reformation and a rogue to the religious hierarchy, he finally became a martyr whose death shook the foundation of English religious society. In his short lifetime, the Bible was no longer only to be read by priests and clergy, but also by the man behind the plow.

## The Juggler and the Spoiler

It was late in the evening when a juggler entered the sixteenth-century market place. Known for his "devilish" magical arts, he claimed to be able to set a banquet table complete with food and wine just by waving his hands wildly. His "reputation" had preceded him. The market filled with inquisitors gathered around the open air table to witness this magician at work. Word of the spectacle reached a curious young scholar, so with books tucked under his arm he rushed to the scene. The juggler began his incantations with "wanton boldness" until his face was as red as a beet and the veins in his neck protruded to alarming size. Finally, sweating and toiling with nothing happening and his enchantments void, he openly confessed that "some man present disturbed my powers." John Foxe who records the story gives credit to Tyndale for being that "some man."[19]

The picture we have of Tyndale is one of a tireless scholar, an uncompromising churchman, and a fearless advocate for the common man's right to explore Scripture in his own tongue. His life and death are a testimony of a man who lived by the unwavering conviction of the Bible in the language of the plow man.

The accuracy and easy-to-read-style of the King James Version of 1611 dwarfed the work of all previous translations. And yet, the work of William Tyndale should be valued as the greatest influence on English translations and its language. Tyndale's use and command of the English language had a positive influence on the works of Shakespeare. Even the famous translators of the 1611 King James Version relied heavily upon the work of Tyndale. It has been estimated that 80 to 90 percent of the King James Version is the direct expression of Tyndale. He was—and is today—without peer.

### Events in the Courageous Life of William Tyndale

1494  Born in Stinchcombe, Gloucestershire (Latin name: Guillaume Hytchins)

1509  Henry VIII ascended to the throne of England (1509–1547)

do it not for any dutye to him, but onely for peace sake, what should I speake here of my dayly reuenues, of my first fruits, annates, palles, indulgences, bulles, confessionals, inhabited and rescripts, testaments, dispensations, priuileges, elections, prebends, religious houses, and such like, which come to no small masse of money? In somuch that for one palle to the Archb. of Mentz, which was wont to be geuen for x.thousand, now it is growen to xxvij. thousand florence, whiche I receiued of Iacobus the Archbyshop not long before Basill Councell: Besides the fruites of other Byshoprickes in Germany, comyng to the number of fifty, wherby what vantage cometh to my coffers, it may partly be coniectured. But what should I speake of Germany, when the whole world is my Diocesse, as my Canonistes do say, and all men are bounde to beleue. 220. except they will imagine (as the Manches do) two begynnynges, whiche is false and hereticall. For Moses sayth: In the begynnyng God made heauen and earth, and not in the begynnynges, 221. wherfore as I begon, so I conclude, commaundyng declaryng and pronouncyng, to stand vpon necessitie of saluation, for euery humane creature to be subiect to me.

*Marginal notes:*
218. Ex lib 6a. iuxta nationis Germanica.
Moue stile bye Prophetes in Germany.

Æneas Syluius.
219. Sext Decret. De penis.cap.Falicis in Glofa.
Ité.De priuilegijs c. Autoritaté in Glofa.
220. Pope Bonifacius.8.Ext. De Maio.& obed.c. Vnam sanctam.
221. Ibid.

*The end of the first Volume of the Booke of Martyrs.*

*A liuely picture describyng the weight and substaunce of Gods most blessed word, agaynst the doctrines and vanities of mans traditions.*

Iustice.

*AT LONDON*
Printed by Iohn Daye, dwellyng ouer
Aldersgate beneath Saint Martins.

*Anno. 1576.*

*Cum gratia & Priuilegio Regiæ Maiestatis.*

This is the final leaf of Foxe's *Acts and Monuments* (popularly known as *Foxe's Book of Martyrs*) displaying the scales of justice balancing God's Word against the traditions of man (1576). John Foxe (1516–87) was an English martyrologist who was exiled during Mary's bloody reign and returned to England when Protestant Elizabeth I took the throne. His work *The Acts and Monuments* recorded the many atrocities of history, possibly exaggerated at times.

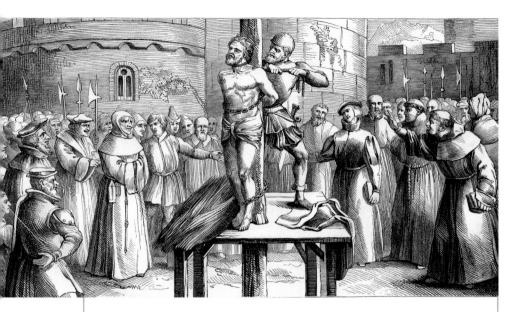

An engraving of William Tyndale's execution. Tyndale was strangled and burned at Vilvorde in October 1536. His final words from the gallows were, "Lord, open the King of England's eyes."
Photo: John Foxe, *Acts and Monuments* (1848), vol. 5, 127.

1512 Bachelor of Arts from Hertford College, where he honed his Latin skills.

1515 Master of Arts from Oxford University and introduction into Lollard theology.

1516 Cambridge—immersion in Lollard movement and continuing studies.

1521 Henry VIII given the title of Defender of the Faith by the Pope.

1522 Little Sodbury—tutor to children of John Walsh and wife Anne (Poyntz); makes vow to translate Scripture into English for the "boye that dryveth the plough."

1523 London—meets with Cuthbert Tunstall seeking permission to translate Scripture into English (1408 *Constitutions* had forbidden translating the Bible into English without permission).

1524 Hamburg, Germany—seeks asylum and freedom to translate; begins life of exile.

1525 Cologne, Germany—learned German in Wittenberg, Luther country. Translated "Cologne Fragment" and paid Peter Quentell to print New Testament (only a portion of Matthew and perhaps some of Mark were completed). The translation of the following words brought condemnation from the Roman Catholics: church—congregation; priest—elder or senior; charity—love; do

## The Real Prize

Only one extant copy of a complete Tyndale 1526 New Testament was thought to exist. However, a few years ago another copy was found in a German library simply marked "Bible." I was happy with my 1552 Tyndale—until I saw a 1536 edition (while not a first edition, it was printed during Tyndale's lifetime) for sale in an auction in New York. The price was a great deal more than I had or could borrow. I called a respected dealer friend and alerted him to the upcoming sale and my opinion that it could go for less than the projected price. Several bidders I knew who could buy it had not made a recent purchase, so I believed that they might not be aware of the sale. I waited for the news.

Very early in the morning two days later I got a call. He simply said, "I got it." My heart raced. I asked him the price, and the price was indeed fantastic. I asked him how much he was going to ask for it. He told me he would let *me* have it for 10 percent over his price if I could buy it within forty-eight hours. After that, he would double the price and offer it to other collectors. I was elated—but wait, I didn't have any money.

I let my mind run wild with possible scenarios under which I could potentially buy such a treasure. I thought of a California friend and collector who would have the resources for such a purchase. Was there some way I could trade him some of my Bibles for enough cash to buy the 1536 Tyndale? But how could I possibly part with anything? I decided to offer him my 1552 Tyndale and a first edition King James Version. That was probably overkill since the value of those two was more than necessary. However, I have always felt if I really wanted something, I would make an offer that the seller couldn't refuse—and I really wanted that Tyndale.

I called him and gave him my "pitch." At first he was skeptical, thinking that I was getting the best deal. I explained the whole situation as straightforwardly and clearly as I could. As a businessman he knew he had me dancing on a string. His counter was to add a leather fourteenth-century Hebrew manuscript written on the skin of a red calf that he knew I had just acquired. I had not planned on including such a wonderful and rare piece.

The next thing that happened can only be explained if you understand a collector's "twisted" mind. The price was just too steep! It didn't make any sense but I acted anyway—I fired my answer back without a moment's hesitation: "I'll take it." He responded just as quickly, "I'll send the check today." We both got what we wanted, a win-win. I was so excited I could hardly dial the phone to tell my dealer friend I had the money. Once I reached him I assured him the check was "in the mail" and as soon as I got it I would pass it on. That is the importance I put on having a Tyndale of 1536, the year he was burned at the stake. With a New Testament whose date was contemporary with the translator in my pocket, I knew I had the "real" prize.

penance—repent. Printing in Cologne led to discovery and threats of confiscation of printed pages, forcing him to flee to Worms.

1526 New Testament printed at Worms (Lutheran stronghold) by Peter Schoeffer.

1526 Henry VIII declared his interest in Anne Boleyn.

1527 Marburg—city ruled by the Lutheran, Philip of Hesse, provided a brief safe-haven.

1528 Tunstall began six-month campaign to arrest Lollards, Lutherans, and those reading Tyndale Bibles.

1528 Tyndale writes *Parable of Wicked Mammon*.

1528 Published *The Obedience of a Christian Man*.

1529 Hamburg—sanctuary where he spent most of the year translating the Pentateuch.

1529 Packington began to buy Tyndale New Testaments for Tunstall to burn in England.

1529 Wolsey surrendered his official office for not accepting Henry's marriage to Anne.

1529 Thomas More became Lord Chancellor of England, the highest office in England.

1530 Antwerp—first verified address since Little Sodbury. Stayed with Thomas Poyntz, relative of Anne Poyntz Walsh. To protect his work and maintain his anonymity, van Hoochstraten published his translation of the Pentateuch rather than the stated Hans Luft of Marburg.

1530 Published *Practice of Prelates* (emphasis on kings over priests).

1530 Wolsey charged with high treason and died as a sick man.

1530 Thomas Cromwell became Vicar General (a powerful position under Henry VIII).

1531 Henry VIII to be supreme head of church, both king and pope.

1533 January, Henry and Anne married; in April Anne was proclaimed queen.

1534 Tyndale revised his New Testament and published it in Antwerp.

1535 May 21 Tyndale betrayed by Henry Phillips and imprisoned in Vilvorde, suburb of modern Brussels.

1536 Tyndale strangled and burned at the stake; Tyndale's "Blankstone" edition printed.

1536 May 19 Anne is executed and eleven days later Henry married Jane Seymour.

# 6

# A Political Pastor Struggles in Exile

## *The Pastor Survives and His Psalms Endure*

William Tyndale's incarceration and subsequent execution in 1536 prevented him from translating the entire Bible. That task awaited another scholar and disciple of Tyndale: Miles Coverdale. Tyndale, the fiery martyr, paved the way for the approval of an English Bible; but it was left to Coverdale, the ever politically astute and mild-mannered scholar, to bring the Bible to every church in England.

As a poet has said, "Immortals never come alone." The work of the immortal William Tyndale might have passed into obscurity had it not been for the politically savvy and capable Miles Coverdale, a Yorkshire man born about 1488 in the home province of John Wycliffe. Educated as an Augustinian monk at Cambridge, Coverdale was admitted to the priesthood in 1514. By 1528 Coverdale abandoned his priestly habit, left his Augustinian order, and embraced Lutheranism.

Coverdale, like Wycliffe and Tyndale before him, believed everyone should have the Scriptures for their own study. He writes, "Sure I am that there cometh more knowledge and understanding of the Scriptures by their sundry translations than by all the glosses of our sophistical doctors."[1]

Coverdale was also a highly regarded preacher. John Hooker of Exeter, a servant of Coverdale, writes of him,

He most worthily did perform the office committed unto him: he preached continually upon every holy day, and did read most commonly twice in the week in some one church or other within this city. He was, after the rate of his livings, a great keeper of hospitality, very sober in diet, godly in life, friendly to the godly, liberal to the poor, and courteous to all men, void of pride, full of humility, abhorring covetousness, and an enemy to all wickedness and wicked men, whose companies he shunned, and whom he would in no wise shroud or have in his house and company.[2]

This is high praise from a man living in his household and observing him daily.

## Coverdale Takes to the Pen

Tyndale was a man uncompromising in his convictions, undaunted by the task before him, and tireless in his pursuit of perfection. Acting independently of others, Tyndale forged his translation from his own self-motivation. Coverdale, on the other hand, passed prosperously through life, politically correct. His ability to move among political enemies without being alienated by any of them enabled him to keep his head while most of those associated with Bible translation were dying for the cause. Coverdale gained some powerful protectors who eventually allowed his translation to become the first Bible authorized in the British Empire. His translation work was motivated by others, rather than a self-motivated effort.

Coverdale's place in history was safeguarded by his willingness to compromise. Thomas More, statesman and humanist scholar, may have encouraged Coverdale to take up the work. More desired an official English translation but could never accept one from his archrival, William Tyndale. Regardless of who suggested it, Coverdale began his translation project. In spite of his willingness to compromise for the sake of a goal, he was exiled in the late 1520s, 1530s, most of the 1540s, and again in the late 1550s. Yet his death was due to natural causes.

Tyndale's translation was governed by his desire for accuracy and style, while Coverdale's was governed by his desire for smooth renderings in English. Tyndale's work was a natural product of his scholarly knowledge of Greek and Hebrew, whereas Coverdale's lack of knowledge of the original languages meant he had to rely on Luther's German and Jerome's Latin translations. His choice of English expression had more to do with aesthetic judgment and linguistic taste. The results of Coverdale's tactics favored a smooth and more stylistic product.[3] Tyndale's translation intentionally highlighted linguistic faithfulness to the original author's intended meaning. Because Coverdale was not as careful with the intended meaning, his translation was not an improvement on Tyndale's work.

A portrait of Thomas More engraved by H. T. Ryall. More is known for his opposition to the work of William Tyndale. Once Tyndale passed from the scene, More supported Coverdale in his translation pursuits.

Photo: George Offor, *The New Testament* (1836), 27.

# The boke of Job.

## What this boke conteyneth.

Chap.   I. II.   The prosperite of Job, and how God geueth Satan power ouer his body &d goodes, which he is content withall

Chap.   III.   The flesh can not suffre: and here is described the vnpacient man, that grudgeth agaynst the iudgment of God.

Chap.   IIII.   Jobs frendes comforte him, and geue his synnes the blame of his punyshmét.

Chap.   V.   That no man is without synne. A prayse off the allmightynesse and louynge kyndnesse of God.

Chap.   VI.   Job excuseth his owne vnpacience, layeth ypocrysie to his fredes charge, &d sayeth they are but dyssemblers.

Chap.   VII.   A frendly contencion that Job maketh with God, shewinge the myserable life and trauayle of man.

Chap.   VIII.   Baldad reproueth Job. The nature of ypocrytes.

Chap.   IX.   All men are synners in the sight of God, and rightuousnesse commeth only of him. He punysheth also whom he will.

Chap.   X.   No man is without synne, nether maye eny man escape the honde of God.

Chap.   XI.   Sophar reproueth Job of synne: and for so moch as no man maye withstonde God, he byddeth him be paciét.

Chap.   XII.   All thinges come off the mightie ordinaunce of God. The wicked haue better dayes then the godly.

Chap.   XIII.   Job speaketh as he thinketh, reproueth the ypocrysy of his frendes, and cõmendeth the wisdome of God.

Chap.   XIIII.   The miserable life off man.

Chap.   XV. XVI.   No man is innocét before God. The conuersacion of the vngodly.

Chap.   XVII.   Job declareth his mysery.

Chap.   XVIII.   Baldad reproueth Job as vngodly, and sheweth the punyshment off the wicked.

Chap.   XIX.   Job sheweth his miserable estate, and reproueth his frendes, in that they increace his payne.

Chap.   XX.   punyshmént off the proude, vngodly and ypocrytes.

Chap.   XXI.   Wicked men haue prosperite in this worlde. God punysheth acordinge to his owne will.

Chap.   XXII.   They tell Job, that is punyshment commeth for his synnes.

Chap.   XXIII. XXIIII.   Job defendeth his innocécy

Chap.   XXV.   No mã is innocét before God.

Chap.   XXVI.   Job mocketh his fredes, because they go aboute to proue the thynge, that he denieth not. The power of God.

Chap.   XXVII.   God punysheth vs not acordinge to oure merites, but is mercifull and sparth euen the vngodly Agayne, he chasteneth the most righteous (as Job was) with aduersite.

Chap.   XXVIII.   The wisdome &d foreknowlege of God.

Chap.   XXIX.   The prosperite that Job was in fore. His innoceney and good dedes.

Chap.   XXX.   He complayneth of his mysery: how the ignoraunt and symple people laugh him to scorne.

Chap.   XXXI.   He rehearseth his innocét life.

Chap.   XXXII.   Jobs frendes are angrie, and forsake him.

Chap.   XXXIII.   God punysheth for synne, yet heareth he a meke prayer.

Chap.   XXXIIII.   Job withstõdeth the wordes of them, which saye, that the wicked only are punyshed.

Chap.   XXXV.   Job is reproued, for holdinge himself rightuous.

Chap.   XXXVI.   An argument, that God punisheth no man, excepte he haue deserued it.

Chap.   XXXVII.   The power of God is here described. Job is reproued.

Chap.   XXXVIII. XXXIX. XL. XLI.   The foreknowlege and wisdome of God.

Chap.   XLII.   Jobs frendes are reproued, and he himself is restored to his prosperite agayne.

## The first Chapter.

 N the lõde of Hus there was a man called Job: an innocent and vertuous man, soch one as feared God, and eschued euell. This man had vij. sonnes, and iij. doughters. His substaunce was vij. M. shepe, iij. M. camels, v. C. yock of oxen, v. C. she asses, and a very greate housholde: so y he was one of the most principall men amõge all them of the east countre. His sonnes now wente on euery man, and made bancketes: one daye in one house, another daye in another, and sent for their iij. sisters, to eate z drinke with them. So when they had passed ouer the tyme of their banckettinge rounde aboute, Job sent for them, and clensed them agayne, stode vp early, and offred for euery one a brentofferinge. For Job thought thus: peraduenture my sonnes haue done some offence, and haue bene vnthankfull to God in their hertes. And thus dyd Job euery daye,

A
Gen. 22. d

Iob. 42. c

Aa

A leaf from the first edition Coverdale Bible (1535). The Coverdale Bible was the first complete Bible in English and was adorned with over 150 woodcuts. Coverdale used most of Tyndale's translation from his New Testament, Pentateuch, and unpublished notes with very little change.

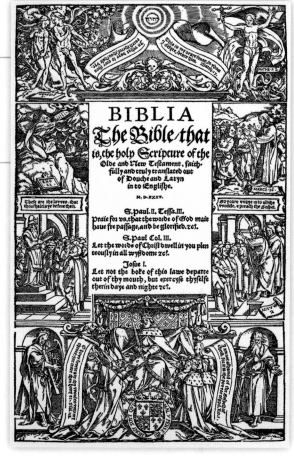

## The Pastor's Legacy: The First Complete Printed English Bible

In 1535, publisher Jacobus van Meteren printed Coverdale's first complete English-language Bible in Antwerp. By this time, the English Bible was in great demand in England. In 1533, a new English law had passed, compelling foreigners to sell their editions to London binderies. This was a blatant attempt to protect the bindery industry in England. Jacobus van Meteren sold the sheets already printed from the Coverdale Bible to another publisher, James Nicholson of Southwark. Although printed in Antwerp, all surviving Coverdale Bibles have English-style bindings.[4]

Any authorized Bible must have the support of the king, so Coverdale attempted to gain support from the royal family. His Bible translation contained an elaborate dedication to Henry VIII, no doubt politically motivated as Coverdale often did to keep in good status with powerful men. Many believe Henry, through Thomas Cromwell and Thomas More, encouraged Coverdale to translate the Bible—hence the dedication. Because of Henry's open opposition earlier, he certainly could not accept the work of Tyndale. Coverdale's support of the influential More and Cromwell helps explain his long and successful life as a translator. His political sensitivity proved his

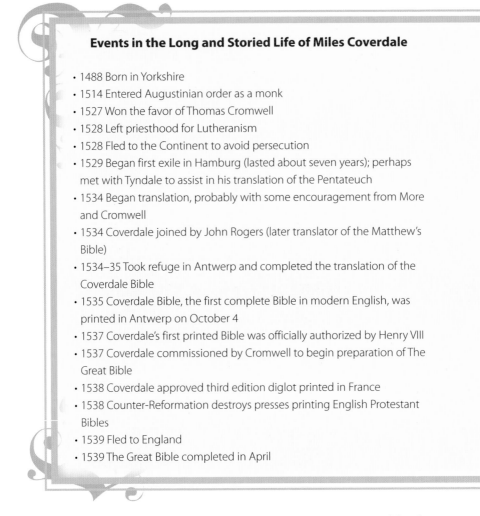

**Events in the Long and Storied Life of Miles Coverdale**

- 1488 Born in Yorkshire
- 1514 Entered Augustinian order as a monk
- 1527 Won the favor of Thomas Cromwell
- 1528 Left priesthood for Lutheranism
- 1528 Fled to the Continent to avoid persecution
- 1529 Began first exile in Hamburg (lasted about seven years); perhaps met with Tyndale to assist in his translation of the Pentateuch
- 1534 Began translation, probably with some encouragement from More and Cromwell
- 1534 Coverdale joined by John Rogers (later translator of the Matthew's Bible)
- 1534–35 Took refuge in Antwerp and completed the translation of the Coverdale Bible
- 1535 Coverdale Bible, the first complete Bible in modern English, was printed in Antwerp on October 4
- 1537 Coverdale's first printed Bible was officially authorized by Henry VIII
- 1537 Coverdale commissioned by Cromwell to begin preparation of The Great Bible
- 1538 Coverdale approved third edition diglot printed in France
- 1538 Counter-Reformation destroys presses printing English Protestant Bibles
- 1539 Fled to England
- 1539 The Great Bible completed in April

most valuable asset as others around him were being persecuted for their faith.

Coverdale made a political gesture to win the favor of Henry. The dedication introducing the Bible and making reference to Henry's wife, Anne Boleyn, was his way of gaining Henry's attention. Anne had long supported Coverdale's work on the Bible and no doubt helped him become acceptable to the king through her court influence. However, after Henry's divorce from Anne and her subsequent execution, some surviving copies show a corrected "Anne" (Boleyn) with "Jane" (Seymour, the new queen) in the introduction.

- 1539 Act of Six Articles signed into law attacking those of the Reformation
- 1540 Deaths of prominent Reformers forces Coverdale into exile again, this time with his new wife, Elizabeth Macheson
- 1540–43 Exile in Strasburg
- 1540–47 Extended exile
- 1541 or 1542 Received Doctor of Divinity degree from Tübingen
- 1546 Coverdale's books condemned by Bishop Bonner and several burned publicly
- 1549 Assisted Erasmus in his paraphrase, Volume II
- 1550 Reprint of his 1535 edition of the Coverdale Bible
- 1553 Death of Edward VI. The ascension of Mary signals another period of exile.
- 1554 Released from prison for tax evasion and returned to Denmark
- 1558 Moved to Geneva where he had a minor role in the translation of the Geneva Bible
- 1559 Returned to his beloved England
- 1563 Contracted the plague but recovered
- 1563 Received Doctor of Divinity degree from Cambridge by incorporating his earlier work from Tübingen
- 1569 Died on January 20 and was buried in the chancel of St. Bartholomew, London. The church was torn down in 1840, and Coverdale's remains were moved to St. Magnus Church near London Bridge.

Coverdale wisely omitted the offensive notes and introductions of Tyndale. His margins contained only alternate readings, interpretations, and references to parallel passages. About 150 small, scattered woodcuts adorned the black letter text of his 1535 first edition. A "black letter" text is sometimes called "Old English" or "Gothic" text.

The apocryphal books were destined to be relegated to a secondary position in the English Bible. Coverdale separated the apocryphal books from within the text and placed them together in a separate grouping between the Testaments, declaring, "The books and treatises, which among the fathers of old are not reckoned to be of like authority with the other books of the Bible, neither are they found in the Canon of the Hebrews."[5] For the first

This is a portrait from an engraving by J. Thomson (1536) of Henry VIII's wife, Anne Boleyn, whose marriage caused Henry to break with the Roman Catholic Church. Photo: George Offor, *The New Testament* (1836), 47.

time, these books were clearly set forth as having lesser value than the canonical books. From this time, all Protestant English Bibles have followed Coverdale's example.

Coverdale only slightly revised Tyndale's translation of the New Testament, Pentateuch, Jonah, and the historical books. His original and most creative translation came in his work on the poetic and prophetic books. Without Tyndale to follow, he was left to his own stylistic contributions. He emphasized the readability of the receptor language rather than the source language in which he clearly was not competent. His translation of the Psalms became the standard for the Psalter for years to come and was used in the Common Book of Prayer (1549–1960).

How could a scholar unfamiliar with Hebrew and Greek handle the intricacies of grammar in a translation? Coverdale did not capture much of the Hebrew structure such as parallelism and rhythmic cadence. It should be noted that Hebraisms are still troublesome to today's translators. A casual comparison will reveal the problem.

*Exodus 2:1–2*

**Tyndale:** And there went a man of the house of Leui and toke a doughter of Leui. And the wife conceaued and bare sonne. And whe she saw that it was a propre childe, she hyd him thre monthes longe.

**Coverdale:** And there wente forth a man of the house of Leui, and toke a doughter of Leui. And the wife conceaued and bare a sonne. And whan she sawe y it was a proper childe, she hyd him thre monethes.

**KJV:** And there went a man of the house of Leui, and tooke to wife a daughter of Leui. And the woman conceiued, and bare a sonne: and when shee saw him that hee was a goodly childe, shee hid him three moneths.

*Psalm 1:1*

**Coverdale:** O Blessed is y man, y goeth not in the councell of y vngodly: y abydeth not in the waye off synners, or sytteth not in y seate of the scornefull.

**KJV:** Blessed is the man that walketh not in the counsell of the vngodly, nor standeth in the way of sinners, nor sitteth in the seat of the scornefull.

It seems fairly clear that Coverdale slightly revised Tyndale in Exodus 2 and the KJV follows both closely. Whereas, Coverdale's Psalm 1 and the KJV vary slightly. This pattern can be observed by simple comparison. Coverdale felt the freedom to emphasize style and English composition more than accuracy based upon the original text.

Coverdale had a few memorable and idiomatic translations:[6]

- Job 19:18 "Ye, the very desert fools despise me."
- Psalm 90:10 "The days of our age are three score year and ten."
- Proverbs 16:28 "He that is a blabbe of his tongue maketh division."
- Proverbs 8:26 "winebibber"
- Jeremiah 22:1 "Graven upon the edge of your altars with a pen of iron and with an adamant claw."
- Exodus 10:14 "Thou shalt not break wedlock."

## Royal Endorsement Meets Opposition

The first royal endorsement led to tragedy. Queen Anne Boleyn's evangelical leanings and her patronage of the 1535 Coverdale Bible signaled its

## Christian Books Forbidden

In 1546 Henry VIII, under the pretense of declaring the truth of the Scriptures, set forth a proclamation outlawing many Christian books. The proclamation states,

"His Majesty straitly chargeth and commandeth, that no person of what estate, degree, or condition soever, he or they be, from the day of this proclamation presume to bring any manner of English book, concerning any manner of Christian religion, printed in the parts beyond the sea, into this realm, to sell, give, or distribute any English book, . . . or the copy of any such book, to any person dwelling within this His Grace's realm . . . unless the same shall be specifically licensed so to do by His Highnesses express grant, to be obtained in writing for the same . . . and therewithal to incur His Majesty's extreme indignation. Hereafter follow the names of certain books: The Whole Bible, the New Testament, a General Confession, the Christian State of Matrimony, Psalms and Songs out of Holy Scripture, Daniel the Prophet, an Apology Against William Tyndale, the New Testament in Divers Prints, The Obedience of a Christian Man, An Answer of Sir Thomas More's Dialogue, The Parable of the Wicked Mammon, A Treatise by John Frith, The New Testament of William Tyndale. . . ."[7]

There were a total of eighty-nine books Henry banned from those who lived in his kingdom.

downfall. Its destiny was completely tied with the queen's fate. Her arrest and execution in May 1536 meant that the king would not authorize the Bible she supported. Coverdale knew his Bible would never receive Henry's authorization. England's long-awaited authorized Bible was once again denied.

A fully accepted and authorized Bible did not have long to wait. In 1537, James Nicholson of Southwark printed a quarto edition, which J. F. Mozley calls "one of the rarest of all English Bibles."[8] It was a slight revision but primarily a reprint of the 1535 Coverdale. The quarto has these words on the title page: "Set forth with the Kynges moost

gracious license." Finally an English translation could be said to have met the requirements of the *Constitutions* of 1408. A licensed, fully approved Bible that could be read without fear of governmental reprisal was finally ready for the English-speaking world. That was undoubtedly the single most important event in the long, eventful history of English translations to that time.

Living for eighty-one years, Coverdale had an eventful life full of accomplishment. From the first complete printed Bible in the English language (1535) to the last edition of his famous Great Bible (1569), Coverdale saw it all.[9] From the forbidden Bible to the bloody work of the Counter-Reformation and the persistent persecutions of Queen Mary, Coverdale's

room, a quick glance around the room revealed treasures I hadn't expected. For the better part of the day, I viewed, drooled over, fondled, and tried to keep in check my envy of some of the most exciting and rare Bibles I had ever seen. The price for most of them sent me into "sticker shock."

He noticed my attention had finally focused on two items: a first edition 1611 King James Version (He) and a second edition Coverdale 1537. Both were priced the same. His delicate and very British inquiry as to my interest was a model of Christian charity. Our conversation went from his recommendation on which I should buy to how to pay for it. My Bible-buying budget was not even close to the asking price of these sacred entrustments. My wife was not with me to encourage me or to inject common sense.

Feeling my pain, Mr. Thomas cracked first when he recommended I purchase the Coverdale, since it was rarer and 1611 editions would come on the market fairly frequently. His next proposition caught me speechless. He offered to allow me to pay for it over a period of a year, and when half was paid he would send the Bible to me.

Speechless maybe, but paralyzed I was not, so I jumped on the deal without a moment to contemplate the impact of the decision on my annual budget. Over the next few months, my entertainment budget was nil and my Bible purchases centered on the 1537 only. The intervening twenty years has proven the advice sound and payment plan generous. The late Alan Thomas, bookseller, has a very special place in our hearts; and for me, a "poor" Bible collector, a friend was made.

life was punctuated with misery, suffering, and multiple banishments. Nevertheless, his accomplishments place him in a unique category of heroes of the faith.

7

# A Royal Court Intrigue

*The First "Authorized" Bible*

The King James Version has been known for many years as the "Authorized Bible" from the title page that states, "Appointed to be read in Churches." The worldwide influence of the Authorized Version has left the impression that the King James Version was a state authorized edition of the Bible. Many are surprised to discover that King James I never authorized the edition bearing his name. Then has there ever been an authorized Bible? If so, what was the first authorized Bible and why was it necessary?

## John Rogers Seeks Royal Approval

The Bible from the pens of Tyndale and Coverdale was not a Bible once for all delivered to the saints. We turn now to the men who would defend and improve the early translations. The turn of the sixteenth century witnessed the birth of John Rogers (ca. 1505–55) near Birmingham, England. Educated at Cambridge, he received his BA in 1525. In 1534 he fled England to Antwerp, where he ministered to merchants and worked in the printing business with printer Jacobus van Meteren.

A portrait of John Rogers, translator of the Thomas Matthew (pseudonym) Bible, by an unknown engraver. Photo: Heaton, *Reformation* (1913), 185.

Fear of reprisals and persecution led some to take false names. Sometime while living in Antwerp, John Rogers took the name Thomas Matthew to conceal the fact that his translation work was closely associated with his friend, the hated William Tyndale. Rogers revised Tyndale's 1535 New Testament and incorporated the books of the Old Testament that William Tyndale had translated into his own Bible. The remaining books came from the Coverdale Bible and his own editorial work.

Rogers's work was primarily one of editing various translations. He viewed Tyndale as superior to Coverdale when the two disagreed. In many cases he simply reprinted entire chapters without alterations. At the end of the book of Malachi, Rogers printed in large letters the initials "WT." No doubt this veiled footnote acknowledged William Tyndale as the primary translator of his revision.

The Matthew's Bible clearly reflects a style of English superior even to Coverdale. Hebrew parallelism is better preserved, its wording is more natural, and its accuracy is apparent. Even Miles Coverdale, when translating the Great Bible (1539), used Matthew's as his primary source rather than his own 1535 edition.

Would anyone dare insert notes in a Bible? John Rogers was just the man. He greatly expanded marginal notes that were developed from his own scholarly pursuits and from contemporary continental commentaries.[1] He included comments from Ambrose, Augustine, and Josephus. The Matthew's Bible notes were expositional in nature, theological in perspective, and practical in orientation. He attempted to explain obscure and difficult passages in order to prove that the biblical text itself was not enough for complete understanding. Unlike Tyndale's notes, Rogers tended to tone down the inflammatory comments relating to church doctrine.[2] However, it should not be concluded that he avoided attacking certain customs and beliefs that would anger the Roman Catholic Church.

Henry VIII was about to make a decision that was to have a positive impact on the English Bible for generations to come. On August 4, 1537, Archbishop Cranmer wrote a letter to Vicar-General Cromwell commending a new Bible translation and seeking his approval. Pollard records the letter:

> That you shall receyue by the bringer herof, a Bible in Englishe, both of a new translacion and of a new prynte dedicated vnto the Kinges Majestie, as farther apperith by a pistle vnto his grace in the begynnyng of the boke, which, in myn opinion is very well done, and therefore I pray your lordeship to rede the same . . . and forasmoche as the boke is dedicated vnto the kinges grace, and also great paynes and labour taken in setting forth the same, I pray you my Lorde, that you woll exhibite the boke vnto the kinges highnes: and to obteign of his Grace, if you can, a license that the same may be sold and redde of every person, withoute danger of any acte, proclamacion, or ordinaunce hertofore, graunted to the contrary, vntill such tyme that we, the Bishops shall set forth a better translation, which I thinke will not be till a day after domesday.[3]

The first edition of the Matthew's Bible (1537) with the signature of William Whipple, a signer of the Declaration of Independence.
Photo: R. Maisel.

Cromwell acted immediately by presenting this new Bible (Matthew's) to Henry VIII for his approval. Henry, after some consideration, granted the request. It was official. A new Bible translation received the "divine" blessing of the king.

Clearly an authorized Bible would be a bestseller. For years the only Bibles one could get were either Latin or black-market Tyndale versions. The prize for printing the first "officially licensed Bible" was still in question. Two men, Richard Grafton and James Nicholson, both from London, directly competed for the "Authorized Bible" market.

Richard Grafton received the license to print the Matthew's Bible (1537) and it is so stated on the title page. He sought to enlist Cromwell to help him receive royal support for permission to be the sole publisher of all "authorized" Bibles (which would have included the Coverdale Bible as well). Cromwell did not grant his petition.

James Nicholson continued to print the Coverdale Bible without a formal license to be printed on the title page. He was granted the license to print the quarto Coverdale Bible as noted on the title page (1537). Nicholson was not prevented from publishing any edition of the Matthew's Bible, but apparently he did not print any editions of it. Perhaps the license was granted for the Coverdale quarto as a concession to the less financially capable Nicholson.

The fact that Grafton requested permission from Cromwell suggests the 1537 Coverdale quarto with the king's license (granted to Nicholson) may have been printed prior to the 1537 Matthew's Bible. From the fear of possessing a forbidden Bible to the commercial fight to gain royal sanction as the exclusive publishers, the Bible was well on its way to becoming a "bestseller."

Returning to England in 1548, Rogers lectured at St. Paul's Cathedral while continuing his association with the printer, Edward Whitchurch, another exile. He was placed under house arrest for seditious preaching in 1553 and burned at the stake in 1555, the first martyr under the reign of Bloody Mary.

Interestingly, the first translation officially authorized by a ruling sovereign was essentially the same version Henry VIII and the church so diligently attempted to destroy. Tyndale's prayer at the stake had been

answered—at least for now. This very version became known as the "primary version" of the English
Bible. All later versions would draw deeply from it.
Its authority is reflected at the bottom of the title
page where it reads, "Set forth with the Kynges
moost gracious licence." The freedom of reading and
possessing a Bible in one's own language had arrived,
but the suffering and persecution was not over. Church-based authority lin-
gered long and did not give up without a fight.

An engraving of John Rogers's
execution (1555) at Smithfield,
England. Queen (Bloody) Mary's
first victim was John Rogers (aka
"Thomas Matthew"), depicted here
being consumed by the flames of
martyrdom.   Photo: John Foxe, *Acts and
Monuments* (1846), vol. 4, 611.

## Henry Bows to the Church for a Licensed Bible

The king paced back and forth, his shoes clicking on the cold stone floor.
Bellowing, grumbling, and peering occasionally into the courtyard below,
he said, "How dare these priests challenge the Bible I have licensed!" He
paused to stroke his beard and then mused sarcastically, "I have given them
permission to print their precious Bible and the archbishop has openly encouraged its reading. Now they want another more agreeable translation."
His thoughts began to turn more reflectively: "I could call on Cromwell to
take up the task. He certainly would be careful not to offend some of these
over-paid, underachieving priests."

## Bloody Mary's First Victim (1555)

Freed from the bonds of prison and its horrors, John Rogers was led to the stake. The bails of sticks soon to be set ablaze promised him the rewards of his faith. He had been delivered long ago from the fear of death. Confident of the promises of the Master he had served for many years, he was soon to meet his Savior. With a mocking in his voice, the sheriff bawled, "Will you recant of your abominable doctrine?"

"That which I have preached I will seal with my blood," the worn, feeble voice replied.

"Then you are a heretic," shouted one of his captors.

"That shall be known at the day of judgment," Rogers confidently spoke by now in a voice no more than a whisper.

"Well, I will never pray for you," the sheriff threatened.

"But I will pray for you," came the same confident reply. They continued their path toward the hideous goal with Rogers quietly singing the Psalms. They were soon met by his wife and eleven children. Rogers showed no sorrow but cheerfully and steadfastly walked to the stake where he was burned to death in the presence of his family and a great number of onlookers giving praises and thanks. Truly a life lived well.

It is estimated that Bloody Mary was responsible for 290 deaths during her reign. None was more impressive than how John Rogers faced his horrible death.[4]

A calmer Henry quietly began praising himself for his ingenious idea. "If they want another Bible, I'll give them one—not translated by that heretic, Tyndale, but by that old standby, conservative, and un-troublesome, Miles Coverdale. Then I won't take the heat from those religious zealots calling themselves bishops. Let Cromwell face them down!"

It was now time for Henry to make a decision. By the end of 1537, England had two authorized Bibles. King Henry VIII and Vicar-General Cromwell encouraged the reading of the Bible. Some preferred the Matthew's Bible while others read the cheaper quarto edition of Coverdale. As is often the case, there were those who felt the reading of the Bible should be from

A first edition of the Matthew's Bible (1537). The Matthew's Bible pays a rather silent tribute to the outlaw William Tyndale by inserting his initials WT prominently in the text. Photo: R. Maisel.

one approved standard Bible. The notes of the Matthew's Bible offended many. A Bible, some insisted, should be placed in every church where it could be chained and proclaimed to the people without confusing or misleading notes.

A portrait of Henry VIII from a picture by H. Holbein.
Photo: George Offor, *The New Testament* (1836), 70.

Cromwell stepped forward to support a standardized text that would be more acceptable to the bishops and clergy. They were also concerned about a variety of translations and accompanying notes that could be confusing or misleading. Cromwell chose Miles Coverdale, a proven friend of the court, to undertake the new translation. So in 1539 the famous "Great Bible"[5] was

This is a portrait of Thomas Cromwell from a picture by H. Holbein. Cromwell's magnificent speech in the House of Commons in Wolsey's defense led to his position as Henry VIII's spokesman before Parliament. Later, accused of treason for not yielding to Henry's marriage to Anne Boleyn, Cromwell was beheaded in 1540. Photo: Heaton, *Reformation* (1913), 211.

published, and another Bible competing for official status sought approval.

Just before the Great Bible appeared, however, a revision of Matthew's Bible surfaced and competed for official recognition. A scholar in both Greek and Hebrew with a master's degree from Cambridge, Richard Taverner (1505–75) set his mind to the task of translation. His version, also published in 1539, would become popularly known as the Taverner Bible, but its official title was *The Most Sacred Bible whiche is the holy scripture, conteyning the old and new testament, translated into English, and newly recognized with great diligence after most fayhtful exemplars by Rychard Taverner.*

Taverner had been in the employment of Cromwell as a clerk. Did Cromwell encourage Taverner's work or did Taverner know of Cromwell's admonition to Coverdale to do a revision? We do not know. Whatever the case, even though Taverner knew Greek and probably had some readings more accurate than his predecessors, his text had almost no influence on subsequent translations. F. F. Bruce points to one rendering that did survive: in Hebrews 1:3 the Son of God is called the "express image" of his person.[6] Taverner also introduced "parable" for Tyndale's "similitude."

Most differences between Taverner's version and Matthew's version are limited to style and idiomatic renderings. For example, 1 John 2:5 in Matthew's reads: "We have an advocate with the Father." Taverner's reads, "We have a spokesman with the Father." While both are acceptable translations, Taverner's use of "spokesman" reflects an attempt to be more idiomatic.

With the royal license settled, the next question was, "Who is going to be selected to print the 'authorized' Bible?" Coverdale's commission to do the new translation was based primarily on the fact that he was a trusted friend of Cromwell and had proven his ability to produce a classic piece of work. Grafton and Whitchurch (who published the Matthew's Bible) received the contract for printing the Great Bible. However, France was chosen over England as the place of production. This was primarily due to its advanced printing techniques and better quality paper. Also, a French location for printing meant the enemies of the English translation would not be able to interfere with its progress. Though English translations had been approved by Henry and his court, the attempts of the enemies of the Reformation to destroy all English Bibles were not slowed down. Those enemies would even try to follow the translation to France.

> Though English translations had been approved by Henry and his court, the attempts of the enemies of the Reformation to destroy all English Bibles were not slowed down.

Thomas Cromwell, aware of the potential dangers to the publication of a prime translation, sent letters to Francis I, king of France, asking him to permit the printing of an official English translation. The king granted permission around the spring of 1538 with the understanding that they "avoid any private or unlawful opinions."[7] This was a reference to the potential anti-Catholic marginal notes that might be included, as appeared in the Matthew's Bible. Catholic France was in the midst of a counter-reformation at the time of the translation, and its printers faced constant dangers.

Danger still lurked at every stage of the work. Coverdale and Grafton continued to send completed sheets of the text to Cromwell in England. While clouds of pending doom loomed over the project, work continued uninterrupted until December 1538. At that time, the inquisitor general for

France, Matthew Ory, issued an order expounding the dangers of Scripture in a vernacular. Fraunces Regnault, the printer, was ordered to appear before the magistrates to answer charges. Coverdale and Grafton escaped to England with some of the sheets from the Great Bible in hand.[8] The printing offices were raided and the remaining copies of Coverdale's diglot of 1538, and perhaps a large number of Great Bibles, were destroyed.

Bishop Bonner, the recently appointed consulate to France (later to become bishop of London), was able to recover some of the copies. Whether or not the copies were returned to Coverdale and Grafton is a mystery. The presses and type were purchased by Cromwell and brought to England, where the remaining pages and subsequent editions were printed.

The arm of the enemy has a long reach. It has been suggested that conservatives in England who feared the translation sponsored by Cromwell led much of the opposition to the "secret" work of Coverdale, Whitchurch, and Regnault on the Great Bible in France. Some historians believe that word was leaked to various autocrats in France who in turn led the attack on Coverdale's work. While facts are scarce, this could very well be the case.

## A Translation Assigned to All Churches

Coverdale's 1539 Great Bible translation was certainly not a translation from the original languages. His translation work depended heavily on Tyndale's English translation, Sebastian Munster's Hebrew Bible with Latin notes and text,[9] and Erasmus's Latin text.[10] It is interesting that he relied more on the Matthew's Bible (1537) than his own 1535 edition. (See timeline on pp. 16 and 17 for more information on the sources of the various translations.)

The Coverdale Bible (1535) was supplanted by a less controversial Bible named for its size, the Great Bible (1539). The title page of the Great Bible had

A portrait of Thomas Cranmer from an engraving by W. Holl. Cranmer found favor with Henry because of his support of the marriage with Anne Boleyn. Later Cranmer suffered arrest for treason under Mary, but he received a reprieve when Elizabeth came to the throne. Photo: George Offor, *The New Testament* (1836), 86.

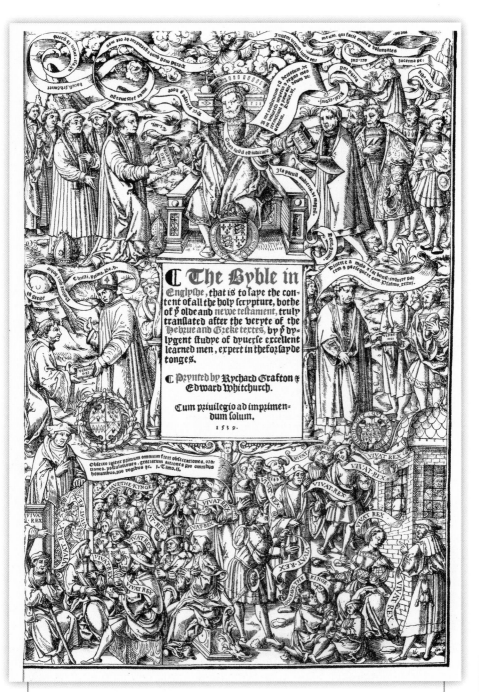

A facsimile of the title page of the first edition of the Great Bible published in 1539 (so named for its large size, 16½ × 11 inches). It depicts King Henry VIII receiving the Bible from the translators and handing it out to Cranmer (left) and Cromwell (right). The priest and the noblemen receive it and are preaching to the people, who are giving praise to the king. The point is obvious: Henry is the head of the church, not the pope.

an elaborate engraving designed by the famous sculptor Hans Holbein. It pictures the Lord in the clouds with outstretched arms. Below is King Henry VIII sitting on a throne with bishops and nobles sitting on each side of the page. The bishops are bare-headed with their miters at the king's feet. The symbolism of Henry's divine right is obvious. The king is holding a book in each hand, presenting them to the bishops and nobles. On the right side, Cromwell is giving a Bible to a layman and on the left Cranmer is handing a Bible to a priest. Both Cranmer and Cromwell are represented by their respective coat-of-arms.

The second edition of the Great Bible (published in April 1540 with Cranmer's preface) became the standard edition and was called "The Cranmer's Bible." The preface appeared in all subsequent editions. Grafton and Whitchurch published the Great Bible in seven different editions within the span of two years.

The fourth edition (dated November 1540 in the colophon and 1541 on the title page) was the first edition with Cromwell's coat-of-arms expunged from the title page. Cromwell's fall from Henry's favor in July 1540 caused this drastic action. This same edition claims Bishop Cuthbert of Duresme as the overseer and pursuer of the edition. This is none other than Bishop Tunstall, who so relentlessly denied Tyndale's New Testament entrance into England. Yet, the Great Bible is nothing more than a minor revision of Tyndale's New Testament! Apparently a few short years and the winds of political change can affect the "thinking" of the politically ambitious.

The production of the Great Bible made it possible for churches to conform to the 1538 Cromwell injunction that the Bible should be placed in every church. Pollard records the decree:

> A proclamation, ordered by the King's majesty, with the advice of his honorable council for the Bible of the largest and greatest volume, to be had in every church. Devised the 6th day of May the xxxiii year of the King's most gracious reign [1541]. Where, by Injunctions set forth by the authority of the King's royal majesty, Supreme head of the church of this his realm of England.[11]

The title pages from the Great Bible of 1541 and 1540. Note the absence of Cromwell's coat of arms in the 1541 edition. After he had fallen out of favor with Henry VIII, his coat of arms was ordered expunged. On the inside cover of this Bible (upper one) was one of the six "Admonitions" placed above the Bibles in St. Paul's Church in London, 1542.

Photo: R. Maisel.

## The Ultimate Price for Bible Reading

A tall young man approached the chained Bible at St. Paul's Cathedral. He was known for his pious character and clear, loud reading voice. As John Porter reverently opened the beautiful Bible and began to read, a group of worshipers gathered to hear this angelic voice. The activity was soon noted by Bishop Bonner and his chaplains who began to fear the disgruntled crowds at the other end of the church who were complaining about these "Godspellers."

The bishop called for Porter and rebuked him sternly, accusing him of expositions upon the text and creating a disturbance. Even though Porter denied he was saying anything contrary to the text, Bonner sent him bound in leg irons and handcuffs to prison. Porter's cousin, serving as his advocate, urged the jailer to release him from the chains. The cruel treatment, he argued, was normally reserved for more serious crimes. After the cousin extended friendship and money to Porter's captors, the jailers unfettered him, took him from the less serious criminals, and put him in the prison with the felons and murderers. Porter took the opportunity to share with the prisoners what he knew from the Scriptures. Some, either prisoners or guards, complained about his preaching. He was taken to a lower dungeon shackled in bolts and irons where, after six or eight days, he was found dead.[12] How many prisoners' souls were saved by this godly man we will never know, but his faithfulness is an encouragement to all who love the Bible.

These were the perilous times of Henry VIII and Bishop Bonner. Cruelty and injustice served their powerful hold on all who would oppose them. John Porter dared to stand up for his Lord and paid the ultimate price.

Various Great Bibles: Open Bible in front, Great Bible (quarto), 1569; Bible standing on left side, Great Bible, 1540; Bible standing on the right, Great Bible, 1541. Great Bibles were published until 1569, and the Psalms were used in prayer books for many years after that.   Photo: M. Brake.

One of six vellum "Admonitions" (1542) hung on the pulpit of St. Paul's Church warning parishioners, under penalty of imprisonment, not to disrupt the church by reading the Scriptures aloud.

CRANMER'S
OR THE
GREAT BIBLE

TRANSLATED
BY
TYNDALE

CORRECTED
BY
COVERDALE

The Great Bible was officially licensed and standardized so that all religious authorities could support its use.

How did the common person react to an authorized Bible available to all? Bishop Edmund Bonner set about to place the Great Bible in every church in England. In the famous Saint Paul's Cathedral in London, Bonner, at his own expense, chained six beautiful Great Bibles on the six pulpits. The Bibles were to be read in orderly fashion "without disputations." Instead, however, people gathered around the Bible and began to act disorderly, reading with irreverence and arguing its meaning. In order to prevent parishioners from reading the Bible during the services and to maintain order, Bonner placed on the front of each pulpit the infamous "Admonitions." The "Admonitions" set certain rules for the use of the Bible. For instance, the Bible was to be read quietly, humbly, and charitably, without disturbance to others during services, and not drawing crowds to listen to the exposition of the text. A people who had been deprived the freedom to read

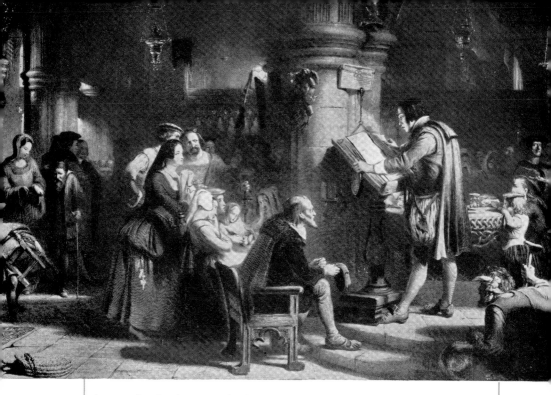

An engraving showing a crowd gathering around a reading of Scripture, and a copy of the "Admonitions" hanging above one of the pulpits at St. Paul's Church.   Photo: Heaton, *The Bible of the Reformation* (1913), 275.

the Scriptures finally had a Bible to read, and they had difficulty in doing so in an orderly fashion.

The Bible in the English vernacular, now "approved to be read," created a lasting thirst for Englishmen of all classes. Everyone was caught up in this new delight. They either read it themselves or had it read to them. Many began the process of learning to read just for the enjoyment of reading the Bible. It is impossible to imagine the first reading of the Scriptures and the impression it made upon their hearts. Some supported the "old school" that argued if the common folk started reading the Bible on their own, it would lead inevitably to religious anarchy. The younger ones, no doubt, were burning with a zeal for spiritual freedom.

## Nuggets of a Bible Collector

The constant pursuit of rare Bibles is driven by the "high" a collector feels each time he lands a treasure. The rare find of something special presses the often-empty hunt deep into the forgetful quadrant of the brain. The chase for a 1537 Matthew's Bible and the ultimate catch was just such an adventure for me.

For the most part, to buy a Bible of the importance of a Matthew's Bible one must look to England or auction houses in New York. While living in Portland several years ago, I waltzed into a rare bookshop downtown, as I often did, just to see what it held. On this particular occasion as I entered, the shopkeeper recalled my publishing a Wycliffe Bible facsimile. He said as a matter of fact, "I just got in a Bible you might have an interest in." He pulled out a large folio Bible with a date of 1535 and the name "Matthew's Bible" on the spine. I knew immediately something was wrong. The 1535 was a Coverdale Bible and the 1537 was the Matthew's Bible. I knew I was in for a delightful time of investigation.

I took it upstairs and started leafing through it. I soon discovered it was indeed a Matthew's Bible. I returned to the shopkeeper, who was also the owner, and began to inquire as to how long he had had it, where it came from, and some other small talk. I had to appear somewhat disinterested because I didn't want him to see me squirm or to reveal how badly I wanted it. I nonchalantly inquired the asking price. To my utter shock, he asked a very low price. I wanted it; but I didn't want to appear too anxious. I won't reveal the price, but I offered him three hundred dollars less than his asking price.

He told me he had received it on consignment from a woman back east. He continued to reveal its origin, history, and owner. The famous Civil War Scofield family came to the Northwest around 1903. By 1906, the last of the family passed away and the house was sealed. In the early 1950s, when the state decided to build a highway through the area, the house was opened and a vast amount of Civil War memorabilia and this Bible were discovered.

As our conversation continued, he pointed out a signature in the middle of the Bible written as "Wm. Whipple" and dated as a gift from Mr. Harris in 1754. William Whipple was a signatory to the Declaration of Independence! By now I was so excited I felt as if I were hopping around while, in fact, I was nonchalantly leaning against the counter. He went on to say he must call the woman and see if she would take my offer.

I agreed and was walking on air as I went home. That night, I tossed and turned in bed, chastising myself until dawn. "What if the shopkeeper offered someone else the same book?" I tortured myself as I rolled over, "For a lousy three hundred dollars I would miss this great treasure." The moment the shop opened, I called to ask if he had contacted the owner. No more keeping my excitement in check, I would not take the chance again. To my utter delight he said she gladly accepted my offer. Fortunately the Banfield freeway was not monitored with radar that morning as I pressed the speed limit to get to the shop. I breathed a great sigh of relief when it was securely tucked away in my arms. It is now one of the central pieces of my collection.

# 8

# Theology Influences Bible Versions

*Notes to Aid the Reader*

Shrouded in the darkness of the early morning hour, eight of England's finest scholars stepped into the mist. Cautiously, silently, moving through deserted streets toward the shipping docks, the leader finally signaled the group to halt. The dense fog enveloped the group and the muffled sounds were eerie. Tensely listening for pursuers, each man stood motionless, barely breathing for fear that his heartbeat would be the one heard by the enemy. In the distance, the salty banter of seamen preparing to set sail calmed the rush of adrenaline. Safety was within reach. These faithful Englishmen were about to embark on their destinies.

These were perilous times indeed. They all agreed they had to leave England for the sanctuary of Europe, where the Reformation could survive and grow. To stay would mean certain arrest and the choice of the hangman's noose or the executioner's fire. They knew they must be free in order to worship and to write about the Reformation hope. The success of the English Reformation rested on these men and those who would follow.

Their fears were well founded, for as soon as the new queen was crowned she instituted far-reaching anti-Protestant reforms. The accession of Catholic Queen Mary I to the throne of England in 1553 signaled a period of intense

Protestant persecution. Mary, the daughter of Henry VIII and Catherine of Aragon, fervently embraced the Catholic faith of her mother and was determined to restore England to loyalty to the pope. Her humiliation with the divorce of her parents in 1533 and the failed plot of John Dudley to give the throne to the great-granddaughter of Henry VII, Lady Jane Grey, further shaped Mary's attitude toward Protestants.

Mary was not satisfied with reform results begun early in her reign, so she dismissed married clergy and attempted to restore Catholic dogma. Thomas Cromwell's destruction of monasteries in the 1530s was so successful that Mary could do little to restore them. Totally frustrated, she began embracing more stringent measures. John Rogers, Thomas Cranmer, Hugh Latimer, and Nicholas Ridley were arrested in Mary's first year as queen. John Rogers, responsible for the famous Matthew's Bible (1537), was the first to suffer martyrdom under Mary (1555). John Foxe records the horrible deaths of Latimer and Ridley as they were burned at the stake. Public reaction to Mary's chancellor and henchman Stephen Gardiner's inhuman burnings and beheadings of Protestants backfired. England's indifference to Protestantism now turned into sympathy to its cause. Foxe's *Acts and Monuments* (1576) popularized and perhaps overdramatized the events under Mary. Her nearly three hundred victims were embedded in the national conscience.

It will not come as a surprise that some of the greatest scholars and theologians in England's history were among those fleeing their beloved homeland. Miles Coverdale (translator of the Coverdale Bible, 1535) and many English Protestant leaders fled England for Switzerland and Germany, where they took refuge. Among the notable continental exiles were: William Williams, William Whittingham, Anthony Gilby, Christopher Goodman, Thomas Wood, Thomas Cole, John Bale, John Knox, John Bodley, William Kethe, and John Foxe. Almost immediately the exiles began

A portrait of Queen Mary by an unknown artist. Mary's Catholic views brought the hatred and fear of Protestants.
Photo: W. J. Heaton, *The Puritan Bible* (1913), 41.

writing books and pamphlets defending their reformed convictions. From this group came the translators of the Geneva Bible.

The Geneva Bible (1557 New Testament and 1560 Bible) was produced by English exiles in a small, Latin letter with verse divisions and notes to assist the reader in understanding the text and thereby to introduce Reformation theology. It was their desire to produce an affordable and readable book to suit the needs of the common person.

We simply cannot blame or credit Mary for the production of the Geneva Bible. Her active persecution of Protestants did provide the context that led to the freedom for publication. Fleeing to the Continent gave the Reformers the opportunity to operate freely in a society that would tolerate academic and religious freedom. The growing need for a new translation, however, became apparent to almost everyone. The English Bibles previously published were large, cumbersome, and expensive; the awkward black letters (often called Old English or Gothic) and the lack of verse divisions made imperative a new translation that would accommodate the growing reading public. The church in England had a desire for a "holy book" and the black letters represented a holdover from the Catholic demand for a Bible only in the "holy language" of Latin. Even today laymen often view the Bible in an archaic language as more "sacred" than a modern idiomatic translation. So too, the large Gothic letters continued to be preferred by the British. Even the Geneva Bibles published in England were often printed in the "Old English blackletter." Even so, a new translation was inevitable.

With the vast writings of the English exiles on the Continent, a thirst soon developed for the Bible in common English that would be affordable and could be read by "the man behind the plow." Nearly two hundred years earlier, Wycliffe, the translator of the first complete Bible in the English language, had seen the need for the common man to have the Bible in his own language to combat the abuses of church dogma. Now it was clear: not

> The English Bibles previously published were large, cumbersome, and expensive; the awkward black letters and the lack of verse divisions made imperative a new translation that would accommodate the growing reading public.

only should the laity have the Bible in their own language, but it must also be affordable, easily readable, and portable. The Reformers strongly favored adding study aids to the biblical text. These famous theologians reasoned that the ancient texts need some explanation and they were just the ones to assist readers in their understanding of these more difficult texts. After all, the Reformation was birthed in an exegetical study of New Testament texts by well-known scholars like Martin Luther, Philipp Melanchthon, and John Calvin.

As might be expected, God began to work. The center of Reformation scholarship was in Geneva, led by the Greek and Latin scholars, Theodore Beza and John Calvin. The English exiles considered Geneva the place to study. It was many of these Geneva scholars who produced French and English Bibles and New Testaments during this period.

Printing came to Geneva nearly a century before the Reformation. The early sixteenth-century writings of John Calvin were instrumental in making Geneva the center of European printing. Dedicated printers flocked to Geneva during these lush economic times. Jean Crespin, Conrad Badius, and Robert Stephanus (Estienne) were the most influential in printing Bibles and theological literature. Stephanus was best known for his printing of a 1528 Latin Bible and the 1550 Greek New Testament. In 1551 he printed a small Greek

The first edition of the Geneva New Testament (1557). It was the first English Bible to insert verse divisions and to use Latin letter.

New Testament with verse divisions, the first to use verses that remain in modern versions. This same verse-division system was used in the English Geneva New Testament of 1557. Stephanus abandoned the heavy black letters in favor of the more easily read Latin letters (also called Roman letter).

It was left to printer Conrad Badius to publish the New Testament as the first step in the production of the complete Geneva Bible just a year before the death of Bloody Mary.[1] The lone translator was William Whittingham, a fellow at All Souls Church and a Greek scholar, who married the sister of John Calvin's wife.

Whittingham's edition was not a new translation but a revision of Tyndale with some help from Beza's Latin. This edition was the first to have verse divisions[2] and to be printed in Roman letter. Words not in the Greek manuscript were printed in italics. It is the first critical edition of the English New Testament rather than a simple revision of previous works.[3]

While this small sextodecimo (16°) is considered the first edition of the Geneva Bible's New Testament, there are a vast number of differences when compared to the 1560 edition. It must not be considered a mere revision of the 1557 New Testament even though it was under the supervision of Whittingham himself. So successful was the so-called "revision" in the Bible of 1560 that there was no need to reprint the New Testament (1557). A facsimile edition by Samuel Bagster appeared in 1842, but it was only for historical study purposes.

## The Geneva Bible Goes to Print

The long exile for the Protestant Reformers was nearly over. The death of Queen Mary on November 17, 1558, and the accession of Elizabeth I to the throne signaled a safe return of the exiles back to England. A few remained in Geneva to complete the translation already under way. While contributors to the 1560 Geneva were Anthony Gilby, Christopher Goodman, William Cole, and Thomas Sampson, the guiding force in its production was William Whittingham.

The complete Geneva Bible was printed in Geneva on April 10, 1560. The title page reads:

> The Bible and Holy Scriptures conteyned in the Olde and Newe Testament. Translated According to the Hbrue and Greke, and conferred With the best translations in divers languages. With moset profitable annotations upon all the hard places, and other things of great importance as may appear in the Epistle to the Reader.[4] At Geneva Printed by Rouland Hall M.D.L.X.

The first edition of the Geneva Bible (1560). It has an additional feature that highlights five large maps. Its prominent Calvinistic notes made it difficult for the Anglican clergy to accept it.   Photo: R. Maisel.

A small woodcut of the crossing of the Red Sea was surrounded by the words of Psalm 34:19: "Great are the troubles of the righteous: but the Lord delivereth them out of all." Below the woodcut was

Exodus 14:14: "The Lord shal fight for you: therefore holde you your peace." Perhaps the title page was a fitting message to remind the English exiles of their struggle under and deliverance from Mary's persecution. The Dedication was to Queen Elizabeth whom the Reformers saw as their "Moses." It reads, "To the moste vertuous and Noble Quene Elisabet, Quene of England, France, and Ireland. . . . Your humble subiects of the English Churche at Geneva, with grace and peace from God the Father through Christ Jesus our Lord."

## The Geneva Bible's Scholarship

When we consider the credentials of the men involved in this translation, there is little room left to quibble about the quality of its production. Some of the greatest theologians in Christian history, including John Calvin (whose Introduction to the 1557 New Testament appeared in English), John Knox, and Theodore Beza (known for publishing several Greek New Testaments), took part in the Geneva Bible project. Modern scholars have no problem admitting that it was one of the finest translations ever made. Charles Butterworth acknowledges the influence of the Geneva Bible when he writes, "In the lineage of the King James Bible, this volume is by all means the most important single volume." He adds, "It was for fifty years (1570–1620) the household Bible of the English people."[5] It was the Bible of Shakespeare[6] after about 1597 and the Bible of the Puritans[7] coming to America. Even some of the translators of the 1611 King James Version continued to use it as late as the mid-1620s.[8]

The sources for the translation of the Geneva Bible can be traced to Greek, Hebrew, Latin, French, and English forerunners. The Greek text of Stephanus (1551) and Beza's Latin (1555) were used in the New Testament. The English text source was primarily the 1557 Geneva with reference to Tyndale's edition published by Richard Jugge in 1552 and the Great Bible (1539–41). The French Bible by Pierre Olivetan (cousin of John Calvin), the Latin Bible of Pagninus, the Hebrew-Latin of Sebastian Munster, and the Latin of Leo Juda were also sources consulted.[9]

## The Man behind the Translation

Behind many great projects and deeds in history, a businessman can be found funding the dreams of scholars and entrepreneurs. The Geneva Bible was primarily financed by the English exiles' benefactor, John Bodley, the father of Thomas Bodley, after whom the famous Bodleian Library in Oxford is named. Bodley was granted an exclusive seven-year printing license in England in 1560, which was renewed in 1565 for twelve more years. However, it was not printed in England. Alfred Pollard, recognized historical scholar, suggests that because the renewal calls for letting the archbishop of Canterbury and bishop of London make conditions, such as the omission of the notes, Bodley did not want to print it under these conditions.[10] It was printed in England for the first time under the license purchased from Queen Elizabeth by Christopher Barker in 1576.[11]

## The Making of the Geneva Bible

The Geneva Bible became the cornerstone of the Reformation, and its influence on the KJV translators makes it one of the most important Bibles in English history. David Ewart writes of its influence on the King James Version, "Next to Tyndale, the Geneva Bible had the greatest influence on the Authorized Bible."[12] This is acknowledged even though the KJV translators used the Bishops' Bible of 1602 as the text to follow.

## Selected Readings and Marginal Notes

A number of interesting readings make the Geneva Bible unique. For example:

A portrait by Cornelius Jensen of Thomas Bodley, the namesake for the Bodleian Library in Oxford. Photo: W. J. Heaton, *The Puritan Bible* (1913), 125.

- Luke 2, "cratch"—NIV and KJV read "manger."
- Luke 4:8, "Hence from me, Satan."—KJV reads "Get thee behind me, Satan."
- John 16:2, "They shall excommunicate you." —NIV and KJV read "They will put you out of the synagogue."

It was not enough to have a readable text; an added feature of providing Reformation notes and study aids became a distinguishable attribute of the Geneva Bible. Most pages have margins filled with notes and references. The Geneva Bible was the precursor to the modern "study Bible."

The notes provide theological commentary, give geographical explanations, record textual variants, and offer clarification of difficult words and phrases. Many passages have notes that attempt to explain the literal sense of the passage. Lewis Lupton compared the Geneva notes with Calvin's *Commentaries* showing Calvin's influence on the notes of the Geneva Bible.[13] The notes, while intended to be the strength of this edition, became the most controversial aspect. The Calvinistic flavor of the notes irritated the Anglicans, and the demeaning of the power of the monarchy upset King James I. It ultimately became the impetus that led to a new translation in 1611.[14]

The Geneva Bible was clearly influenced by Calvinistic teachings. But it would be a mistake to believe that the Geneva is only a "Calvinistic Bible." Its notes are far more extensive and helpful than that. While there are several notes from the Geneva Bible of 1560 that express the distinctive Calvinistic teaching on predestination, election, and reprobation, John Eadie points out that "a mere fraction of the notes is decidedly Calvinistic" and estimates that of the 250 explanatory notes in the 1560 edition "not more than ten of them are unmistakable Calvinistic utterances."[15]

The moderate Calvinist Charles Ryrie likes to point out to the zealous Calvinists an embarrassing reading in Luke 10:31: "And by *chance* there came down a certain Priest that same way." The marginal note tries to minimize the non-Calvinistic term *chance*: "For so it seemed to man's judgment, although this was so appointed by God's council and providence."[16] Later expansions on the notes by Laurence Tomson in 1576 showed a greater tendency toward the Calvinistic doctrines. Some typical expressions from the notes of the 1560 edition are:

Exodus 2:8: "Man's counsel can not hinder that which God hath determined shall come to pass."

Proverbs 16:4: "So that the justice of God shall appear to his glory, even in the destruction of the wicked."

Acts 13:48: "None can believe, but they whom God doth appoint before all beginnings to be saved."

Romans 9:15: "As the only will and purpose of God is the chief cause of election, and reprobation: so his free mercy in Christ is an inferior cause of salvation, and the hardening of the heart an inferior cause of damnation."

Romans 11:29: "To whom God giveth his spirit of adoption, and whom he calleth effectually, he cannot perish: for God's eternal counsel never changeth."

Titus 1:2: "Hath willing, and of his mere liberality promised without foreseeing our faith or works as a cause to move him to this free mercy."

Many of the notes simply attempt to explain difficult terms or concepts in the text:

> Isaiah 7:14: "Immanuel." Marginal reading, "Or, God with us, which name can agree to none, but to him that is both God and Man."
>
> Hebrews 11:21: "Jacob leaning on the end of his staff." Marginal reading, "Or worshiped toward the end of his staff."
>
> Genesis 3:7: "made themselves breeches." Marginal reading, "Ebr. things to gird about them to hide their privates."
>
> John 16:2: "They shall excommunicate you." Marginal reading, "Greek, put you out of the Synagogues."
>
> Acts 10:6: "by the sea side." Marginal reading, "He shall speak words unto thee whereby thou shalt be saved and thine house."

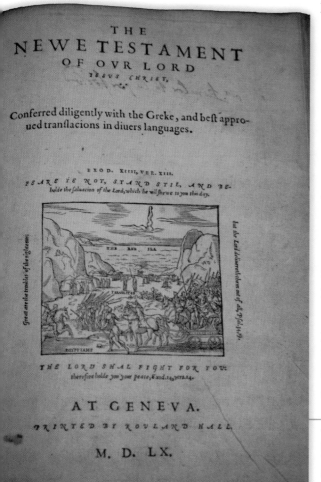

## The Popularity of the Geneva Bible

From the first printing in 1560 in Geneva to the last printing in England in 1616 (many editions were printed by Joost Broerss in Amsterdam until 1644) at least one Geneva Bible edition was printed each

The title page to the Geneva Bible's New Testament. The Geneva Bible of 1560 was extremely popular because of its extensive notes. The notes were greatly expanded in a 1599 edition.

year. Between 140 and 200 editions were printed during these years. Author J. R. Dore suggests that 150,000 copies were imported from Holland after it ceased to be printed in England. However, these copies were so poorly printed that Archbishop Laud finally put a stop to these imports.[17] It was ordered in an Act of the Scottish Parliament passed in 1579 that every household with a minimal family worth purchase a pre-publication of the Geneva Bible. Its first printing was a reprint of the 1562 edition of the Geneva Bible printed by Thomas Bassandyne and Alexander Arbuthnot in 1579.[18]

## Curiosities of the Geneva Bible

The popular name for the Geneva is "Breeches Bible" for its reading in Genesis 3:7, "They sewed fig tre leaves together, and made themselves

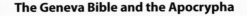

### The Geneva Bible and the Apocrypha

The Coverdale Bible was the first English Bible to separate the Apocrypha from the rest of the Bible and to suggest it did not have the same authority as the rest of Scripture. The Geneva Bible described it with even more restrictions. The Introduction to the Apocrypha reads:

"These books that follow in order after the Prophets unto the New Testament, are called Apocrypha, that is books, which were not received by a commune consent to be read and expounded publicly in the Church, neither yet served to prove any point of Christian religion, save in as much as they had the content of the other Scriptures called Canonical to confirm the same, or rather whereon they were grounded: but as books proceeding from godly men, were received to be read for the advancement and furtherance of the knowledge of the history, & for the instruction of godly manners: which books declare that at all times God had an especial care of his Church and left them not utterly destitute of teachers and means to confirm them in the hope of the promised Messiah, and also witness that those calamities that God sent to his Church, were according to his providence, who had both so threatened by his Prophets, and so brought it to pass for the destruction of their enemies, and for the trial of his children."

breeches." It is not a reading unique to the Geneva. The Wycliffe New Testament (1382) and Caxton's edition of Jacobus de Voragine's *Golden Legend* (1483) also used the term "breeches."

There are five editions of the Geneva Bible dated 1599. In these editions Franciscus Junius's notes replaced Tomson's in Revelation. It should be noted that in England the Geneva was not permitted to be printed after 1616. However, several editions dated 1599 were actually printed in 1633 by Robert Barker. Because printing them was prohibited in England, the date of 1599 was used since that was the last year of Christopher Barker's printing license. This insured that Robert would not be criticized for producing a Geneva Bible. The earliest of these editions was perhaps actually printed in 1599; we know this because "it abounds more than any others in gross errors."[19]

By 1642 the King James Version was overtaking the Geneva in popularity. This led Joost Broerss in Amsterdam to print the KJV with the Geneva notes in the margins.

## Description of the Geneva Bible

There were a number of unique innovations associated with the Geneva Bible: the five woodcut maps, the author's argument at the beginning of each book, twenty-six woodcuts scattered throughout, memory devices at the top of each page, a dedication to Queen Elizabeth, the Apocrypha attached to the end of the Old Testament (a practice begun with the Coverdale Bible), various tables, extensive notes, and cross-references. It was printed in Roman type in a small quarto size (9½ × 6½ inches), with italics for words not in the Greek text,[20] numbered verses, and paragraph markers.

Pre-Geneva Bibles were printed with paragraph divisions. But with the new use of verse divisions, paragraphs became less important. Paragraph marks (¶) were placed in the margins for the first time to mark larger divisions of the text. Later translations omitted the paragraph mark but noted the divisions. The practice of using the mark was retained and expanded in the King James Version. Interestingly, no paragraph marks occur in the 1611 KJV after Acts 20:36.

## Significant Geneva Bibles

*1557 Geneva New Testament.* The Whittingham New Testament was the first new translation since the Great Bible of 1539. Published without notes, it was not a primary translation, but a revision of Tyndale with minor word changes. The differences between the 1557 New Testament and the 1560 Geneva New Testament can be observed on nearly every page. The 1557 was never reprinted until a facsimile edition was undertaken in the nineteenth century. There were only a few printed in 1557, and since they were never again reprinted they are very rare.

*1575 Geneva Version.* The first Geneva Bible printed in England was a small octavo Latin letter edition. It is significant to note that the Geneva Bible was designed to be in small format, in the easier-to-read Latin letter, and divided by verses so that the Bible would be accessible to all. In Geneva the Reformation was in full swing and the principal tenet of the movement was the freedom to read and study the Bible.

*1577 Geneva Version.* My copy is an association copy belonging to Sir Richard Knightly (1533–1615), patron of the Puritans. He was knighted at Fortheringay in 1566 by the Earl of Leicester and was present in his official capacity as Sheriff of Northampton at the execution of Mary Queen of Scots (see sidebar "The Oath of a Queen" in chapter 10). A short essay relating to a man's sin is inscribed and signed by him at the beginning of the Bible. His second wife was Elizabeth Seymour, youngest daughter of the protector of Sumerset, uncle to Edward VI and therefore related to Queen Elizabeth I. Several pages of manuscript detailing this history are well preserved. Bibles clearly traceable to relatives of the Tudor royal family are very rare.

*1578 Geneva Version.* This is the first large-folio black-letter (often called Old English or Gothic) edition of the Geneva printed in England. The English preferred their Bibles to be in the formal black letter, believing it was in some way more respectful or pious. However, it violated the original intent of the Geneva. The larger volumes in black letter were difficult for laymen to purchase.

*1579 Bassandyne Bible.* Robert Lekprevik received license to print the Bible in Scotland on April 14, 1568: "Lord Regent to Robert Lekprevik . . . give, grant, and commit to him full license privilege and power to imprint

THE
NEWE TESTAMENT
OF OVR LORD IE-
SVS CHRIST.

Conferred diligently with the Greke, and beſt approued
tranſlations in diuers languages.

GOD                                            SAVE

THE                                            KING,

AT EDINBVRGH.
PRINTED BY THOMAS
BASSANDYNE.
M.D.LXXVI.

CVM PRIVILEGIO.

The title page of the Bassandyne Bible 1579.

## A Collector's Folly and a Soul Mate Found

I eagerly scanned through a London dealer's personal letter offering me a first edition Geneva Bible published in 1560. This wonderful treasure, offered at two thousand, was undervalued in my opinion. However, as a teacher with a family of five to feed, it was an enormous price.

My wife entered my office sensing an atmosphere of gloom and doom. She lovingly inquired of my troubled spirit. I lamented in a sullen monotone the wonderful Bible offered me and recounted its virtues. It contained an inscription from the famous eighteenth-century bibliophile Francis Fry to his daughter, and included the entire original fold-out maps. But we were simply unable to acquire it!

She interrupted me quickly with sympathetic words. Calmly, she persuaded me of this once-in-a-lifetime opportunity and urged me to buy it. "We will find a way," she said with a tone of confidence in her voice. Although in total denial I began to rationalize: "Of course we can." The atmosphere suddenly changed from gloom and doom to exhilaration and excitement! I wasted no time in phoning the dealer to place my order.

We knew we had a treasure: a Geneva Bible that belonged to Francis Fry (1803–86). Fry was a very important nineteenth-century bibliographer, scholar, Bible collector, and businessman. A plate on the first blank page in Fry's hand reads, "Priscilla Anne Fry from her loving Father, Francis Fry. Tower House, Cotham Bristol 1881." Apparently the Bible remained in the Fry family at least to the mid-twentieth century.

The Frys were a prominent English Quaker family who made their living in the chocolate business. In addition to joining the family chocolate business as

all . . . the English Bible imprinted before at Geneva."[21] For some unknown reason Lekprevik did not immediately print the Bible. By 1574 an edict went out reversing the favor found previously and Lekprevik fell into disgrace and spent time in the Edinburgh tower for printing without a license.

The responsibility for printing the first Bible in Scotland fell to Thomas Bassandyne. The lack of profitability in the printing business forced Bassandyne to take a well-connected partner of means, Alexander Arbuthnot. They concluded it would be less expensive to print in folio format rather than the usual thick quarto Geneva Bible.

a young man, Francis later became a director and then chairman of the Bristol waterworks, served on the board of directors of the Bristol and Gloucester Railway, and served on committees of the Bristol Philosophical Society.[22]

Fry was arguably the greatest Bible collector of the nineteenth century. His grandfather Joseph Fry's interest in printing Bibles may have piqued Francis's interest in his lifelong hobby of Bible collecting. Fry's reputation as a Bible collector and scholar is his greatest contribution to history. In a visit to Munich in 1860 to study books printed by Peter Schoeffer, the sixteenth-century German printer, he discovered that the first complete Tyndale New Testament was published by Schoeffer in 1526 (no extant copy of Fry's time had this information).[23]

Fry visited many private and public libraries collating pages in the various copies of the Great Bibles and the King James folios. His labors were marked by accuracy, great bibliographical acumen, and profound acquaintance with the history of English Bibles.[24] He published *A Description of the Great Bible—1539, Cranmer's Bible 1540–41, King James Bible 1611–40* (1865), *A Biographical Description of the Editions of the New Testament* (1878), and *The Bible by Coverdale, MDXXXV* (1867). In addition, he published facsimile editions of *The Souldiers Pocket Bible* (1862), *A Bibliographical Description of the Editions of the New Testament* (1878), and *The First New Testament printed in the English Language 1525–26* (1862). Unfortunately Fry's work has mixed reviews. His enthusiasm for perfecting copies of incomplete Bibles and producing facsimile leaves resulted in confusion for modern scholars. Today it is very difficult to examine available copies of the six editions of the Great Bible (1539–41) and the five editions of folio King James Versions (1611–40) and conclude what leaves belong to the original copies.

In March 1575 Arbuthnot presented to the General Assembly a proposal for printing the English Bible. The petition included a plea that would compel every person (bishops, superintendents, and commissioners) to buy a Bible for his parish church and pay for them in advance. The Assembly gave permission but included a condition that every book be overseen before it was printed. The individuals paid for the Bibles in advance nearly three years before delivery. A formal license to print Bibles was obtained in 1576.[25]

The printers promised to deliver the Bibles within nine months or to refund the money collected. Because Bassandyne continued to encounter delays, he was ordered to give up the printing office and Alexander Arbuthnot became the printer of record. Bassandyne died early in 1577, and in July of that year the first Bible printed in Scotland was finished and circulated. The New Testament printed first bears the name of Bassandyne, who failed to turn over the office immediately. The Old Testament title page bears the name of Alexander Arbuthnot, who soon became the official printer of the king. By 1580 the Assembly and local magistrates commanded every home to have Bibles in their houses. To enforce the order, every house in the kingdom was searched to assure their compliance.[26]

*1599 Geneva Bibles.* The 1599 Barker edition was the first to have the Huguenot divine Franciscus Junius's notes replace the notes in Revelation written by a Theodore Beza disciple, Laurence Tomson (1539–1608). However, the most important aspect of this edition is that five different printings claim the date of 1599. The last folio was printed in England in 1616 and the last quarto in 1615. After 1616 Joost Broerss and other Dutch printers printed many Geneva Bibles in Amsterdam. The advent of the King James Version in 1611 signaled the end of the endorsement of the Calvinistic Geneva in England. From 1616 England forbade the Geneva Bible to be printed. It is believed that the 1599 editions were actually done in 1633 and probably by Robert Barker but dated to the printer Christopher Barker so as not to blame Robert Barker for printing a banned Bible. Many of these quartos actually printed by Robert Barker are filled with printing errors and were not welcomed in England.

*1642 Geneva Notes in King James Version.* This Bible was the first King James Version printed outside England. Interestingly, it contained the notes of the Geneva Bible. The King James Version by 1642 had gained control of the Bible market. On the Continent, however, the Geneva notes were still the commentary of choice. From this time Joost Broerss of Amsterdam printed a number of these Bible combinations.

*1776, 1778 Geneva.* It has been understood by many authors that the 1644 folio of the Geneva Bible was the last to be published. However, two more Geneva editions were published in 1776 and 1778. Because the 1776 edition reprinted Bishop Parker's Preface, which accompanied the Bishops' Bible, it was often identified as a Bishops' Bible.

# 9

# The Clergy's Version

*A Bible Longing for an Audience*

Queen Elizabeth's ascension to the throne of England in 1558 brought reform in the church. Only five of the bishops appointed by King Edward VI survived Mary's bloody reign of terror. Queen Mary's appointments reflected her own survival instincts as much as her spiritual desire. Thanks to Mary, the Bible had been banned for five years. With Elizabeth on the throne, men and women everywhere could start reading the Bible again. A Bible in the British Museum records Queen Elizabeth's words, written in her own hand:

> August. I walke many times into the pleasant fields of the Holy Scripture where I plucke up the goodiesome herbes of sentences by pruning: eate them by reading: chawe them by musing: and laie them up at length in the hie seate of memorie by gathering them together: that so having tasted theire sweeteness I may the lesse perceave the bitterness of this miserable life.[1]

Church divisions and controversies were sure to resurface. Early in Elizabeth's reign, the Act of Uniformity was relaxed. As time passed, confusion surfaced, and Elizabeth charged Archbishop Parker with reestablishing the authority of the Act. He drew up a list to regulate the services and the prayer

A portrait of Queen Elizabeth I by artist Zucchero. She was one of the most powerful monarchs in English history. Elizabeth's ascending the throne after the short and bloody reign of her sister, Catholic Queen Mary, meant the Protestant church could live peacefully and safely again while the Catholics lost political favor. Photo: Heaton, *The Puritan Bible* (1913), 137.

time of the church, and to govern clerical dress. Rebellion surfaced as nonconformists took a stand and the division between the Church of England and the Puritans widened. While the controversy centered on church practice, the division spilled over into a fight over which translation was to survive. Elizabeth's desire to maintain a strong hold on her sovereignty forced her to seek the support of Protestants. Her support of the Protestant Bible gained Elizabeth widespread approval. Although not giving official sanction, she apparently was willing to be hailed as a patron of the Bible.

There was still a lingering distaste for the note-infested Geneva Bible. A scholar named Matthew Parker filled the theological seat of Canterbury as archbishop. Born in Norwich in 1504, Parker was educated at Corpus Christi College in Cambridge. He became dean of Lincoln and was a chaplain to Queen Anne Boleyn, Elizabeth's mother. His unassuming and quiet reformed ideas enabled him to escape the wrath of Mary. He was a great candidate for a new translator.

Archbishop Parker initially supported the reading of the Geneva Bible but later, as he became more anti-Calvinistic, he began to support a new translation. He saw the success of the Geneva Bible as an attack on the authority of the bishops. All religious authorities universally condemned Tyndale's version. Since Coverdale's translation and the Great Bible were not translated from the original languages, they were considered inferior. Matthew's and Taverner's versions did not gain general acceptance. However, Tyndale's New Testament was printed by the queen's printer, Richard Jugge. This may account for some of Tyndale's readings surviving in the Bishops' Bible.

The widespread popularity accorded the Geneva Bible after 1560 did not include the majority of the clergy in the Church of England. Although

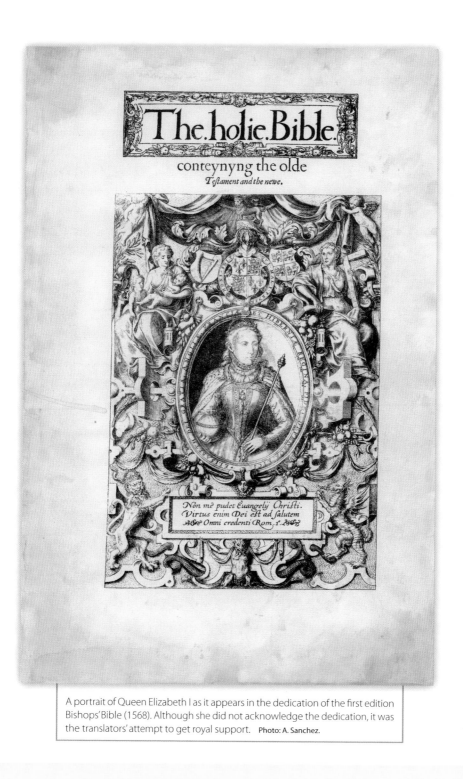

The.holie.Bible.

conteynyng the olde
Teſtament and the newe.

Nòn mẽ pudet Euangelij Chriſti.
Virtus enim Dei eſt ad ſalutem
Omni credenti Rom, 1.

A portrait of Queen Elizabeth I as it appears in the dedication of the first edition Bishops' Bible (1568). Although she did not acknowledge the dedication, it was the translators' attempt to get royal support.  Photo: A. Sanchez.

they recognized the superiority of the translation, the Calvinistic notes were offensive. Recognizing the inadequacies of the Great Bible, someone suggested an official translation be undertaken that could complete the task previously given to Coverdale.[2] Even Cranmer wanted the bishops to join together and complete a translation.

In 1563 a massive translation project was launched, and Archbishop Parker was selected as the chief editor. The following men were given the task to complete various parts of the Bishops' Bible: W. Allen, bishop of Exeter; R. Davies, bishop of St. David's; E. Sandys, bishop of Worcester; A. Pearson, canon of Canterbury; A. Perne, canon of Ely; R. Horne, bishop of Winchester; T. Bentham, bishop of Litchfield; E. Grindal, bishop of London; J. Parkhurst, bishop of Norwich; R. Coxe, bishop of Ely; E. Guest,

Two important Bishops' Bibles: Open in front is the 1568 first edition, and standing in the back is the 1572 first revision.

Photo: R. Maisel.

bishop of Rochester; G. Goodman, dean of Westchester; and Giles Lawrence, professor of Greek at Oxford.

On September 22, 1568, a copy of the Bishops' revision of the Great Bible was sent to Queen Elizabeth. The cover page had a large portrait of the queen, a very distinguishable characteristic of the first edition of the Bishops' Bible.

Church endorsement attempted to force the use of the new translation. The Bishops' Bible translators used Stephanus's Greek New Testament (1550), Pagninus's Latin (1528) and Munster's Hebrew (1535). They omitted any marginal notes that they thought might cause offense. Some of the notes in the Bishops' Bible were word for word from the Geneva Bible, including a predestination section at Romans 9.[3] In 1571 the Convocation of Canterbury ordered every bishop to have a copy of the Bishops' Bible translation at his house for use by servants and strangers.[4] In 1572 the Bishops' New Testament was extensively revised. While the 1568 edition reads "love" in 1 Corinthians 13, the 1572 revised New Testament reads "charity." King James translators in 1611 followed the revised Bishops' Bible and used "charity."

> Although the Bishops'
> Bible was never
> officially licensed
> as the authorized
> Bible, the church and
> state enthusiastically
> received it.

Although the Bishops' Bible was never officially licensed as the authorized Bible, the church and state enthusiastically received it. Clearly superior to the Great Bible, its actual translation fell short of the quality and simplicity of the Geneva translation. It never gained the popular support that many had hoped it would.

Sheer beauty alone will not bring popularity. Published by Richard Jugge, it was the most beautifully illustrated and finely printed edition of the

Engraving of Matthew Parker. Photo: Heaton, *The Puritan Bible* (1913), 161.

sixteenth century. Adorned by finely carved woodcuts, it remains a marvel of printing. With the war for its legitimacy over, printers could concentrate on making a fine printed Bible with illustrations to enhance its appearance. Parker's extensive preface is one of the defining elements of the Bishops' Bible.

Fear seems to have prevented a truly revised text that conformed to standard language of the day. The Bishops' Bible was no more than a slight revision of the Great Bible. Parker's theological persuasion meant that he refused to acknowledge superior readings from the Geneva text. Even with all its faults, many editions of the Bishops' Bible were published from 1568 to 1602. Yet it was not a Bible for the people but rather for continued theological debate. Its primary influence came when it was selected by the King James translators to be the standard version to be followed in the new translation.

## Important Editions of the English Bible

*1536 Tyndale's First Quarto New Testament.* There are three editions with variations of woodcuts of the apostle Paul's foot resting on a stone that introduces eleven epistles. In one edition his foot is on a stone that has the word "mole," in another the engraver's mark, and one is blank. The text of these editions follows closely the 1535 edition, the last edition revised by Tyndale himself. This edition is also known as the GH edition; GH refers to Guillaume Hytchins, the assumed name of William Tyndale.

*1538 Coverdale Diglot.* In 1538 three Coverdale diglots were published. In that year, Coverdale decided that Nicholson should publish a diglot with English and the Latin Vulgate in parallel columns. Coverdale felt that if the church hierarchy and the king could see his English translation side-by-side with the church-sanctioned Vulgate, they would conclude that his translation was faithful to the text of the Vulgate.

It was published in a very small, handsome format. However, this edition was so full of misprints and errors that Coverdale would not sanction it. He decided to have it done again, this time in France with Fraunces Regnault,

### A Collector's Nightmare

*Only three more first editions left to fill my collection*, I thought as I tried to justify the purchase of a first edition 1568 Bishops' Bible. While not exactly rare, they don't appear on the market very often. I was offered a copy of the Bishops' in exchange for my 1611/13 second edition of a folio King James and a 1522 Erasmus Greek New Testament. Both of my copies were highly sought after.

The King James 1611/13 version is desired because it is an early edition rather than for its significance as an important edition. The third edition of the Erasmus New Testament is important because of its influence on the King James Version. It was the edition used by Tyndale and has the infamous Johann Comma[5] in 1 John 5:7, the reading in the KJV. I have had a number of both editions, so I assumed they were easier to get and less expensive. Suffering from that delusion, I decided to make the deal. *Now only two first editions left*, I thought.

Several months later, while bargaining with another collector over trading various editions, I concluded that his asking price was too much. I didn't want to make the trade. He responded, "How can you say I am asking too much when you traded a 1611/13 KJV and a 1522 Erasmus for a 1568 Bishops' Bible?"

His point, of course, was that I didn't really know the value of Bibles. While embarrassed and feeling hurt over the implication, I realized he was quite right—I did pay too much for that Bishops' Bible. As with most collectors, I try to only make trades or purchases that are "collector smart" or "good deals." I had been bested. Making what peer collectors believe is a poor deal is a collector's nightmare. Although I later replaced both the "She" Bible and the Erasmus, the hurt of a sour deal still lingers. "Oh, get over it!" you might say. Well, I just can't. My nightmare has become my daydream that haunts my every future deal.

who was printing the Great Bible. This edition was done under Coverdale's own supervision and was ultimately approved. In the meantime, Nicholson edited and reprinted his mistake-ridden copy. While it was a vast improvement, many misprints remained.

*1541 Great Bible.* The 1539 Great Bible had on the title page a woodcut showing Henry VIII passing a copy of the Bible to his vice-regent Thomas Cromwell and to Archbishop Thomas Cranmer, and each distributing the Bible to the laity. Both Cromwell and Cranmer's coat of arms are affixed to their side of the sheet. The people are shouting, *"Vivat Rex* and God save the King." The design of the title sheet was to show a unified nation under Henry's authority that was derived from the Bible in which the church and state were working harmoniously. The turmoil over Henry's work at destroying the Bible, his fight with the Roman pontiff, and his personal problems set the stage for something to help unify the nation. In 1540 Cromwell fell out of favor and his coat of arms was chiseled out of the woodblock title page in the editions of 1541. The title pages in all subsequent editions actually have a blank space where Cromwell's coat of arms once appeared.

*1548–49 Erasmus's English Paraphrase of the New Testament.* These two small folio volumes (Gospel of John translated by Princess Mary before becoming "Bloody Queen Mary") were often used by clergy as a substitute for sermons.

*1552 Tyndale New Testament.* In 1552 Richard Jugge produced a revised Tyndale New Testament in quarto size with more than a hundred woodcut blocks. Although some of the blocks were used previously, for the first time Satan is pictured with a wooden leg in Matthew 13. Published under the reign of King Edward VI, the title is a portrait of Edward and later the edition was called Edward's New Testament. This edition claims to be with the "advice and helpe of godly learned men" and contains new introductions with notes.[6] Two other Jugge editions appeared in 1553 and 1566.

*1553 Great Bible.* "Queen Mary's Bible." This edition of the Bible was the last one printed before Mary Tudor became queen of England. Catholic Mary took her wrath out on Protestant Bibles by destroying them and persecuting those possessing them. The 1553 edition in the British Library has a note stating that Mary had destroyed the greater part of these Bibles. Complete copies of this Bible are very rare. One story is that many of the copies were gathered together for burning. As they were being fed to the fire, Protestant sympathizers gathered up torn, partial copies of the Bible and later bound them together. This story accounts for the many surviving but very incomplete copies of the 1553 edition. No Protestant Bible was printed in England during the reign of "Bloody Mary."

*1569 Great Bible.* The last Great Bible ever printed. In violation of its name, it was a thick quarto edition in handy size printed by John Cawood. The Psalter is divided into days for readings and has Latin chapter summaries. The Great Bible Psalter became the preferred form for many editions for several generations.

*1576 Bishops' Bible.* This small and rare folio Bible edition was the first Bishops' Bible to be authorized "Set forth to be read by the churches," by the Church of England.

*1602 Bishops' Bible.* The 1602 Bishops' Bible was the last folio of this version. With the success of the King James Version, the Bishops' Bible had no appeal to English readers. Yet this Bishops' Bible edition was the base version used by the King James translators.

*1619 Bishops' New Testament.* This very small octavo measures $5\frac{1}{2} \times 3\frac{1}{2}$ inches and is the last edition of the Bishops' New Testament. Printed by Bonham Norton and John Bill, printers to the "King's most excellent Majesty," it does not agree with any of the previously printed Bishops' editions. It most closely resembles the 1602 folio edition. The notes are neither from the Bishops' Bible, the Geneva version, nor any edition of the Matthew's version. It most closely follows Jugge's notes in the Tyndale New Testament of 1552. The extensive notes sometimes are greater than the text itself.[7]

There are no clues about who may have authorized Norton and Bill to use Jugge's notes rather than the expected Bishops' notes. It is interesting that the Bishops' notes were less controversial to the church than Jugge's. In the table of "The Epistles of the Old Testament according as they be now read," the day's readings follow no known Bishops' translation, but unpredictably follow the Matthew's version of 1537, with some exceptions. This strange and rather unusual edition has escaped the notice of scholars for some time.

*1722 King James Version, Edinburgh.* The first King James Version was not printed in Scotland until 1628 at Edinburgh. Scots imported Bibles printed in England and printed their own in Scotland after 1628. The common thread in printed Bibles was the excess of errors. The General Assembly of 1717 instructed the Commission to take steps to stop importing copies of Holy Scriptures that were filled with printing errors. The purpose of this 1722 edition was to have corrected all the mistakes that characterized so many Bibles. One quite noticeable mistake that did not get corrected was in Psalm 53:1, which reads "on God" for the correct "no God."[8]

# 10

# The Catholic Church Responds

*From Sacred Latin to Vulgar English*

The Bible in the vernacular fueled the fires of the Reformation. Without the English Bible, reform would have been impossible. The Reformation began in the early part of the sixteenth century and came at the expense of the established Roman Catholic Church. The controversy was not that the Bible could be read by the masses but that its interpretations sidestepped the received opinions and teachings of the church.

The Roman Catholic Church could not stand by and let the Protestant Church gain popular support. Protestants were attempting to interpret the Scriptures from their own reasoning powers devoid of help from the informed clergy and tradition. Reformed opinions were condemned as private and without any accountability to the church body worldwide. The Bible and its innate interpretation spread to the illiterate throngs without theological guidance. According to the Roman Catholic Church, this could not be tolerated.

## The Need for a Roman Catholic English Bible

The uneducated Roman Catholics saw no need for an English Bible, since it was not self-explanatory. Yet the barrage of Protestant translations in the period of free expression of thought under Edward's reign began to have an effect on the Catholic Church. The production of the Geneva Bible in 1560 with sectarian theological notes set the stage for a Catholic translation with its own doctrines explained in extensive footnotes and marginal notes.

Finally, a justification for a vernacular Bible had surfaced. While a translation of the Bible alone was a threat to the church's authority, a Bible with a full interpretation, expressing Catholic doctrines with full church authority behind it, proved to be the impetus necessary for its approval.

The Roman Catholic Church had to act—in self-defense really. The Reformers' emphasis on Greek and Hebrew as the source for the English Bible, with some disdain for the Catholic-sanctioned Latin Vulgate, also helped make the decision to commence a Catholic translation. As with the Protestant Bible under Henry VIII, the Douay-Rhemes was a product of exiles fleeing persecution—this time from Protestant Elizabeth.

Of course the Latin Vulgate would be used, but if it was to be sanctioned, which Vulgate would be officially recognized? In 1547, at the Council of Trent, the Louvain edition of the Vulgate became the official authorized Bible of the Roman Catholic Church. It soon became imperative that an English translation be made with church-sanctioned notes based on the recently approved Louvain text.

A new Roman Catholic translation now seemed imminent. Accepting this challenge, Roman Catholic scholar Gregory Martin took up the task of an English translation in October 1578 and completed it in March 1582. William Allen, Richard Bristow, and William Reynolds aided Martin. All four men met at the English college of Douay in France, where they were colleagues. (The effort moved to Rhemes, France, in 1578.) While Martin is usually given credit for the entire work, it appears the other men provided financial assistance and contributed some of the translation help.

## The Douay-Rhemes Bible

The first English translation of the Roman Catholic New Testament was published in 1582 in Rhemes, France. Because of financial difficulties, the

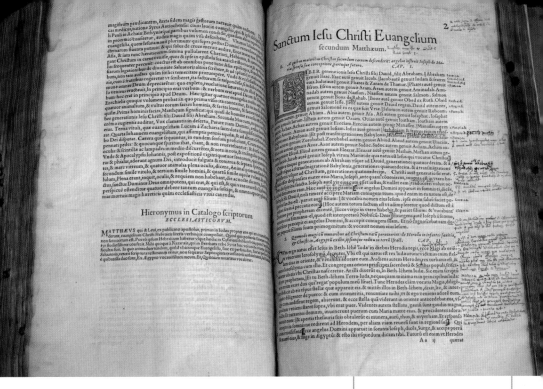

Old Testament did not get published until 1609/10 at Douay, France, where the college had relocated.

Would the new translation use Greek and Hebrew or Latin as the source for the new translation? The translators of the Douay-Rhemes consulted the Latin Bible (not the Greek) primarily, but they also drew from the English Geneva Bible and Coverdale's Regnault (France) edition of the diglot of 1538. Coverdale's diglot placed in the text his English translation side by side with the Latin to show his faithfulness to the Latin text beloved by Roman Catholics. The Rhemes New Testament adopted some of Coverdale's readings. For example, "the Son of man hath not where to lay his head" (Matt. 8:20) and "I see men as it were trees, walking" (Mark 8:24).[1] From the Geneva Bible, the Rhemes adopted "the wicked generation" (Matt. 12:45) and "whited tombs" (Matt. 23:27).

It is generally agreed that the end product was quite good. The Douay-Rhemes's weakness lies primarily in its lack of vernacular expressions and normal English word order, not unlike many early English translations.

## The Controversy: Catholic versus Protestant

Now it was the Protestants' turn to react to a Roman Catholic English version. In 1589, the Protestant scholar William Fulke (1538–89) published *The Text of the New Testament of Jesus Christ, translated out of the vulgar Latine by the Papists of the traitorous Seminarie at Rhemes. . . . Whereupon is Added the Translation out of the Original Greeke, Commonly used in the Church of England. . . . A confutation of all such Arguments, Glosses, and Annotations.* Dedicated to the Protestant Queen Elizabeth, this prodigious work laid side by side the text of the Bishops' and the Rhemes New Testament. Fulke blasts both the translation and the notes in the Rhemes New Testament. He refers to the pope and the church in the most vulgar of terms: "The Babylonical harlot and the spouse of the Antichrist."

The Reformation divided the Roman Catholic Church from the Protestant Church, but the battle over the Bible in English took the

First editions of the Rhemes New Testament (1582) and the Douay Old Testament (1610). The Roman Catholic response to the popular Protestant Geneva Bible with Calvinistic notes was to produce an English translation from the authorized Latin Vulgate with its own sectarian notes. Photo: R. Maisel.

battle to pen and ink. The Fulke-Martin controversy over the Roman Catholic Rhemes and the Protestant translations became intense. Later, the King James translators could not avoid the "blood spilt" over the issues of notes added, language used, and methods employed. Martin used disparaging language to discredit Protestant translations, such as: "manifold corruptions," "foul dealing," "false translations," and "heresies." He said, "[Translators were] corrupting both the letter and sense by false translation, adding, detracting, altering, transposing, pointing, and all other guileful means."[2]

As might be expected, Fulke was ready to respond. He shot back equally inflammatory accusations about the Rhemes translators: "They [translations, glosses, and annotations] contain manifest impieties, heresies, idolatries, superstitions, profaneness, treasons, slanders, absurdities, falsehoods and other evils."[3]

The war of words and insults revolved around the comparison of details in the texts. In four editions of his *Defence* (*A Defence of the Sincere and True Translations of the Holy Scriptures into the English Tongue*) (1589, 1601, 1617, and 1633), Fulke attempted to set the Rhemes New Testament against the Bishops' New Testament refuting each argument, gloss, and annotation point by point and word by word. As indicated above, one major target for Fulke was Martin's use of the English language. He consistently accused Martin of using ecclesiastical terms instead of words used by common people. To Martin, as to most Roman Catholics of the time, the English language was not capable of fully expressing the theological language, as was the sacred Latin. Martin argues, "As when you affect new strange words, which the people are not acquainted withal, but it is rather Hebrew to them than English" [e.g., Jeshuah for Jesus].

Fulke responds, "Seeing the most of the proper names of the Old Testament were unknown to the people before the Scripture was read in English, it was best to utter them according to the truth of their pronunciation in Hebrew, rather than after the common corruption which they had received in the Greek and Latin tongues."[4]

The Roman Catholic Rhemes met the same opposition under Elizabeth as the Protestant translations under Mary. The Rhemes New Testament was produced during the reign of Protestant Queen Elizabeth (1558–1603).

Like Tyndale New Testaments just thirty years earlier, the Rhemes New Testament had to be smuggled into England. English Catholics faced the same dangers experienced by Protestants earlier. The English desire to spread the Bible to the common people did not, of course, include the Catholic Rhemes New Testament. The Catholics' concerns for suffering are expressed in the notes to Revelation 22:23: "Lord Jesus Come quickly and judge betwixt us and our adversaries, and in the mean time give patience, comfort, and constancy to all that suffer for thy name, and trust in thee O Lord God our only helper and protector, tarry not long."

The strategy employed by Fulke clearly backfired. It was Fulke's intention that his rather inane and ad hominem arguments would destroy the credibility of the Rhemes. Instead, the interest in the Rhemes New Testament increased and ultimately influenced the Protestant King James Version.[5] The following Latin terms used by the King James translators in the book of Romans

The Fulke's first edition New Testament (1589; front, open) was a side-by-side comparison of the Rhemes New Testament and the Anglican Bishops' Bible. The Fulke's New Testament was to demonstrate the superiority of the Bishops' Bible, but the strategy backfired because it encouraged reluctant readers to look at the Rhemes (1582). Also pictured are the first edition Rhemes (right rear, open), and the King James Version (1629; left rear, open), the first edition published at Cambridge. Photo: R. Maisel.

came from the Rhemes edition: "consent," "impenitent," "approvst," "propitiation," "remission," "grace," "commendeth," and "confession is made."

## The Influence of the Roman Catholic Bible

The Catholic Bible was here to stay. The Rhemes New Testament went through four reprints (1582, 1600, 1617, and 1633) but was not revised for over 150 years. In 1738, Bishop Richard Challoner (bishop of the London district including the thirteen American colonies) began editing the New Testament and published a large-folio edition. As a pastor, Bishop Challoner observed the need for a Bible people could understand. He took to the task of revising using some of the same reasons and principles that had produced the King James Version. His desire for revision led him to publish

*continued on page 180*

## The "Gentle Madness" of a Bible Collector

The serious pursuit of any collectible—regardless of its cost or value—requires a bit of madness.

My relentless pursuit of that next treasure has kept my bank account at alarmingly low levels throughout the years. My wife has "enjoyed" my library whose fragrance is *eau de cologne musty* and a house that functions as a public storage unit. Her years of embracing the "gentle madness" of a collector have gained my admiration.

My ability to purchase rare Bibles and manuscripts has to a large extent been possible by trading with other collectors, selling rare and valuable copies that have little significance to my collection, or by selling second copies. In some cases the financial pressures have led me down a "dangerous path" of selling a rare or important copy to justify a family expenditure. With such madness, I purchased a car named "Cromwell," the down payment on a house called "Gutenberg," and recently an English Tudor dubbed "Stuart." A little imagination will suggest what I sacrificed to obtain these family "necessities." After all, the highly contagious disease called "Gentle Madness" afflicts only bibliophiles, bibliomaniacs, and those with an eternal passion for books.[7] Maybe you are safe—or maybe not.

The auction at Swann Galleries was somewhat disappointing. I was casually previewing the various Bibles coming up for auction the next day. There were a few things of interest: an incomplete 1539 Great Bible, two Geneva Bibles, and a manuscript. As I was looking at the Great Bible, a man approached me and inquired of my interest in Bibles. Once I reluctantly revealed my interest in Great Bibles, he offered me a 1540 Great Bible he had tucked away in his modest inventory in his home in Brooklyn. It certainly gained my interest since the 1540 edition of the Great Bible was the first edition to have Archbishop Thomas Cranmer's prologue, from which the Bible was dubbed "Cranmer's Bible." I needed to see it before the auction, because if I bought it I would not be able to buy anything at the auction the next day.

Brooklyn, New York, then the home of the Dodgers, the archrival of my beloved Yankees, was not a city I longed to see. My first adventure on a New York subway to Brooklyn was about to begin. As we sped along about five o'clock that evening, the culture shock began with the graffiti on the subway walls at each stop, cluttered fences beyond the subway, and the scruffy subway interior. Fellow travelers also reinforced my preconceived idea that New Yorkers were "interesting," to put it mildly.

We walked from the train station to a quaint Italian section of town with houses lined up in a row, all looking the same with ten steps to the front door. Children ran back and forth across the street, garbage cans neatly sat on the sidewalk, and cars lined the curb, parked tightly. It was a picturesque view I had not expected, right out of a Norman Rockwell painting.

Inside, my new friend introduced me to his wife, who enthusiastically invited me to dinner. After a fine Italian meal, Lawrence took me to his study where he began pulling out copies of Erasmus's third edition (1522) Greek New Testament, his first edition (1516) of the annotations, several other important Bibles, and books about the Bible. Then, he pulled out a Bible draped in a cloth that was the finest 1540 copy of the Great Bible I had ever seen. It was a "perfect" copy complete and with a binding by the famous nineteenth-century binder Riviere. This copy was printed by Richard Grafton, while most 1540 editions bear the printer's name Edward Whitchurch, and on the title page it spells Archbishop Cranmer's title "Cantorbury," where other copies have "Canterbury."

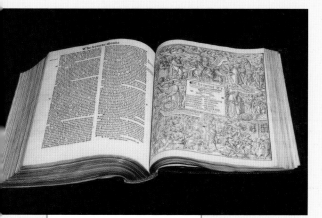

The Great Bible (April 1540). It was printed by Richard Grafton, with Riviere binding. This is the earliest Great Bible containing Cranmer's Prologue and one of only a few known copies to have the name Richard Grafton as the printer.

We began to negotiate immediately. The price was really out of my range, as was so often the case. Negotiations centered not just on price but on how payment could be made. Racing through my mind was the incriminating thought that this may be the last chance to buy this very important copy in such fine condition. I thought carefully about the price, weighed the potential negative financial consequences and the impact of bringing such an item into my home without prior notice, and then concluded that I just couldn't pass it up.

We had just met so he was not very comfortable with me taking the valuable treasure without the money. I left without it in hand, but in a few days it arrived and I have never looked back. It still is one of my most prized items. By the way, I also eventually bought the 1516 Erasmus Annotations and the 1522 Erasmus Greek New Testament I saw that night. It was one of the most memorable and exciting trips I ever made to purchase a Bible—and in Brooklyn of all places!

a small four-volume revision of the Douay-Rhemes in 1749–50. This edition became the standard edition for Roman Catholics for the next two hundred years.

The decades of Protestant persecution and the denial of a Catholic Bible was near an end. Freedom of the "press" finally won the day. By the nineteenth century, Protestant religious fervor waned and the years of Catholic Bible suppression gave way to public approval of religious tolerance. The change in the religious climate gave Thomas Haydock opportunity to revise and extend the notes of the Challoner revision of the Douay-Rhemes in his 1811 edition. The new edition included commentary and apologetics from patristic writings and later Catholic scholars.[8] Haydock Bibles in large, family folio editions became very popular in Ireland, England, and America. As modern Roman Catholic historian Sidney K. Ohlhausen reminds us, "The first Catholic president of the United States [John F. Kennedy] would take his oath of office on a Haydock Bible. This was in 1961, the one hundred and fiftieth anniversary of its appearance."[9]

Finally, all Christians—both Protestant and Catholic—could read God's Word in their beloved English language. Protestants and Catholics alike could feed their souls from the Living Word of God without dependence on a reader or expositor. The winds of reform and controversy would continue for many years as both religions struggled for reform.

## Significant Roman Catholic Bibles

*1589 Fulke's Counterblast to the Rhemes New Testament.* Although not a Catholic New Testament itself, apologist William Fulke placed the Bishops' New Testament side by side with the Catholic Rhemes New Testament and systematically refuted it issue by issue. His ungracious attacks on the Catholic Rhemes gained it more attention than he expected. It was reprinted in 1601, 1617, and 1633.

*1633 Rhemes New Testament.* The 1633 edition, probably produced at Rouen, includes engraved portraits of the four writers of the Gospels before each book, Paul before Romans, and John before Revelation, as well as a presentation of the day of Pentecost.

*1738 Rhemes New Testament in folio.* The folio edition of 1738 is the only Rhemes New Testament ever published in folio form.

*1547 Louvain Latin Bible.* The Louvain Bible was the first authorized Roman Catholic Bible and was not revised until the Clementine edition in 1592. At the time of the Council of Trent (1546), the Catholic Church had no authorized edition. By imperial edict all suspected Latin Bibles had been prohibited, and the theological faculty of Louvain was ordered to prepare an authorized edition.[10] The Latin edition appeared in 1547.

*1609 Latin Bible.* My copy is a curious edition. It is from the authorized edition of the Latin Vulgate known as the Sistine Clementine edition of 1592. Even though the 1547 had official church sanction, it was not an authorized edition; that awaited the 1592 edition. The Latin term *authentica* was used for official approval to indicate both authorized and accurate.[11] Scholars would of course want to use an authorized version for study.

This 1609 has the royal arms of James I and in the center of the arms the date 1615. The Bible was in the collection of Paul Schmidtchen in the 1960s. Schmidtchen believed this copy was the personal copy of King James I of England and had his personal handwriting in the margin of one of the leaves. He also notes the Latin title is missing and in its place is the woodcut title and genealogies in English. He theorizes the staunch Protestant King James attempted to hide the identity of the censured Roman Catholic Bible to prevent criticism for his secret use of the Latin Vulgate. My attempts to identify the handwriting took me to the British Library, which forwarded the writing to the Folger Shakespeare Library. I waited with great expectation for the arrival of the news from Washington, DC. But when it arrived, I read the letter with a bit of disappointment when they declared that in their "non-professional" opinion the handwriting was enough different that it did not appear to be that of James I. I tucked the Bible away in my safe and concluded it was still a mystery.

# 11

# A Royal Translation

*Splendors of the Stuart Court*

The angry shouting from the emotionally charged hall began to subside as the gavel banged repeatedly on the podium. His Majesty King James I of England could scarcely be heard as he stood to address the court and confidently proclaim, "We have assembled here today for a conference that shall change the Church of England. Not only do we want to clarify a number of Church teachings, but it is time to seek new interpretations of the Holy Scriptures."

Immediately, Puritan John Rainolds rose to his feet to be recognized, knowing full well he might be reprimanded for such a bold act. However, he was also aware that unlike Her Majesty Queen Elizabeth, King James was not known for his forceful character. "May your Majesty be pleased," John shouted above the roar in the room. All eyes turned toward John as he continued: "If it pleases your Majesty . . . If it pleases your Majesty," he repeated, "may a new translation be made that will answer to the intent of the original." A hush crept slowly around the room as everyone waited to hear the reaction of His Majesty at such a suggestion.

Before the king could respond, the haughty bishop of London, Richard Bancroft, leaped to his feet and blurted out in disagreement, "If we humored

A portrait of John Rainolds by an unknown artist. Rainolds was the main Puritan spokesman at Hampton Court (1604) and introduced the idea of a new translation, which led to the King James Version.

Photo: W. J. Heaton, *The Puritan Bible* (1913), 291.

every special interest, there would be no end of translations." Bancroft knew Rainolds supported the Puritan translation in the Geneva Bible. Here was his chance to belittle the Calvinistic, note-infested, sectarian version and support his favorite, the Bishops' Bible.

The churchmen in attendance now anticipated a full floor fight over the support of the Geneva Bible against the Bishops' Bible. James's hatred for the notes in the Geneva Version and the Bishops' Bible's support of church over state made the fight a certainty. They were stunned when James calmly cleared the air: "I confess I have never seen a Bible well translated, and the worst is the Geneva." With that admission, the door for a new translation swung wide open. The room buzzed at the prospect.

It was Monday, January 16, 1604. From these outbursts of emotion, a writing project began that would change the world of literature in English forever. Rainolds had no idea he would become the father of the King James Version. The seed he sowed that day soon gave birth to the most influential book ever published in the English language.

## The New Version Gets Under Way

The Reformation that swept England and the Continent was sweeping Scotland. The reign of Catholic Mary Queen of Scots, James's mother, now became tenuous. Her inept ability to rule wisely signaled her imminent abdication. In 1567, Protestant lords declared James VI king of Scotland. Mary was deposed as queen and after a failed plot to regain power, she fled Scotland to England, where she was imprisoned as an alleged accomplice to her husband Darnley's murder. After several Catholic plots to place Mary on the English throne, Queen Elizabeth had her beheaded (1587). James (later King James I), Darnley's son by Mary, raised no serious protest to her execution. This denial was a fact that caused resentment in the years to come.

King James VI of Scotland ascended the throne as King James I of England in 1603. Elizabeth had been sick for some time both mentally and physically. She sat with her feet propped up with pillows and her eyes fixed on the floor without a word. For a week she refused to change her dress. On March 22, 1603, the Privy Council was summoned to clarify the succession to the throne. When asked who was to ascend the throne, she cried, "Who but our cousin of Scotland, I pray you trouble me no more."[1]

The next morning, Elizabeth, the most powerful monarch in England, passed away. James of Scotland was proclaimed king of England, France, Scotland, and Ireland. From Henry VII (the first of the Tudors) through the "Virgin" Queen Elizabeth I (the last Tudor), the House of Tudor maintained a very powerful monarchy. When it passed from Henry VII through Mary Queen of Scots to James, the monarchy came to reside in the House of Stuart.

James's classical education in the tenets of the Reformation brought a reign that would bring the church and state, still trying to define itself, into close proximity. Declared head of Scotland's church and state in 1584, James soon began a long history of interference. The lords who brought him into power withdrew their support when they could not force their will on him. His enthusiastic claim of divine right to rule over the throne in both civil and spiritual matters ultimately brought his reign into deep conflict.

The way James handled the deeply divided problems of the Protestants and Catholics would define his reign. James's ascent to the throne of England gave hope to previously persecuted Catholics and Puritans.[2] Catholic hope rested on James's following his Catholic

A portrait of King James I by an unknown artist. The fame of King James I was more due to his influence in the production of the King James Version than his ineffective and often controversial reign. Photo: W. J. Heaton, *The Puritan Bible* (1913), 263.

mother, Mary Stuart. The Puritans' hope grew from the recognition of James's thoroughly Calvinistic education and his previous thirty-seven years as head of the Presbyterian Church in Scotland. He soon disappointed them both.[3]

King James was notorious for interfering with the affairs of both church and state. A petition by the Puritans complaining about the plight of their party in England circulated at Hampton Court and was presented to James.[4] In 1604 James I convened a conference at Hampton Court to discuss flaws in church practices and to consider the complaints of the Puritans.[5] His participation in church affairs in Scotland spilled over into his new kingdom in England. James, hailed as "a living library and a walking study," gave strength to his questions on issues of papal power versus regal power, communion, amusements on Sunday, and the removal of images from churches. James was critical of both the Roman Church and the Geneva Bible because of their critical attitude toward kingship.[6] The conference was about to embark on a mission unexpected by its participants. Safe from the recent plague infesting London, the Hampton Court conference would continue as if the world was as intent on the king's church matters as the men of the church were.

In the midst of the anti-Puritan tone of the conference, John Rainolds, a distinguished Puritan representative, boldly suggested that a new translation be undertaken. Rainolds's suggestion may have risen out of impure motives. He may have tried to use the conference to authorize his beloved Puritan Geneva Bible instead of taking the time, effort, and expense of an actual new translation. Nevertheless, the king's imagination quickly pounced on the idea. He now had another reason to attack the Puritans and could publish a translation without their sectarian and very objectionable notes. The Geneva Bible circulated widely, especially among the Puritans, but it was not approved by the church. Yet the

A TRVE AND

PERFECT RELA-

TION OF THE WHOLE

proceedings against the late moſt
barbarous Traitors, *Garnet* a Ieſuite,
and his Confederats :

*Contayning ſundry Speeches deliuered*
by the Lord Commiſsioners at their Arraign-
*ments, for the better ſatisfaction of thoſe that were*
*hearers, as occaſion was offered ;*

The Earle of Northamptons Speech hauing
*bene enlarged vpon thoſe grounds which*
*are ſet downe.*

*And laſtly all that paſſed at Garnets*
Execution.

¶ IMPRINTED AT
*London by* ROBERT BAR-
KER, Printer to the Kings moſt
Excellent Maieſtie. 1606.

The title page to *The Gun Powder Plot* (1606), with a confession from Guy Fawkes (leader of the plot to blow up the parliament building) along with his faint signature possibly after torture (lower right). This is probably a carefully crafted facsimile of the document, although it was represented to me as the original.

Bishops' Bible, authorized by the church, had not gained popularity or general acceptance.

A new translation was now a certainty in everyone's mind. James, after appointing teams to begin the work of translation, enacted a reign of terror when the infamous "Gunpowder Plot" of 1604 failed. This Roman Catholic plot to blow up the House of Lords by planting more than a ton and a half of gunpowder in thirty-six barrels concealed under coal and wood brought the full wrath of the king. The plot was discovered through an informant who had just become a loyal subject to James.[7]

King James was not "Saint" James. His cruelty extended to the persecution of Puritans. Deprived of work and the possibility of advancement, many Puritans fled to Amsterdam and then on to Plymouth in America, where the Geneva Bible remained as the favored Bible. But that story will be told later.

## Who Translated the King James Version?

Why were early English translations the work of individuals and later works by cooperative efforts? Today publishers select committees of scholars to translate modern versions. It is true that most pre–King James Bibles of the sixteenth century were primarily the work of individuals. During the early years the political dangers of translating the Bible into English prevented collaboration among those qualified to translate. By the time there was some degree of safety, translations became a team effort. James chose to produce a translation by using fifty-four highly qualified translators from England's finest scholars to embark upon the new project.[8] A division of six groups emerged that would be responsible for translating various books: two from Westminster (Genesis through 2 Kings, Romans through Jude), two from Cambridge (1 Chronicles through Song of Solomon and the Apocrypha), and two from Oxford (Isaiah through Malachi, Matthew through Acts and Revelation). Upon completion of the initial translation, they met in an equally represented committee of twelve to revise the total work. Miles Smith contributed the introduction, and Thomas Bilson added the headings to chapters.

thankes, and gaue it to them, saying,
Drinke ye all of it:

28 For this is my blood of the new Testament, which is shed for many for the remission of sinnes.

29 But I say vnto you, I will not drinke henceforth of this fruite of the vine, vntill that day when I drinke it new with you in my fathers kingdom.

30 And when they had sung an hymne, they went out into the mount of Oliues.

31 Then saith Iesus vnto them,*All ye shall be offended because of mee this night, For it is written, *I will smite the Shepheard, and the sheepe of the flocke shall be scattered abroad.

32 But after I am risen againe, *I will goe before you into Galilee.

33 Peter answered, and said vnto him, Though all men shall be offended because of thee, yet will I neuer bee offended.

34 Iesus said vnto him, *Verily I say vnto thee, that this night before the cocke crow,thou shalt deny me thrise.

35 Peter said vnto him, Though I should die with thee, yet will I not deny thee. Likewise also said all the disciples.

36 ¶*Then commeth Iudas with them vnto a place called Gethsemane, and saith vnto the disciples, Sit yee here,while I goe and pray yonder.

37 And hee tooke with him Peter, and the two sonnes of Zebedee, and began to be sorowfull, and very heauie.

38 Then saith hee vnto them, My soule is exceeding sorrowfull,euen vnto death: tary ye here,& watch with me.

39 And he went a little further, and fell on his face, and prayed saying, O my Father, if it be possible, let this cup passe from me: neuerthelesse, not as I will, but as thou wilt.

40 And he commeth vnto the disciples,and findeth them asleepe,and saith vnto Peter, What,could yee not watch with me one houre?

way againe, and prayed the third time,saying the same words.

45 Then commeth hee to his disciples, and saith vnto them, Sleepe on now, and take your rest, beholde, the houre is at hand, & the Sonne of man is betrayed into the hands of sinners.

46 Rise, let vs be going: behold, he is at hand that doeth betray me.

47 ¶ And *while he yet spake, loe, Iudas one of the twelue came, and with him a great multitude with swords and staues from the chiefe Priests and Elders of the people.

48 Now he that betrayed him gaue them a signe, saying, Whomsoeuer I shall kisse,that same is he,hold him fast.

49 And foorthwith he came to Iesus,and saide, Haile master, and kissed him.

50 And Iesus said vnto him,Friend, wherefore art thou come? Then came they, and layde handes on Iesus, and tooke him.

51 And beholde, one of them which were with Iesus, stretched out his hand, and drew his sword, and stroke a seruant of the high Priests,and smote off his eare.

52 Then said Iesus vnto him, Put vp againe thy sword into his place:* for all they that take the sword, shall perish with the sword.

53 Thinkest thou that I cannot now pray to my Father,and he shall presently giue mee more then twelue Legions of Angels?

54 But how then shall the Scriptures be fulfilled, * that thus it must be?

55 In that same houre said Iesus to the multitudes.Are ye come out as against a thiefe with swords and staues for to take mee? I sate dayly with you teaching in the Temple,and ye layd no hold on me.

56 But all this was done, that the * Scriptures of the Prophets might be fulfilled.Then all the disciples forsooke him,and fled:

57 ¶*And

*Mar.14. 43.luke 22. 47.ioh.18. 3.

*Gen.9.6. reuel.13. 10.

*Esay 53. 10.

*Lamen.4. 20.

In the 1613 King James Version, Matthew 26:36 reads, "Then commeth Judas with them unto a place called Gethsemane" instead of "Jesus."

The qualifications of the translators were impeccable. In King James's commission to the council at Hampton Court, the king stated the need for the finest scholars of the day. *The Summe and Substance* of 1604 records, "Whereupon his Highnesse wished, that some especiall paines should be taken in that behalfe for one uniforme translation . . . and this to bee done by the best learned in both the Universities, after them to bee reviewed by the Bishops, and the chiefe learned of the Church . . . and lastly to bee ratified by his Royall authoritie."[9]

It may be surprising to learn that the King James translators did not work directly from the Greek and Hebrew texts. The King James Version revised the many previous English versions and was guided by the Greek and Hebrew.[10] By now a fully developed philosophy of translation had emerged from previous work on translations. Richard Bancroft, bishop of London, set the ground rules for the new translation. Unlike Wycliffe, these men incorporated various established rules and principles for guiding the style and accuracy of their work. Bancroft constructed fifteen translation principles to govern the work.

The first of these stated that the Bishops' version would form the foundation Bible to act as the guideline and would be altered only when the truth demanded it.

> The King James Version revised the many previous English versions and was guided by the Greek and Hebrew.

It is well known today that the King James Version is not in modern English. But neither did the translation of 1611 use the common language of its day. The application of translation rule fifteen prevented the use of extensive modern language (the English used in 1611). This rule lists the earlier English versions to be used when they agree and represent the original text. They included Tyndale's (1526), Matthew's (1537), Coverdale's (1535), the Great Bible (1539), and the Geneva (1560). The injunction to use previous translations assured that before it came from the quills of the translators, the language employed was not the English commonly used in the seventeenth century.[11] They did modernize some expressions and words but felt compelled to retain many. To eliminate the offensiveness of several previous translations, marginal notes were omitted, except for notes relating to explanations of Hebrew or Greek words.

The work began in 1607 and was completed and published in 1611 by the king's own licensed printer, Robert Barker. The printing and publication of the King James Version is filled with mystery and intrigue. Scholars have been occupied for many years trying to unravel the mystery in the printing of the various editions of the King James Version. Let's take a glimpse at that story.

## Early Storm Clouds Threaten the Distribution of the New Version

Printing monopoly remained in the hands of the Barkers for many years. The printing license for the 1611 edition went to Robert Barker, the son of Christopher Barker, the established and official printer to Queen Elizabeth. Richard Jugge, an early printer to the queen, died in 1577. His license to print Bibles passed to Thomas Wilkes, who in turn sold a portion to Christopher Barker. In 1589, Christopher obtained the full license exclusively. His son, Robert, took over the business in 1600.

The reader will not be surprised that with a successful printing business, lawsuits played a big part in the production of the King James Version. Robert Barker paid 3,500 pounds sterling to begin printing the Bible in 1611. To ease the burden, Barker took on three partners: his cousins, John and Bonham Norton, and John Bill. Constant quarreling soon led to persistent litigation. In 1615 the court ordered Barker to give a portion of the patent to Bonham Norton and John Bill for one year. Years of litigation began. In 1618 Barker sued Norton for a portion of the office he had lost earlier and for stock in the printing house. For the next years the lawsuits favored first one man and then the next. After years of fierce infighting, Barker joined Bill and regained possession of the printing license. Norton was imprisoned for bribery in 1630 and died in 1635. Barker was now free to pursue the printing of the Bible. However, the years of litigation put Barker into heavy debt.[12]

It was Barker's successful printing and his arguments with Norton that may have led to the printing of the infamous "Wicked Bible." In 1631, Barker published a Bible that had the greatest possible error. In the Ten Commandments, the word *not* is removed from, "Thou shalt *not* commit adultery." It now

## William Shakespeare and the Bible

It may seem strange that the most recognized English literary figure was not involved in the literary production of the King James translation. There is a bizarre theory that links Shakespeare with the translation of Psalm 46. If you count forty-six letters from the beginning of the psalm, you come to the word "shake," and if you count forty-six letters from the end of the psalm, you arrive at the word "spear." This suggests to some that this is a veiled reference to the psalm as a work of William Shakespeare. Notwithstanding this attempt to associate Shakespeare as a translator, there is no evidence he had anything to do with the work on the King James Version.

By 1604 as the Hampton Court conference was in session, Shakespeare had already written many of his works. His comedies, *Merry Wives of Windsor*, *Measure for Measure*, and the *Twelfth Night* were plays James I is said to have enjoyed a great deal. It has been popularly thought that the Geneva Bible was the source of his quotes in his literary works. However, the Bishops' Bible, Geneva Bible, and the Great Bible were all used in various plays. Many of the Tudor translations were so similar it is often difficult to determine which one he used. Shakespeare quoted more from Psalms than any book other than, perhaps, Matthew. When he quoted the Psalms, he more than likely quoted from the Psalter (part of the Prayer Book, generally the Great Bible version) which was frequently bound with the Geneva Bible.

*Twelfth Night* II.v.188: "Wilt thou set thy foot o' my neck?"

Geneva Bible—Joshua 10:24: "*set* your feete upon the neckes of these Kings: . . . and *set* their feete upon their neckes." The Matthew's, Taverner's, Great Bible, and Bishops' Bibles have "*put* your feete."

*Othello* II.iii.296–97: "Give place to the devil."

Geneva Bible—Ephesians 4:27: "Give place to the devil." Earlier versions (Matthew's, Taverner's, and the Great Bible) said, "Give place unto the backebyters."

*Richard II* I.iii.202: "My name be blotted from the book of life."

Bishops' Bible—Revelation 3:5: "I will not blot out his name out of the booke of life." No other version used "blot out."

The conclusion of Shakespearian scholar Naseeb Shaheen is that the Bible most commonly used by Shakespeare was the Geneva version, but he was not limited to it. By the time the King James Version was actually published, Shakespeare's career was about over. He did, however, write **The Tempest** and *King Henry VIII* between 1611 and 1613. Shakespeare died of a fever in 1616, well before the King James Version became the dominant version.[13]

read, "Thou shalt commit adultery." Not only was Barker fined three hundred pounds, but his reputation suffered. Some today believe that Norton broke into Barker's printing office (he had set a precedent of dishonesty by stealing stock and implements a few years earlier) and sabotaged the printing of his 1631 edition.[17] Barker died in 1643, penniless and with a ruined reputation.

The printing controversy of the early King James Version centers around two editions claiming to be printed in 1611. One copy is known as the "He" Bible and the other as the "She" Bible for their readings in Ruth 3:15: "And *he/she* went into the citie." Although both readings have their support in the Latin and Hebrew Bibles,[18] most scholars today maintain that the "he" reading belongs to the first edition. Other differences also exist between these two editions. In the "She" Bible, for instance, Matthew 26:36 substitutes "Judas" for "Jesus" ("Then commeth *Judas* with them unto a place called Gethsemane").

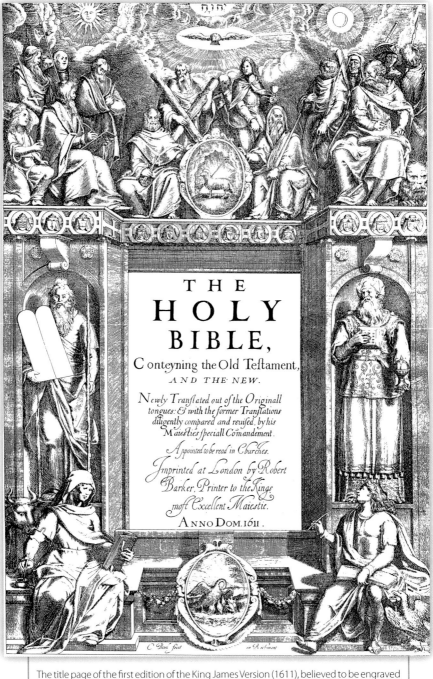

The title page of the first edition of the King James Version (1611), believed to be engraved by Cornelis Boel. It depicts Moses with the Ten Commandments on the left, Aaron on the right, and the four Gospel writers at the corners.

The first edition was a large folio, about $16 \times 10\frac{1}{2}$ inches, printed on a linen and rag paper in large black letter type with the chapter titles, summaries, parallel passages, and marginal references in a more readable Roman print. The title page signed by Cornelis Boel, an Antwerp artist who had painted portraits of Princess Elizabeth and Prince Henry, was engraved with Moses and Aaron standing in ornate niches with the apostles seated below the Tetragrammaton (the Old Testament name for God "YHWH").

If the King James Version was not officially "authorized," then what was its standing? The title clearly stated that it was "Appointed to be read in Churches."[19] While no official license was ever given to the King James Version, its sheer magnitude expressed its own authority. The claim for official authority was an attempt to fulfill the provisions of the *Constitutions* of 1408, which

The title page of the first quarto edition of the King James Version (1612). While the first two editions of the King James Versions were in large folio format for pulpit reading, the printers soon produced these small quartos for personal use.

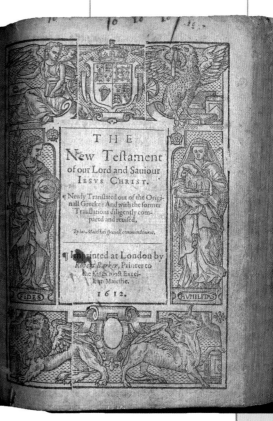

forbade the reading of an unauthorized translation. Thus it became known as the "Authorized Bible." The woodcut New Testament title page depicting the twelve tribes and twelve apostles was taken from the title page of the 1602 Bishops' Bible, whose title page read, "Authorized and appointed to be read in Churches."

Why was the word *Authorized* omitted from the title of what has become known as *The Authorized Version*, that is, the King James Version? Why does the King James Version have two editions with different readings, but both dated 1611? Why do small quarto Bibles in 1612 and 1613 have "he," "she," and "hee" readings in Ruth? Which title page dated 1611 was first, the copper plate or the woodcut?[20] These questions remain a mystery, but perhaps, when someone finds that manuscript copy from the hands of the original translators, a full explanation will be with it. Or maybe not!

The first edition "He" King James Version (1611) and the first edition second printing "She" Bible (1611/13). It is opened here to Ruth 3:15 at the "He" reading of the 1611 edition. Photo: R. Maisel.

How were the two distinct editions conceived? The two impressions of 1611 with the "he" and "she" readings may be partly explained by the fact that the need for copies for every church in England could not be met at one printing office. The second printing office may have set its own type. If the first office had completed its type set, a new setting could be constructed for the manuscript copy by the second office. The fact that the respective readings of "he" and "she" occur in a resetting of the type in the smaller editions of quartos can be explained if there were two separate printing houses all under the authority of Robert Barker. Perhaps originally the printers believed they could do the whole run themselves but later discovered that one shop could not complete the task and therefore set up another shop to help with the vast project. It may be that the second printing office did not complete its run until a year or more later. That would make the date of its publication 1613.

Differences abound in the various copies. The many editions of the King James Version differ in many of their leaves, in spelling, in type set and woodcuts, and their two different title pages. Errors in some copies do not occur in others. The obvious conclusion is that there were two or more different issues.[21] Another difficulty arises from the lack of paragraph markers after Acts 20:36. Why? Did the printers run out of paragraph type casts?

There were a total of five folio editions, all with many interchangeable leaves word for word: 1611, 1613, 1617, 1634, and 1639/40. A smaller folio edition printed in 1613 had seventy-two lines per page instead of the fifty-nine lines of the other folio editions. The smaller edition reduced the total pages from 738 to 508. The printing of each page of the fifty-nine-line editions used the same number of lines, line for line and word for word, enabling the printer to substitute reprinted pages when errors surfaced.[22] In the event additional copies needed some leaves, those left over from a previous printing could be used in the new printing. The nineteenth-century scholar and Bible collector Francis Fry observed 244 reprints of the second issue.[23] Of the two title pages dated 1611, one has a beautiful copper engraving signed by C. Boel, and the other has a woodcut identical to the 1602 Bishops' Bible.[24]

Demand soon dictated production. Sometime near the end of 1611, sufficient demand required a new printing. The numerous copies using the copper plate soon began to wear it out.[25] The popular woodcut carving could be used by a simple alteration of the inside frame. It is worthy to note that many King James Versions since 1611 also used this same woodcut title page. Therefore, copies can be found with either title page. The New Testament titles of all the folio editions continued to use the woodcuts. Today the copper engraved title is considered to be the original and is thus the most prized by collectors.

The confusion of the surviving copies of the KJV makes the reconstruction of the Bibles very difficult. If, as some scholars assume, there were as many as five printing presses printing these pages, it is not difficult to see how pages could get mixed and even omitted.[26] Each printer would, of course, want to use up any previous pages left over from an excessive overrun, or replace only those damaged by water or carelessness. Alfred W. Pollard theorizes that an accident must have happened early in the printing of the 1611 run that destroyed 119 of the 138 sheets (signatures Aa–Zz and Aaa–Zzz). Between 1611 and 1613 many of the editions exhibit combinations of the two printings bearing these signatures. During this period almost no two copies agree.[27] This would help explain why a corrected page does not necessarily mean a later whole copy. New mistakes entered when reprints were made.

The determination of which reading is from the original printing is problematic. However, in some instances, one can explain clearly which copy preceded the other. If a page has corrected an error, it most likely represents a later printing. This is the case with Ruth 3:15 where the first edition reads "he" and the later edition "she." Most feel "she" is the correct reading. The familiar error in Matthew 26:36 in the first edition reads correctly "Jesus" while the second issue reads incorrectly "Judas."[28]

The first edition of the King James Version (1611). The King James Version is a royal monument of English literature. It helped to stabilize English vocabulary, grammar, and spelling. While its printing history may be uncertain, it was a very well-printed Bible.   Photo: B. Bahner.

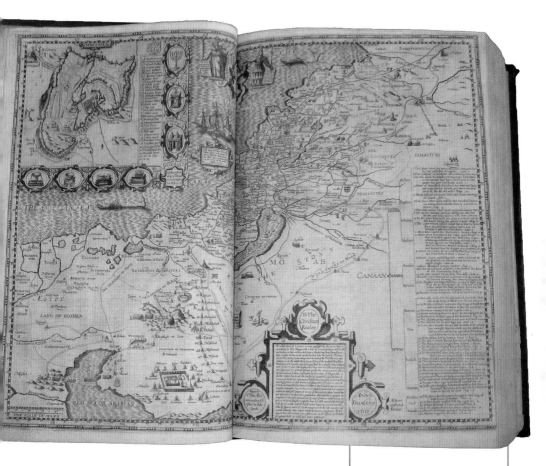

The introduction may shed some light on the printing corrections. The initial page of the genealogies that contain an introduction "To the Christian Reader" is blank on the reverse in one instance, while the reverse of others has the royal coat of arms. Presumably the blank was printed prior to the one containing the coat of arms under the assumption that, once the royal coat of arms was included, they would not be removed. The coat of arms is present in some copies dating to 1611, but it appears regularly in the 1613 second issue.

Two other major features in the 1611 issue help point to reprint leaves or corrections. The 1611 first issue spells "LORD" with all capitals of the same print size in the book of Genesis. From Genesis 40 through the remainder of

A 1611 King James Version engraved map by Elstrack. Photo: J. Hellstern.

the Old Testament it is spelled "Lᴏʀᴅ," with the word in all capitals also, but the "L" is a larger font. Noting this print in Genesis easily and quickly identifies the 1611 "He" Bible.

Even the maps tell a tale of mystery. There are two distinct maps of Canaan in the 1611 first issue. The characteristics of the first one printed are as follows:

1. The seas are stippled (i.e., multiple dots make an appearance of gray coloring).
2. There is no authorship name attached.
3. The original plate used to reproduce the map is copper.
4. Other minor differences are observable with careful comparison.

The characteristics of the second map are:

1. The seas are shaded using fine lines to make the gray coloring.
2. The author's name, Elstrack, is printed on the lower right corner of the right page.
3. The plate used to reproduce the map is a letterpress.

It is probable that the map with Elstrack's name is the second one printed since it occurs in the folios dated 1613, 1617, and 1634. The 1611 first edition, first issue can be found with different title pages, different maps, and different "To the Christian Reader" verso leaves (one blank and one with the royal coat of arms).

There are some specific details that help in understanding the variations in pages. Evidence that pages were intentionally printed in such a fashion so as to always read page for page can be seen from Exodus 14:10, where the *editio princeps* (term used of the first edition first issue) reads,

> And when Pharaoh drew nigh,
> the children of Israel lift up their eyes,
> and behold, the Egyptians marched after
> them, and they were sore afraid: and
> the children of Israel lift up their eyes,
> and behold, the Egyptians marched

after them, and they were sore afraid:
and the children of Israel cried out unto
the LORD.

Lines 2, 3, and 4 are repeated in lines 5, 6, and 7. When the error was discovered, the three lines were omitted. This left three empty lines in the reprinted page. But instead of bringing material forward and filling in the lines in the 1611/13 "She" Bible, the blank lines were inserted at the beginning of chapter 15 on the recto, or front side of the leaf. The leaf remained intact and could simply be inserted in any future folio edition.

Francis Fry, after comparing a hundred copies, leaf by leaf, believed he could determine which leaves belonged to the *editio princeps* and which belonged to the 1613 ("She") and its variants. Fry, a recognized nineteenth-century scholar, spent much of his academic energy and research to understand the process of printing. He believed he understood which signatures and reprinted leaves belonged to the first and second issues. Over the course of many years, he gathered copies and exchanged leaves according to his theory. Although this was a worthy project, he destroyed copies that could have been used for research today.[29]

Fry is not the only one to be blamed for this reprehensible practice. At least he did it for historical and scholarly purposes. Today people put together various copies of the folio editions and call them *editio princeps* in order to sell them as first editions of 1611. It is still possible to detect the displaced leaves after careful examination of these made-up copies. Mixed copies came from the printer's office when the 1613 printing took place. Perhaps leaves and partial copies were left from the 1611 printing and were used in the new edition. Determining which edition of the 1611 folio or 1612 quarto was used as the text form for the 1613 folio is difficult.

Portrait of Francis Fry
Photo: Theodore Fry, *A Brief Memoir of Francis Fry* (1887), Frontispiece.

## Early Reception of the King James Version

The King James Version was not immediately accepted as the standard English Bible. A well-established scholar of the period, Hugh Broughton, who was ignored by the translation assignment committee, was a vocal critic. He counted hundreds of words that he confidently condemned as totally erroneous, and he warned that the translators would answer for their corrupt work on the day of judgment. Broughton's criticisms were somewhat dulled by his history of behavior.[30] He had sharply criticized the Bishops' Bible thirty years earlier.

The Geneva Bible continued to be the popular Bible of the masses. Many of the translators of the King James Version used the Geneva Bible, which continued to be printed outside England until its last edition in 1644.[31]

Just as it is hard to give up on an old pair of shoes, the old familiar version of the Bible did not easily give way to the new translation. Miles Smith, in his introduction to the King James Version, quoted from the Geneva and continued to quote it in sermons. However, the staunchly Calvinistic archbishop of Canterbury and KJV translator George Abbot and the great preacher and poet John Donne made frequent use of the new version almost immediately.[32]

Many assume that because the king of England supported the King James Version, it received official sanction. There is no evidence that the new version ever received any official pronouncement or that the king even accepted it as the Bible of the kingdom. The title page's statement "Appointed to be read in the Churches" is quite different from saying "Authorized to be read in the Churches." In fact, several editions omitted the phrase altogether (1612 octavo, 1612 quarto, 1612/13 quarto, 1616 small folio, etc.). It is more likely that the phrase was used simply to refer to the larger folio editions as the appropriate ones to rest on the pulpits in the churches. The original intent was not to state that this version was the one officially licensed. Official sanction was more probably assumed since the king's printer, Robert Barker, published the translation initiated by the king himself. Whatever the case, the "Authorized Version" continued to be published and its authority was soon established.[33]

## A Surprise Blessing

I longed for a first edition King James ("He") Bible (1611). They are expensive and difficult to find.

A fellow collector called me one evening to tell me about a King James Version being offered for auction at a little-known California auction house. He was in the same predicament as I, an appetite for collecting without the nourishment to fill it. The next day, I sent for a full description, date of the auction, and estimated hammer price.

When the information arrived, I poured over the description. It was not clear. It sounded as if the full text of the Bible was incomplete and perhaps much of it from another copy. The price was estimated from ten to twelve thousand dollars. While that would be a good price for a complete copy, this one was suspicious. After getting over the disappointment of the description and the fact the price was too high for the Bible described, I mailed off an impossible offer of seven thousand dollars.

Normally the seller has a reserve usually about 10 percent below the low bid estimate; in this case it would be nine thousand dollars. My offer was primarily to alert the auction house of my interest in such things so they would send me a notice of any Bible they might get in the future.

Two weeks later, after I had forgotten about my bid, I received a bill in the mail for seven thousand dollars. I had won the bid! I was confused to say the least. On the one hand I did not have seven thousand dollars, and on the other hand I felt there was a mistake. I phoned the auction house to inquire as to why I was the winner of the bid. The person on the other end said there had been no interest in the Bible and only my bid came by mail before the auction. The auctioneer contacted the woman who owned the Bible and told her of my bid and asked if she would be willing to sell it for that price if no one attempted to buy it at the auction. Her answer enabled me to have my first 1611 ("He") Bible. I had to go deep into my savings and credit cards to get it, but with joy and excitement, I sent a check off in time to save my reputation as a legitimate collector.

When I received the copy, to my utter surprise, it was a complete copy without mixture. The description had been misleading, but as I reread it, I felt it was quite accurate. It was describing the condition of some of the ragged edges—not the absence of leaves, undoubtedly the reason no one pursued the bid. While the price tag dipped deeply into my pocket, the blessing more than matched the depleted bank account.

Just as those old shoes must finally give way to a new fit, the King James Version finally gained a full share of the buying market. By the end of its second decade of printing, the Authorized Version had established itself as the version of nearly every household. It took about thirty years for it to displace the popular Geneva Bible completely. Scotland began printing the King James Version in 1629 and officially recognized it by 1634. A. S. Herbert points out that the Authorized Version continued to be printed in great numbers from 1616 on.[34] The Geneva Bible, however, was not printed after 1616 in England, although an English edition of the New Testament bears the date 1619 on the title page, and the entire Bible was printed in Amsterdam until 1644.

> By the end of its second decade of printing, the Authorized Version had established itself as the version of nearly every household.

Progress could not be halted. The King James Version ultimately triumphed for several reasons.[35] First, the scholarly men translating the Bible placed a great deal of emphasis on literary as well as linguistic considerations. The literary beauty made it acceptable to a wide range of readers. Its flowing patterns and rhythmic style also made the text memorable. This was, after all, the period of Shakespeare, when the English language itself was at its apex. No other period in English literature venerated the English language as did the late sixteenth and early seventeenth centuries.

Second, the King James Version found acceptance among English-speaking clergy and theologians. Because it did not contain objectionable notes as the Geneva Bible did, various theological positions embraced it.

Third, the new version won over its readers by sheer merit. Its faithfulness to the original languages and its fluid expressions as literature guaranteed its success. By the middle of the seventeenth century, the entire English-speaking world read it as the Word of God. So dominant did the King James Version become that for 270 years it had no peers. It was not until the English Revised Version of 1881 that any version seriously challenged its supremacy. The challenge, however, was more of a token than substantial, but it opened the door to the twentieth century with its plethora of translations.

# 12

# The King's Bible Revised

*From King James to Queen Victoria*

W hen we carefully compare the modern King James Version with the original 1611 edition, we will discover a number of departures the modern King James Version makes from that first edition. Some of these differences are deliberate changes to correct errors of previous editions. From the first year of publication, errors crept into the text. Subsequent editions attempted to eradicate printers' errors. Each revision, however, corrected old errors and introduced new ones. These errors include spelling, vocabulary, and many errors introduced by using a later edition rather than going back to the original 1611 edition. The financial windfall of printing the popular version in the seventeenth century encouraged unskilled editors to print Bibles hurriedly and without much attention to proofreading. Soon printers, being aware of the misprints, undertook to revise and correct the readings.

Not all differences between the two distinct 1611 and 1613 issues can be attributed to printers' errors, however. There seem to have been distinct differences in the translations. Where did they come from and who made the changes? These are difficult questions to answer. There may have been several places of printing, and each printer took some liberties with the manuscript he received from the translators as previously suggested.

In addition to the most heralded difference of "he" and "she" readings in Ruth 3:15 in the two first issues of 1611/13, there are several other differences. A few are mentioned here.

| Text | 1611 "He" Bible | 1611 "She" Bible |
| --- | --- | --- |
| Matthew 26:36 | "Jesus" (1617) | "Judas" |
| John 20:25 | "put my finger into the print of the nails and . . ." | Omitted |
| 2 Timothy 4:16 | "may not bee laid to their charge" | "may be layd to their charge" |
| 1 Kings 3:5 | "and offered peace offerings" | Omitted (1617) |
| 2 Chronicles 25:12 | "children of Judah" | "children of Israel" |
| Song of Solomon 2:7 | "till she please" | "till he please" |
| Habakkuk 2:5 | ". . . nations, and heapeth unto him all . . ." | Omitted |

## The First Attempt to Correct the Text—1616

The small 1616 folio edition of the King James Version in Roman type revised the text in many places. While some minor revisions occurred in a 1612 black letter (old English style) New Testament and a 1612 Roman type (Latin letters), the first serious attempt was made to edit the complete Bible in 1616. This rare edition, not particularly intended for church reading, was a very accurate editing of the original 1611 printing and only occasionally adopted 1613 folio or 1612 quarto readings. However, it had almost no influence on the subsequent folio editions of 1617, 1634, and 1640, which continued to be set from the 1611 printing. The setting of these large black letter editions was so difficult and costly that the corrections were ignored. A few of the revisions are listed here:

| Text | 1611 "He" Bible | 1616 "She" Bible |
| --- | --- | --- |
| Leviticus 26:40 | "the iniquity" | "their iniquity and the iniquity" |
| Deuteronomy 16:5 | "the gates" | "thy gates" |
| 2 Chronicles 32:5 | "prepared Millo" | "repaired Millo" |
| Job 39:30 | "there is he" | "there is she" |
| Jeremiah 49:1 | "inherit God" | "inherit Gad" |

## Original Translators Seek a Revision—1629

Translators appear to be their own critics. The credit for the first thorough revision of the King James Version belongs to two of the original translators of the 1611 edition. Recognizing the need for the extensive revision, Samuel Ward and John Bois set to the task of revising the text.

Up to this time, the printing of the king's version was left in the hands of Robert Barker, "Printer to the King's most Excellent Majesty." For the first time, two Scottish printers from Cambridge, Thomas and John Buck, "Printers to the University of Cambridge," began to print the King James Version. The first edition, in a small folio format, made major revisions. No evidence exists that any official authority was ever granted for such a project. Nevertheless, it was still referred to as the Authorized Version and the title page reads, "Appointed to be read in Churches."

In spite of the king's desire to reduce the number of marginal notes in the 1611 edition, the 1629 revision began to expand on the marginal notes. This beautiful Roman type set took careful note of the words printed in italics, spelling, punctuation, and marginal references. These notes, however, were not objectionable like those of the Geneva Bible. Most notes were references to the meanings of particular Hebrew or Greek words. Second Kings 23:33 reads, "that he might not reigne in Jerusalem." The marginal note says, "Or, because he reigned." Romans 6:13 reads, "as instruments of unrighteousness" and the note, "Gr, arms or weapons." Other variations are:

| Text | 1611 | 1629 |
|------|------|------|
| Exodus 26:8 | "and the eleven" | "and the eleven curtains" |
| Deuteronomy 5:29 | "My commandments" | "all My commandments" |
| Deuteronomy 10:10 (marg.) | "fortie" | "former" |
| 1 Samuel 1:20 (marg.) | "revelation" | "revolution" |
| Mark 15:41 | "Galile" | "Galilee" |
| 1 Corinthians 12:28 | "helps in governments" | "helps, governments" |
| 1 Timothy 4:16 | "unto the doctrine" | "unto thy doctrine" |

## The Revision Process Finds Success—1638

During the first few decades of the seventeenth century, Bible printing was a major economic boom. No wonder attention was given to printing Bibles and preparing revisions. In 1638, Ward and Bois, joined by Thomas Goad and Joseph Mead, continued the revisions they began in the 1629 edition. Printers Thomas Buck and Roger Daniel printed the very accurate revision in a large folio similar in size to that of the original 1611 folio. Special attention was paid to render the italics uniformly. In addition to improvements in the margin and italics, new readings were also introduced into the text itself. These new readings can be compared as follows:

| Text | 1611 and 1629 | 1638 Revision |
|------|---------------|---------------|
| Matthew 12:23 | "Is this the sonne of David?" | "Is not this the sonne of David?" |
| 1 John 5:12 | "hath not the Sonne" | "hath not the Sonne of God" |
| Acts 6:3[1] | "whom we may appoint" | "whom ye may appoint" |
| John 14:6 | "the truth" | "and the truth" |

This revision became the standard edition until 1762. Scholars have applauded its accuracy for many years. Generally speaking, the editions produced in Cambridge were more accurate than the Barker editions. However, all the errors were not corrected, nor were some of the corrections made in 1629 retained in 1638.

## Printers Sacrifice Accuracy to Become Entrepreneurs

The text between 1638 and 1762, apart from printers' errors, remained stable. The revision of 1638 formed the text that most printers followed. It must be pointed out, however, that printers often followed texts that were not necessarily "standard." It is possible to find many variants in the editions between the publications of these two major revisions.

The real problem from 1630 to 1762 was the carelessness of printers. Public demand for Bibles caused printers to shortcut careful proofreading

The Wicked Bible (1631). This Bible with the most improbable error in Exodus 20:14, "Thou shalt commit adultery," is perhaps the most famous Bible ever produced. During this period the Bible was in great demand and printers anxious to take advantage of the market began printing Bibles quickly and cheaply.

procedures. This period is notorious for its number of error-ridden editions. In 1631, the eighth commandment in Exodus 20:14 read, "Thou shalt commit adultery." This edition became known as the "Wicked" Bible. (See sidebar "Famous Editions of the Bible" for other Bible nicknames.) In 1638, one edition read in Luke 7:47, "her sins which are many are forgotten" (rather than "forgiven"). In 1653, a small Bible known as the "Unrighteous" Bible read in 1 Corinthians 6:9, "Know ye not that the unrighteous shall inherit the

The Unrighteous Bible (1653). This Bible is known as the "Unrighteous" Bible for its reading "Know ye not that the unrighteous shall inherit the kingdom of God" (1 Cor. 6:9).

## Famous Editions of the Bible

Many Bibles received unusual nicknames for the way publishers printed certain passages. It usually revolved around the size ("Great Bible"), a publisher (Aitken Bible), a quaint expression ("Bugge" Bible), a special woodcut ("Blankstone" Bible), a misprint ("Wicked" Bible), or omitted words ("Unrighteous" Bible). These Bibles have been highly sought after by collectors.

The Geneva Bible is most commonly known by its nickname, the **"Breeches" Bible** (1560), for its reading in Genesis 3:7: "They sewed fig tre leaves together and made themselves breeches" (King James Version "aprons"). Some other examples are:

**"Bugge" Bible** (1535). Psalm 91:5: "Thou shalt not nede to be afrayde for anye bugges by nyghte." This reading can be found in the Coverdale, Taverner's, and Matthew's Bibles.

**"Treacle" Bible** (1535). The Coverdale Bible was the first to render Jeremiah 8:22 as ". . . for there is no triacle at Galaad. . . ." This can be found also in the Bishops' Bible (1568).

**"Wife-beater's" Bible** (1549). A note in 1 Peter 3:2, in Daye and Seres's edition of the Matthew's Bible, says, "And yf she be not obedient and helpfull unto hym, endeavoreth to beate the feare of God into her heade."

**"Whig" Bible** (1562). A printer's error in Matthew 5:9, in the second edition Geneva Bible, wrote "placemakers" for "peacemakers," which was later facetiously associated with the political methods of the Whig party in England (1678).

**"Leda" Bible** (1572). In the third and first revised editions of the Bishops' Bible, the woodcut initial before the epistle to the Hebrews was borrowed by the printer from an edition of Ovid's *Metamorphoses*, and represented Jupiter appearing to Leda as a swan.

kingdom of God?" Another very infamous Bible in a long list of "error Bibles" was the "Vinegar Bible" of 1716–17. The top of the page heading in Luke 20 reads, "Parable of the Vinegar" instead of "Parable of the Vineyard." The printer, John Baskett, had so many misprints in the printing of this Bible that it was dubbed a "Baskett-full-of-errors."

The great demand for the Scriptures and the English Civil War of 1642 compounded the problem of production. Bible publication slowed

**"1495" Geneva Bible** (1594). A transposition of figures in the New Testament title date of this Geneva Bible seems to make it one of the incunabula Bibles (1456–1500).

**"Judas" Bible** (1611). The "She" Bible and the New Testament of the 1611/13 folio misprint "Judas" for "Jesus" in Matthew 26:36. A similar error occurs in the first issue of the 1610/11 Geneva Bible in John 6:67.

**"Wicked" Bible** (1631). Barker's octavo edition of the King James Version made a colossal mistake in Exodus 20:14: "Thou shalt commit adultery."

**"Forgotten Sins" Bible** (1638). A pocket-size (duodecimo) edition of the King James Version errs in Luke 7:47: "her sins which are many are forgotten" (where "forgiven" is intended).

**"More Sea" Bible** (1641). An octavo edition printed by Barker renders the last sentence of Revelation 21:1, "and there was more sea" (for "no more sea").

**"Unrighteous" Bible** (1653). Printer John Field's small pocket edition of the King James Version renders 1 Corinthians 6:9, "Know ye not that the unrighteous shall inherit the kingdom of God?"

**"Vinegar" Bible** (1716–17). John Baskett's folio edition of the King James Version misprints the page heading over Luke 20 as the "Parable of the Vinegar" (instead of "the Vineyard").

**"Murderers" Bible** (1801). An Oxford University Press octavo of the King James Version misprints "murderers" for "murmurers" in Jude 16.

**"Standing Fishes" Bible** (1806). A London quarto by the king's printers says in Ezekiel 47:10, "the fishes shall stand" (where "fishers" was intended).

**"Wife-hater's" Bible** (1810). An Oxford University Press octavo of the King James Version renders Luke 14:26, "If any man hate not his father . . . , and his own wife also, he cannot be my disciple" (where "wife" was substituted for "life").

considerably in England during this period. Less carefully prepared editions were imported from Holland to meet the demand.

## The Revision That Restored Accuracy—1762

It seems that people can tolerate inferior quality printing, outdated language, and inadequate text only so long. In 1762, Dr. F. S. Paris edited the

King James text for publisher Joseph Bentham at Cambridge with the intent of updating the language and minor grammar issues. It had been more than one hundred years since a serious attempt had been made toward a revision. Several editions had revised various aspects of the text, but none had taken a careful look at the text itself. A committee had been appointed as early as 1657 to do a revision, but nothing came of it.

This edition, more than any since 1611, formed the basis for the King James Version we use today. Dr. Paris made a serious attempt to correct the text in spelling, punctuation, italics, and printers' errors. Its influence extended to the mind-set that scholarly criticism was necessary for an accurate English translation, and it paved the way in 1769 for Benjamin Blayney's Bible, which ultimately became the standard for all future Bibles.

Paris introduced a rather interesting marginal note in Acts 7:45. The text reads, "Which also our fathers that came after, brought in with Jesus . . ." Paris's note says, "or having received." No notice is made of the alternate rendering of the Greek phrase in the 1881 Revised Version or the 1901 American Standard Version. However, the 1979 New King James Version published by Thomas Nelson picked up the same rendering when it placed in the text itself, not in the margin, "which our fathers, having received it in succession . . ."

The new revision was not without criticism. Several noticeable errors occurred in the revision of italics.[2] In 2 Kings 25:4, the 1611 edition correctly reads, "of warre *fled* by night," whereas the 1762 reads, "of *war* fled by night." In Psalm 13:3, Paris correctly reads, "the *sleep* of death" for the 1611 reading of "the sleep of *death.*" Some other differences between 1762 and 1611 follow:

| Text | 1611 | 1762 |
|---|---|---|
| Matthew 16:16 | "Thou are Christ" | "Thou are the Christ" |
| Luke 19:9 | "the son of Abraham" | "a son of Abraham" |
| John 15:20 | "than the Lord" | "than his Lord" |
| Romans 4:12 | "but also walk" | "but who also walk" |

## The Revision Becomes Standardized—1769

A standardized Bible finally became a reality. Benjamin Blayney edited the King James Version in 1769, and Thomas Wright and W. Gill of Oxford printed it. Incorporating and expanding Paris's work, Blayney's text became the standard King James Version for the next one hundred years. Spelling, italics, and marginal notes were at the heart of Blayney's contribution. Bishop William Lloyd's chronology, first used in the 1701 Oxford edition, had been incorporated into Paris's edition and it remained in the text of Blayney. (The Oxford edition used the dates of AD and BC after James Ussher [1581–1656] for the first time and it is still used today.)

Despite the careful attempt to eliminate errors, Blayney repeated some errors in 1769. This is evidence that Blayney used the text of Paris in his work; however, in some cases Blayney corrected Paris and returned to the reading of the 1611 King James Version. The following chart illustrates these readings:

| Text | KJV 1611 | Paris 1762 | Blayney 1769 |
|------|----------|------------|--------------|
| Deuteronomy 10:2 | "brakest" | "brakedst" | "brakedst" |
| Psalm 135:5 | "our LORD"[3] | "our Lord" | "our Lord" |
| Jeremiah 40:1 | "the word that" | "the word which" | "the word which" |
| Nahum 3:16 | "flieth" | "fleeth" | "fleeth" |
| Acts 7:28 | "diddest" | "killedst" | "diddest" |

Most scholars agree that the work of Blayney was not of equal quality in scholarship with Paris's edition. However, these two editions changed the diction of the English Bible and set the stage for future work in the nineteenth century. With a few exceptions, the notes, and especially the italics, remained the same in subsequent editions. David Norton has observed ninety-nine textual variants from Paris and fifty-eight from Blayney's 1769 edition that have survived in today's King James Version.[4]

| Text | 1611 KJV | 1769 Revision |
|------|----------|---------------|
| 1 Corinthians 5:2 | "earnestly, desiring" | "earnestly desiring" |
| Revelation 13:16 | "to give" | "to give them" |
| Proverbs 6:19 | "and him that soweth" | "and he that soweth" |

## The Standard Revision Revised after One Hundred Years: The Cambridge Paragraph Bible—1873

For many years, the Blayney edition—even with its imperfections—continued to be published in essentially the same form by the official printers. It was not until 1831, after revision critic Thomas Curtis began to complain about the "modern" editions of Scripture not accurately reflecting the 1611 King James Version, that a real controversy began to emerge. Curtis published his findings in 1833 in *The Existing Monopoly: An Inadequate Protection of the Authorized Version of the Scripture.*[5] Dr. Turton of Cambridge and Dr. Cardwell of Oxford took up the challenge to defend "modern" translations. As a result of the controversy, Oxford published an exact reprint of the 1611 King James Version in 1833. It was their intention to produce a reprint

> . . . so exact as to agree with the original Edition page for page, and letter for letter; retaining throughout the ancient mode of spelling and punctuation, and even the most manifest errors of the Press. Without this extreme degree of accuracy the Reader would not have been able to judge by its means, whether the original Standard can still be exactly followed, and how far the deviations introduced at different periods, and which have now had possession of our Bibles for many years, can reasonably be abandoned.[6]

Would the 1611 edition actually be resurrected? The publication of the 1833 facsimile of the 1611 translation demonstrated the impossibility of going back to

THE

**CAMBRIDGE PARAGRAPH BIBLE**

OF THE

AUTHORIZED ENGLISH VERSION,

WITH THE TEXT REVISED BY A COLLATION OF ITS EARLY AND OTHER PRINCIPAL EDITIONS,
THE USE OF THE ITALIC TYPE MADE UNIFORM,
THE MARGINAL REFERENCES REMODELLED,
AND A CRITICAL INTRODUCTION PREFIXED

BY

THE REV. F. H. SCRIVENER, M.A., LL.D.
RECTOR OF ST. GERRANS, EDITOR OF THE GREEK TESTAMENT, CODEX AUGIENSIS, &c.
ONE OF THE NEW TESTAMENT COMPANY OF REVISERS OF THE AUTHORIZED VERSION.

Edited for the Syndics of the University Press.

Cambridge:
AT THE UNIVERSITY PRESS.

LONDON: CAMBRIDGE WAREHOUSE, 17, PATERNOSTER ROW.
CAMBRIDGE: DEIGHTON, BELL AND CO.
1873.

[*All Rights reserved.*]

1873 Cambridge Paragraph Bible. This edition may be the most accurate King James Bible ever published.

the 1611 version with all its misprints and errors. In the intervening two hundred years, great strides had been made in the art of printing and the accuracy of proofreading. There certainly was no need to return to the misprints of 1611. In addition, commonly accepted spelling and language of the day had changed throughout the years.

The controversy did not support the popularity of the 1611 version but rather fueled the fires of revision that ultimately led to the Cambridge Paragraph Bible being published in 1873. Even though the 1769 King James Version edition was considered the finest text of its day, it was collated sometime later for the edition to be published by George Eyre and William Spottiswoode and found to have 116 errors. A new revision to satisfy all readers had to be attempted.

As we might expect with scholars debating the virtues of revision, unanimity was impossible. The schools at Cambridge and Oxford argued for the validity of English translations in modern form and style. The American Bible Society attempted a separate revision of the Authorized Bible between 1847 and 1851. A carefully chosen committee headed by Edward Robinson spent three and a half years using a system of carefully crafted translation procedures to produce a version acceptable to the academic and buying public. When presented to the committee that appointed them, it was rejected because of a few readings considered unacceptable.[7]

The Cambridge Paragraph Bible was an attempt to bring the two universities of Oxford and Cambridge together to support one accurate edition. They were unaware of the difficulty of achieving such a worthy goal. For the first time, modern paragraphs were about to be introduced to the Bible. The nineteenth-century Greek textual critic F. H. A. Scrivener took great care to produce a truly critical edition of the Authorized Bible. Scholars, for many years, praised his success. Scrivener's edition was the most accurate of all the Authorized Bibles. He carefully and laboriously compared each word in the 1611 edition, improved the marginal notes, and modernized the spelling of archaic terms. The text, arranged in paragraph form, afforded the reader the luxury of complete thoughts grouped together. This enabled one to read in context rather than in fragmented and even partial segments, as was often the case in the verse divisions in the 1611 and revisions of it.

Scrivener was fully aware that the Revised Version (completed in 1885) had been underway for about three years when he completed the Cambridge Paragraph Bible in 1873. He felt an accurate, critical edition of the 1611 was necessary if there was to be a competing translation. Scrivener himself was on the committee for the Revised Version. The translators of the Revised Version undoubtedly consulted the Cambridge Paragraph Bible.

Scrivener put together in appendix form a complete comparison of all the major and minor revisions of the King James Version from 1611. He included places of departure from the King James Version and texts restored in the Cambridge Paragraph Bible that were abandoned in revisions between 1611 and 1873. A few comparisons are listed below:

| Text | KJV 1611 | Cambridge 1873 |
| --- | --- | --- |
| Matthew 14:32 | "Gethsemani" | "Gethsemane" |
| Matthew 10:18 | "there is no man good but one" | *there is* none good but one" |
| Mark 6:53 | "Genesareth" | "Genesaret" |
| Matthew 23:24 | "Strain at a gnat" | "Strain out a gnat" |

Passages restored from 1611 and omitted in revisions between 1611 and 1873:

| Text | 1611 | Revisions | 1873 |
| --- | --- | --- | --- |
| Genesis 37:36 | "Medanites" | "Midianites" | "Medanites" |
| Genesis 34:3 | "to her heart" | "to the heart of damsel" | "to her heart" |
| 1 Corinthians 4:9 | "approved unto death" | "appointed to death" | "approved unto death" |
| 1 Timothy 2:9 | "Shamefastness" | "Shamefacedness" | "Shamefastness" |

The controversy over the style of the King James Version and the obvious love for that version came to a head. While nearly every scholar acknowledged the accuracy and the smooth expression produced by the King James Version translators, it became obvious that a new translation was necessary. Changes in language, spelling, and scholarship all pointed to this conclusion.

HARPER'S WEEKLY.

## The King James Version Abandoned—1881

The distinguished group of scholars who revised the King James Version in 1885, pictured in *Harpers* magazine.   Photo: A. Sanchez.

A new version that took seriously the principles of revision was about to take center stage. In February 1870 both houses of the Convocation of Canterbury unanimously passed a resolution to appoint a committee of scholars to begin the task of a new translation. It was designed to be a revision of the Authorized Version, but in effect, it became more than originally proposed. Completed in 1885, the Revised Version (along with the American Standard Version variations in 1901) became the first genuine text revision—instead of just editorial changes—since the 1611 edition. Not everyone accepted the new revision at first, nor has it gained universal acceptance in the intervening years. Scholars delighted in it, but the general public could not pull themselves from the established and familiar King James Version—its minor revisions and problems notwithstanding.

Many of us may have many modern translations sitting on our bookshelves. We hope that each new addition to our shelves will bring clarity to our understanding of the sacred Scriptures. Since 1881 denominations, individuals, committees, and religious sectarians have made numerous translations. While some want their work to be known as revisions of the King James Version, others wish to be considered new translations from the original Greek and Hebrew texts. The continued popularity of the King James Version bears witness to its living legacy and cannot be dismissed.

## Can We Really Call a New Translation a "King James Version"? The New King James Version—1982

One of the latest attempts to produce a revision of the King James Version and yet maintain a close affinity to the 1611 edition was done by Thomas Nelson Publishers in 1982.[8] It is primarily an attempt to update the language and to make it conform to current usage. The noticeable differences occur in the change of the pronouns denoting singular and plural (e.g., "ye" and "thou" to "you").

The facsimile of the 1611 King James Version published in 1982 was packaged in a matching cover along with the 1982 revision. This allowed the readers to compare the editions to see for themselves that no major changes in substance had taken place. While the Greek text type used for the New King James Version was the same used by the translators of 1611, it primarily was the Greek text edited by F. H. A. Scrivener published in the nineteenth century.

The King James Version will not be retired to dusty shelves with other archaic books. After nearly four hundred years, it still has a market share of more than 15 percent of all American Bibles purchased. In addition, it is very popular in other English-speaking countries around the world.[9] Its proponents are steadfast in their vocal support of it. Constant attacks upon other versions, incessant defense of its reading, and the Greek text underlying its translation will probably guarantee the King James Version's viability well into the twenty-first century.

## The King James Version Modernized: The New Cambridge Paragraph Bible—1994

Cambridge University began a project of modernizing the text of the King James Version in 1994. Under the able scholarship of New Zealander and

English language scholar David Norton, the Cambridge Paragraph Bible of 1873 was revised. The publisher's desire was to modernize the English of the 1611 King James Version without making it a revision. The new text would be that of the 1611 translators and not subsequent revisers. Any modernization of the text would not interfere with the original text or translation. Modernization related to spelling, punctuation, and vocabulary. Norton, using the basic text of the original 1611 King James Version, used three guidelines in the revision of the New Cambridge Paragraph Bible. He sought to:

1. modernize unless the meaning of the text is changed or obscured; be wary of transgressing against etymology;
2. preserve genuine forms of words but not variant spellings;
3. where possible, use variant acceptable forms to represent clearly identifiable semantic variations.[10]

Readings of the New Cambridge Paragraph Bible compared with the 1611:

| Text | 1611 King James Version | New Cambridge Paragraph Bible |
|------|------------------------|-------------------------------|
| Matthew 1:5 | Boos | Booz |
| Matthew 2:1 | Hierusalem | Jerusalem |
| Matthew 9:34 | Casteth out the deuils | Casteth out the devils |
| Acts 7:35 | By the handes | By the hands |

Some passages in the New Cambridge Paragraph Bible retain archaic forms of the 1611 even though the modern form might be better understood by modern readers:

| Text | 1611 King James Version and New Cambridge Paragraph Bible | Modern form |
|------|-----------------------------------------------------------|-------------|
| 1 Samuel 30:13 | agone | ago |
| Matthew 13:21 | dureth | endures |
| Exodus 28:36 | grave | engrave |
| 2 Kings 9:26 | plat | plot |

The New Cambridge Paragraph Bible will be welcomed by those who love the King James Version and do not want a mere retranslation of the 1611. Its strength lies in its recognition of the value of the most-used Bible since 1611, and it uses the traditional *Textus Receptus* as its Greek New Testament instead of the critical Greek New Testament used by most modern translations. Its weakness is that it is not considered a Bible in the language of modern English-speaking peoples and it does not consider readings used in modern critical Greek New Testaments.

## Why All the Controversy over the King James Version?

The beautiful words, smooth flow of translation, and poetic marvel of the King James Version face the modern scalpel. Those who wish to make it an icon to be worshiped have forced many in the moderate camp to diminish the value of such a wonderful and historically important work. The argument is often over the archaic language rather than a serious investigation of its merits.

How should the usefulness of the King James Version be viewed in modern culture? Two extremes have drawn the line in the sand and each dares the other to cross. One says the King James Version is the only version inspired by God. Others simply view it as an old-fashioned version unable to speak to the modern Christian community.

0 Inches     1     2     3     4     5

A Visual History of the English Bible

There are compelling arguments for the superiority of the King James Version, and there are compelling arguments for the modern translations. These arguments are legitimately based on two questions: (1) Which Greek New Testament (the *Textus Receptus* that is the basis for the King James Version or the critical text that supports the modern versions) is the best? and (2) Should we read the Bible in modern English or retain the four-hundred-year-old traditional language?

Dare we prescribe a dose of common sense? The King James Version is a revision, so stated in the Introduction to the King James Version, of the seventeenth-century Bishops' Bible. Even scholars who were on the King James Version translation team were reluctant to use the new translation for several years. There is some evidence that the Roman Catholic Rhemes edition actually influenced some minor readings in the King James Version.[11] This should not, however, diminish its value. The term *inerrant* should not be used in its normal sense about any translation or version. It technically refers to the original manuscripts.

> The term *inerrant* should not be used in its normal sense about any translation or version. It technically refers to the original manuscripts.

The King James Version was the translation of the English-speaking church for more than three hundred years. The work of modern textual criticism and the Revised Version of 1881–85 sought to improve upon the Greek text underlying the King James Version and to produce a new translation (which, by the way, was a self-proclaimed revision of the King James Version).

It is clear from "The Translators to the Reader" that the translators of the King James Version saw the original Scriptures in Greek and Hebrew as inspired: "If trueth be to be tried by these tongues, then whence should a Translation be made, but out of them?" Their expressed goal was to make former good translations better. There was no thought at all that they were inspired and that their translation was a product of God's breath. Their defense of a new translation was always

Special miniature King James Versions: Finger Prayer Book, Thumb Bible, and the smallest printed complete Bible, 1895.

argued from sound principles and not an appeal to their own God-inspired labors.

## A Balanced Approach to the King James Version

The more balanced approach to the defense of the King James Version argues not for its inerrant property but for the Greek text used by the 1611 translators. This argument maintains that the Greek text known as the *Textus Receptus* is superior to the text used by modern translations. Roughly 85 to 90 percent of the more than five thousand extant Greek manuscripts represent the same Greek text used by the King James Version translators. This position does not view the work done by the seventeenth-century scholars as a translation to be unchanged for all generations of English readers, but rather encourages modern revisions.

One of the complaints against modern translations such as the New American Standard Bible, New International Version, and the Revised Standard Version is that the current Greek text used by these translators has undergone so many textual critical adjustments through the application of textual principles that it represents no known manuscript. The random selection of variant readings reduces the modern critical Greek New Testament to a mere eclectic text—one that mathematical probability suggests would prohibit the possibility of having an actual inspired text. Such a text could never satisfy a doctrine of inerrancy or inspiration unless one simply takes refuge in applying the designation of inspiration to the original documents (which, by the way, is technically correct).

Where then does the truth lie? What should we think of the King James Version of 1611? Its influence on Christianity, its historical significance, and its literary beauty and accuracy of translation must not be ignored. The appreciation for the work done by dedicated, scholarly men who spent a significant number of years in laborious work for God and the church will continue on in history books and in the hearts of all caring Christians.

The King James Version came along in history when the English language was in its golden age. It was the period of the greatest English writer in history, William Shakespeare. Language was the mark of an educated man, and

## My "Charing Cross Road" Experience

My first collectible Bible (1569 Great Bible) was purchased from Nelson's Bookroom in Wales. After that, I purchased many Bibles from its owner, Les Walker. His bookroom was licensed to sell by post only. Every month I received his catalog and he always had some Bibles and books about the Bible that I also began to collect. I wrote back and forth and called regularly. He sent me a gift every Christmas to remind me of his appreciation of my "monthly contribution" to the success of his business.

My desire to make a trip to Wales became overwhelming. Les had invited me to come to visit his place on several occasions. I could no longer resist. With plane ticket in hand, I was off to an adventure that would change me forever.

The day I arrived, I spent the entire afternoon viewing shelf after shelf of books and Bibles I had not seen before. By nightfall, I was tired and ready to find a bed and breakfast. Les and his wife insisted I spend the night with them. After a vegetarian dinner, they ushered me into a room with a marble fireplace, a quaint four-poster bed, and a view outside of rolling hills, green pasture, and sheep grazing on its lush grass. The house was built in 1776 and had the feel of colonial America. I was thrilled with the hospitality.

The next morning I woke to a beautiful sunrise and headed down the large winding staircase serenaded by the most beautiful sounding classical opera music I had ever heard. Classical music had not been a part of my repertoire, but from that visit on I have been an avid fan of classical music and opera arias.

After a fine vegetarian breakfast, Les took me upstairs to one of the quarters formerly reserved for house staff. There he kept other treasures he had not cataloged. He encouraged me to look through the books and I came across a large folio London Polyglot (Walton's Polyglot) 1657 bound in ten volumes. It was the most important polyglot ever published. It did not take me long to agree to his reasonable price. Although I pulled quite a few books and Bibles to be sent to me that day, the London Polyglot is still a valued part of my collection.

Les Walker's death a few years ago put a big void in my collecting experience. He was a book dealer who genuinely worked for the love of seeing collectors thrilled with what he could provide for them. The Great Bible of 1569, first edition Geneva New Testament 1557, and the London Polyglot 1657 are only a few of the treasures he provided for me over the twenty years that I knew him. It was indeed my own "Charing Cross Road" experience.

his use of the language displayed his intelligence and enabled him to enhance the thoughts and dreams of others. Yes, the King James Version is the
crown jewel of English literature. Let's revere it without worshiping it, enjoy
it without glorifying it, preserve it without mystifying it, and love it without
sanctifying it.

> Splendors of the court of St. James furnish the setting for the celebrated First Au-
> thorized Version. This is perhaps the most brilliant gem in the diadem of that Mon-
> arch. Down through the ages the Bible had held its sway due chiefly to the tireless
> efforts of noted individual translators. But the year 1611 was to mark a new epoch
> in Bible history. That year witnessed the creation of the celebrated *Authorized King
> James Version* of the English Bible printed by Robert Barker in London.[12]

These are glowing and, indeed, deserving words of testimony to the most
recognized Bible in the English language for nearly four hundred years. Its
influence on the English-speaking world is as much due to the beauty of its
expression as its accuracy of translation. God save the King James Version,
but let's enjoy the modern translations for reading and comprehension.

# 13

# The Source for English Translations

*The Battle for a Standard Greek Text*

The cool evening in 1520 could not mask the intense heat of the argument inside the aged stone home. "I tell you there is no Greek manuscript that has the phrase, 'In heaven, the Father, the Word, and the Holy Ghost: and these three are one. And there are three that bear witness in earth . . .'" (1 John 5:7–8). The stocky man shouted as if the volume of his voice would win his argument.

The stately Catholic scholar and Complutension Polyglot prime editor retorted, "Our sacred Latin text has it and that is regarded by the church as the inspired edition." The fierce battle over the text of 1 John continued well into the night. When neither debater seemed to get the upper hand, the Greek scholar finally blurted out, "Well then, if you can find a single Greek manuscript with this reading in it, I will include it in my third edition of the Greek text." The thick atmosphere of the struggle came to a sudden halt. With a last evening toast to the agreement, both men retired for the night.

The challenge Desiderius Erasmus blurted out to Lopez de Stunica that evening was met when Stunica later presented Erasmus with a Greek manuscript with the reading in it. It has been the only Greek text ever found with this reading. Since the manuscript is dated ca. 1520–21, the origin of its production is questioned. Keeping with his word, Erasmus included it in his 1522 Greek New Testament, and the same reading found its way into the King James Version.[1]

This first Greek New Testament to be published suffered from an over-anxious businessman, a text based on a few handwritten manuscripts, and an incomplete text translated from Latin into Greek. Nevertheless, once the text was printed, with all its imperfections, it remained the standard text throughout the history of translations. In fact, it still hinders some modern scholars from arguing rationally about the imperfections of that first published text.

## The Greek Text Used in English Translations

1543 Erasmus Greek New Testament and Latin translation. For the Reformers, any Greek New Testament was divine revelation because the science of textual criticism was not yet developed.

The Word of God as produced originally was most likely handwritten by human authors on papyrus or parchment rolls. Generally speaking, most biblical writings throughout the manuscript period were in codex (book) form. Scrolls were used widely for nonbiblical literature. The words of Scripture were in the languages of Hebrew and Aramaic (Old Testament) and Greek (New Testament). These manuscripts have long since perished. Because they were hand copied, errors crept in. One can imagine copying the entire modern English Bible by hand on notepaper. How many errors would occur? Then imagine someone copying from your hand copy. How many more errors would be incorporated? If this were done many times, and if each time the preceding copies were destroyed (eliminating the possibility of checking and correcting copies), it is little wonder the surviving manuscripts have errors of spelling, poor penmanship, omissions, and insertions.

The story of this chapter recounts how the search for the "pure" Greek text was recovered between the manuscript period and the era of printed Bibles. It will also help us understand some of the differences among modern English Bible translations.

## The Text Defined: Erasmus's Greek New Testament—1516

From the printing of the Gutenberg Bible (1455–56) until Erasmus's Greek New Testament (1516), sixty years passed. During this time the church was quite content with reading and studying the papal-authorized Latin Vulgate. Even Wycliffe's version of the English Bible was translated from the Latin Vulgate.

Greek was little known in the West until the middle of the fifteenth century. The fall of Constantinople (the capital of the eastern empire in 1453) and the dominance of the Turks forced Greek scholars to flee to the West. Greek learning began at once to spread in the West. By the turn of the sixteenth century, most universities offered the study of Greek.

> The production of these ancient books was a strenuous and endless task.

The official status of the Latin Vulgate undoubtedly slowed the production of the Greek New Testament. Bible translation in other spoken languages brought no threat to the Vulgate. However, a Greek New Testament meant the possibility of critical evaluation of the Vulgate. With the winds of the Reformation blowing, and Greek scholarship on the rise, the church was ready for a Greek New Testament.

The production of these ancient books was a strenuous and endless task. The first printed Greek New Testament came from the press in 1514 as a part of a massive polyglot Bible. This magnificent work in Hebrew, Aramaic, Latin, and Greek was the work of Cardinal Francisco Ximenes de Cisneros and was printed in Complutum, Spain. While several highly qualified scholars worked with Ximenes, the work—called the Complutensian Polyglot—became identified with the cardinal.

The Polyglot Greek New Testament text is styled after the hand-printed text of the eleventh and twelfth century. It lacks smooth or rough breathings and is accented after an unknown system.[2] The editors recognized the absence of accents in the earlier manuscripts and chose to keep the printed text free from clutter. The manuscripts used to produce the text are unknown. But in his dedication to Pope Leo X, Ximenes expresses his indebtedness to the pope for sending manuscripts from the Apostolic Library. The famous manuscript Vaticanus (written about AD 325–350 and considered by many modern scholars to be the most important manuscript in existence) is believed to have been in the Vatican since sometime before 1475.

The polyglot text itself, however, shows no dependence on Vaticanus. Some people suggest the manuscripts he used at the University of Complutum were sold to a pyrotechnic to make fireworks in celebration of the arrival of a dignitary.[3] This is not likely. The sale of the manuscripts probably took place, but the librarian at the time was a careful scholar and he would not have made such an error. The text bears little variation from the same text produced by Erasmus, whose manuscripts are well known. Ximenes's manuscripts were probably a collection of documents held by friends. The overwhelming numbers of manuscripts lying around would be almost entirely the text represented by Erasmus's text.

Although the Complutensian Polyglot was the first printed Greek New Testament (1514), it was not published until 1522. The first actual publication of the New Testament was to be under the editorship of Desiderius Erasmus in 1516.

Printers were well aware of the importance of printing the first Greek New Testament. The first one to reach the marketplace gave it a significant advantage over its competitor. Froben, the printer at Basel, heard a polyglot was in preparation in Spain. He wanted to beat Ximenes to the punch by publishing the Greek New Testament first. He knew Erasmus had a great interest in the Greek New Testament and sought to enlist him in producing it.

Enlisting an enthusiastic scholar was vital to its success. The energetic Erasmus arrived in Basel in the summer of 1515 and began work

# NOVVM IN

strumentũ omne, diligenter ab ERASMO ROTERODAMO
recognitum & emendatum, nõ solum ad græcam ueritatem, ue-
rumetiam ad multorum utriusq; linguæ codicum, eorumq; ue-
terum simul & emendatorum fidem, postremo ad pro-
batissimorum autorum citationem, emendationem
& interpretationem, præcipue, Origenis, Chry
sostomi, Cyrilli, Vulgarij, Hieronymi, Cy-
priani, Ambrosij, Hilarij, Augusti-
ni, una cũ Annotationibus, quæ
lectorem doceant, quid qua
ratione mutatum sit.
Quisquis igitur
amas ue-
ram
Theolo-
giam, lege, cogno
sce, ac deinde iudica.
Neq; statim offendere, si
quid mutatum offenderis, sed
expende, num in melius mutatum sit.

APVD INCLYTAM
GERMANIAE BASILAEAM.

CVM PRIVILEGIO
MAXIMILIANI CAESARIS AVGVSTI,
NE QVIS ALIVS IN SACRA ROMA-
NI IMPERII DITIONE, INTRA QVATV
OR ANNOS EXCVDAT, AVT ALIBI
EXCVSVM IMPORTET.

A title page to the first edition of the Erasmus Greek New Testament (1516). It was the first Greek New Testament to be published and became the standard Greek New Testament for more than 350 years.

immediately. In March 1516 the project was completed. The pressure of a short deadline forced Erasmus to produce a very imperfect and perhaps inferior edition. Using only a few actual manuscripts all preserved in the library at Basel, he completed the better portion of the New Testament. For the book of Revelation he borrowed a very mutilated copy of *Codex Reuchlinianus* in which the commentary and text were so mixed it was necessary to translate portions of Revelation (22:16–21) from the Latin Vulgate back into Greek.

It should not be disturbing to learn that the original Greek New Testament was quite imperfect. In addition to Revelation, other texts scattered throughout the New Testament were also translations from the Latin. This is clear in Acts 9:5–6 where the English translation of Erasmus reads, ". . . 'it is hard for thee to kick against the pricks,' and he, trembling and astonished,

Erasmus Greek New Testament (1522). This later Greek edition contains the famous "Johann Comma" from 1 John 5:7: "For there are three that bear record in heaven, the Father, the Word, and the Holy Ghost: and these three are one." This text was ultimately printed in the King James Version of 1611. Photo: R. Maisel.

said, 'Lord, What wilt thou have me to do?' And the Lord said unto him . . ."
(KJV). This reading occurs in the Latin but not in the Greek manuscript used
by Erasmus. In his annotations accompanying this 1516 edition, Erasmus confesses this phrase is not in the Greek codex he is using, and yet he includes it
entirely.[4] It may be a bit disturbing for Protestants to find that such a quotable
text as Acts 9:5–6 came from the Roman Catholic Latin Vulgate.

Many greeted Erasmus's Greek Testament with excitement, while others condemned it as Erasmus's own critical work, especially where there
were variances with the Latin Vulgate. Erasmus's publication of a Latin New
Testament side-by-side the Greek was viewed as a direct assault against the
venerated Vulgate. Had he published the Vulgate New Testament instead of
his own translation, his critics probably would have accepted it more readily.
This edition did not have the famous Johann Comma[5] with the text of the
three heavenly witnesses in 1 John 5:7: "For there are three that bear record
in heaven, the Father, the Word, and the Holy Ghost: and these three are
one." The most famous of Erasmus's editions was his 1522 third edition. It
did contain 1 John 5:7.[6]

We should not be alarmed with the differences between the readings of
the Greek manuscripts. Regardless of which manuscript was considered
the best, the differences were minor compared to the size of the New Testament. Erasmus's third edition of 1522 differed from his preceding editions
in 118 places according to nineteenth-century Greek textual critic Samuel
Tregelles. Many of these corrections came in Revelation where the Latin
version had been translated back into Greek. His fourth edition of 1527
was amended by the Complutensian Polyglot and became the established
edition of Erasmus. In 1535, another edition was printed but varied in only
five places from the 1527.[7]

### The Text Standardized: Stephanus's Greek New Testaments—1546–51

By the end of Erasmus's editions in 1535, Christianity was more concerned with theology than the analysis of textual criticism. The text was
fixed and no one dared tamper with it. The world had to contend with

The title page of the Stephanus Greek New Testament (1550). This edition became the standard Greek New Testament. This copy has a 1588 Greek inscription inside the back cover identifying the owner as Jacques Malenfant of Toulouse, France, who was the almoner (chaplain) of Queen Marguerite de Navarre (1492–1549).

the struggles of the Reformation, which proved a hindrance to the development and investigation of textual purity. It was many years before manuscript authority was challenged.

It was the French printer Robert Stephanus who standardized the text of Erasmus. In 1546 and 1549, he printed two very small editions of the Greek New Testament based upon Erasmus. It was not a critical edition—that is, one in which the text was compared with other manuscripts. The fact that previous editions, along with Colinaeus's edition done in Paris in 1534, did some comparisons opened the door for future critical examination. Stephanus in 1550 issued a beautiful royal folio that almost exclusively relied upon Erasmus. Any acknowledgment of Complutensian readings was placed in the margins while Erasmus's text reigned. Stephanus's popular 1550 folio quickly became the accepted text and is still a respected text today.

Soon after the publication of the folio edition, Stephanus secretly fled Paris for Geneva, where he published a small edition in 1551 using verse divisions. The mythological story is told that on his journey from Paris to Geneva he placed a verse division mark every time the horse bounced. This highlights the fact that the verse divisions seem to be arbitrary rather than planned or methodically placed marks in a natural or thematic fashion. More likely, however, the divisions were inserted for convenience of reference in light of his plan to publish a concordance. The Greek text on each page was sandwiched between Erasmus's Latin New Testament and the Vulgate.[8]

Another French printer, Jean Crespin, reprinted Stephanus's 1550 folio in Geneva in 1553. Crespin altered Stephanus in five or six minor places. He also printed the variant readings of the 1550 edition without acknowledging their sources. It was either Stephanus's or Crespin's edition which William Whittingham, the brother-in-law of John Calvin, used in the famous 1557 Geneva New Testament,[9] the first English version to use verse divisions.

The importance of Robert Stephanus as a printer was that he assured the dominance of the text begun by Erasmus for the next several generations. England especially embraced the text later to be known as the *Textus Receptus*.

## The Text Popularized: Beza's Greek New Testaments—1565–98

Theodore Beza was the successor of John Calvin as the leader of the Calvinistic teachings in Geneva. He published five major editions of the Greek New Testament and several more minor editions. Beza had at his disposal the famous Codex Cantabrigiensis (more popularly known as Beza) and Codex Claromontanus. However, he referred to them only in his written comments.

Beza's text was essentially that of Stephanus. Any departures generally were not on textual authority but the arbitrary choice due to his theological persuasion. Luke 2:22 reads, "And when the days of *her* purification according to the Law of Moses were accomplished . . ." No manuscript evidence exists for "her" in Greek or Latin. The correct reading from the manuscript evidence is "their." Beza chose "her" from the Complutensian Polyglot. Unfortunately, the reading of "her" found its way into the King James Version as well.[10] This suggests the view that the true *Textus Receptus* is not the Stephanus of 1550 but actually the text of Theodore Beza.

The impact of the Beza editions can be measured by their popular use among Protestants during his lifetime. It was this popular use that really cemented the text first published by Erasmus. From this time the *Textus Receptus* was virtually unchallenged among scholars, clergy, and the populace. The 1589 (or possibly the 1598) Beza edition became the Greek text used by the translators of the King James Version in 1611.

Collage of Greek New Testaments. The open New Testament is a 1550 Stephanus edition. Sitting on top of the open New Testament is a 1551 Stephanus New Testament edition with verse divisions. The books standing in the rear are from left to right: 1598 Beza (perhaps the edition used by King James Version translators), 1516 Erasmus first edition, 1589 Beza (another possibility as the edition used by the King James translators), 1565 Beza first edition, and 1528 Pagninus Latin Bible (first Bible divided into numbered verses, although they were placed in the margins). Photo: R. Maisel.

Even the King James Version fell under the power of the Beza domination. By the time the King James translators began their historical task of producing the most famous and influential Bible in English history, the text of Erasmus expressed in Beza's text, with all its faults, was firmly entrenched as the standard Greek New Testament text.

## The Text Commercialized: The Elzevir "Brothers"—1624–42

Business, profit, and printing played an important part in establishing the Greek text for years to come. Bonaventure Elzevir and his nephew (often

### Significant Editions of Erasmus Greek New Testament

**Erasmus Greek New Testament 1516.** The first edition of the Greek New Testament was made from five manuscripts. Alongside the Greek was placed Erasmus's own Latin New Testament. A full volume of annotations to the text and corrections of the Latin New Testament was published with the text. Erasmus attacked the abuses of the church and encouraged Bibles in the language of the people. Even though this edition was the first, its hurried production brought criticism later.

**Erasmus Greek New Testament 1519.** Martin Luther based his translation of the "September" German New Testament on the second folio edition of the Erasmus Greek New Testament. This edition corrected many of the first edition's errors, but he made no real attempt to improve the Greek text or to use other manuscripts. The annotations from this edition had their own pagination and were usually bound separately.

**Erasmus Greek New Testament 1522.** Following the 1519 edition, the third edition included the famous Johann Comma in 1 John 5:7 that Erasmus promised to include if it could be found in any Greek manuscript. It was; he did. Tyndale used this edition and so he included 1 John 5:7, the Trinitarian phrase. Ultimately the phrase made its way into the King James Version.

**Erasmus Greek New Testament 1535.** This was the fifth of Erasmus's folio New Testaments and the last published in his lifetime. It is considered to be the best, and yet it differs very little from the 1527 fourth edition.

erroneously referred to as his brother), Abraham Elzevir, were printers in the Netherlands. They initiated the term *Textus Receptus* in the second edition of their small edition of 1633. In the introduction, they declared the text they were printing as the "universally accepted text free of alterations and corruptions."

The enterprising printers were not as concerned with the "purity of the text" as with the marketability of a self-described universally recognized text. Why wouldn't one buy a text that claimed to be *the* text over other texts? The term *Textus Receptus* attached itself to this text, which was basically a close reprint of Beza's 1565 edition, and even today is the term most often used in referring to the texts of Erasmus, Stephanus, and Beza.

True, the Elzevirs were interested in the commercialization of the Greek text, but their first edition of 1624 not only was beautifully printed, it also standardized wording of the previously fluctuating text. These editions provided a text that remained consistent for a hundred years without being exposed to further alterations.

## The Text Criticized: Walton's Polyglot (1657) to Griesbach (1775–77)

After the publication of the text by Stephanus and Beza in the sixteenth century, most clergy ceased from inquiry into the authorities upon which the printed text was based. For the most part the Elzevir editions sealed the text from scholarly criticism. Most men simply accepted the Greek text as the inspired, inerrant Word of God and spent little time questioning the possible variants in the sources. Other theological battles seemed more important than a pedantic search for the minutia of variant readings in the Greek New Testament.

### Walton's Polyglot—1657
### (Pioneer in textual criticism)

The first real attempt to collect and classify variant readings remained for Brian Walton in his famous polyglot. This massive six-volume edition included the languages of Latin, Ethiopic, Greek, Syriac, Samaritan, Chaldean, Arabic, and Persian. The fifth volume contained the New Testament and consulted the important Greek manuscript Codex Alexandrinus, which had just come into the possession of the Royal Library. Walton placed variant readings in the margins. The valuable critical apparatus in the sixth volume collated an additional fifteen manuscripts. Walton, known for his scholarly abilities, with the aid of other contemporaries, prepared this extraordinary piece of scholarship. Upon the able shoulders of Archbishop James Ussher fell the responsibility of preparing the critical sixth volume. Ussher prepared a valuable critical analysis of Stephanus's and Erasmus's Greek manuscripts as his first attempt at collating a variety of manuscripts. Walton's work was the first important collection of the variant readings.

Allegations of deviating from the doctrine of inspiration hindered critical work. Shortly after the publication of the London Polyglot (another name for Walton's Polyglot), Stephanus Curcellaeus (1586–1659) published his Greek New Testament with a preface detailing his critical apparatus. While not listing the sources of his variant readings, it was seen as a real or supposed threat to the theological world. Many saw the attempts to view the "Word of God" in a critical light as detraction from the doctrine of inspiration.[11] Textual criticism met its first major obstacle, and it resulted in impeding the progress of scholarship.

Τ Η Σ
ΚΑΙΝΗΣ ΔΙΑΘΗΚΗΣ
ΑΠΑΝΤΑ.
Novi Teftamenti
*Libri Omnes.*
ACCESSERUNT
Parallela Scripturæ Loca,
NEC NON
Variantes Lectiones ex plus 100 MSS. Codicibus,
*Et Antiquis Verfionibus Collecta.*

E Theatro SHELDONIANO.
Anno Dom. M. DC. LXXV.

John Fell's Greek New Testament was the first published in England (1675). The chief feature of this edition is its elaborate critical apparatus.

## Fell's Greek New Testament—1675 (The practice of manuscript collation)

John Fell, bishop of Oxford, anonymously published the first Greek New Testament in England in 1675 in an attempt to prevent the theologians from tampering with the text. Using footnotes, he listed support for individual readings by classifying manuscripts rather than individual manuscript readings. This led ultimately to the science of textual criticism. Although the famous Codex Vaticanus was known, it appears that Fell did not specifically cite it. In addition to those variants already known, Fell collected readings from about one hundred sources, including eighteen from the Bodleian Library and others from the Barberini

Library collection in Rome. Fell, never viewed as a great textual critic, paved the way for one of the greatest textual critical scholars of the next hundred years, John Mill.

### Mill's Greek New Testament—1707
### (Textual criticism enters adulthood)

John Mill completed his monumental work just two weeks before his death. He collected all available evidence from Greek manuscripts, early versions (in various other languages like Syriac, Coptic, and Armenian in handwritten manuscripts), the church fathers, and all thirty-two printed editions of the Greek New Testament. Prefixed to his text was an extensive introduction in which he explained the canon, transmission, and his theory of evaluation and use of the patristic citations, manuscripts, and printed texts of the New Testament. Mill made no attempt at a new text but printed Stephanus's 1550 text. All variants or superior readings, according to his theory, were placed in the margins or footnotes. His work was so thorough that it became the standard-bearer for one hundred years. Tregelles suggests Mill commenced the "age of manhood" in textual criticism of the New Testament.

The thirty long years during which Mill prepared his edition of the Greek New Testament were plagued with financial difficulties. Parts of the work show development in his thought and changes in his positions, while in other parts he shows an unsophisticated stage of thought. Nevertheless, the work is invaluable for New Testament textual studies. Mill's death prevented him from completing his textual critical views. It would be many more years before someone would attempt a genuinely critical text.

### Wettstein's New Testament—1751–52
### (Age and quality of manuscripts weighed)

The first major work that produced an important textual critical apparatus was the work of Jacob Wettstein of Basel. He published a beautiful two-volume folio work representing forty years of research in textual criticism. Although he printed the text of Elzevir, the margins clearly noted his

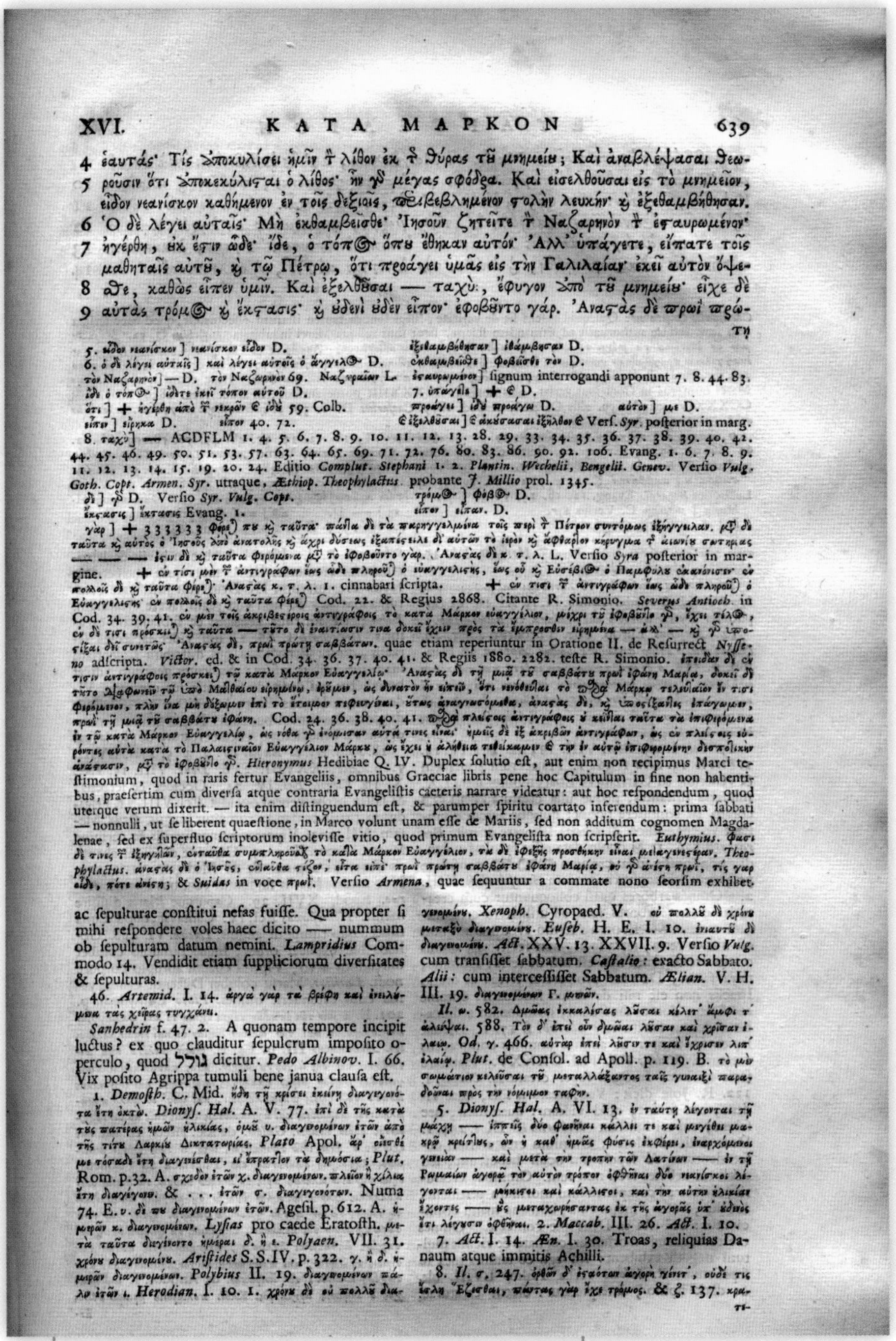

4 ἑαυτάς· Τίς ἀποκυλίσει ἡμῖν τ λίθον ἐκ τ θύρας τῦ μνημείυ; Καὶ ἀναβλέψασαι θεω-
5 ρῦσιν ὅτι ἀποκεκύλισαι ὁ λίθος· ἦν γ μέγας σφόδρα. Καὶ εἰσελθῦσαι εἰς τὸ μνημεῖον,
   εἶδον νεανίσκον καθήμενον ἐν τοῖς δεξιοῖς, περιβεβλημένον στολὴν λευκήν· κ ἐξεθαμβήθησαν.
6 Ὁ δὲ λέγει αὐταῖς· Μὴ ἐκθαμβεῖσθε· Ἰησῦν ζητεῖτε τ Ναζαρηνὸν τ ἐσαυρωμένον·
7 ἠγέρθη, ἐκ ἔσιν ὧδε· ἴδε, ὁ τόπος ὅπυ ἔθηκαν αὐτόν· Ἀλλ' ὑπάγετε, εἴπατε τοῖς
   μαθηταῖς αὐτῦ, κ τῷ Πέτρῳ, ὅτι προάγει ὑμᾶς εἰς τὴν Γαλιλαίαν· ἐκεῖ αὐτὸν ὄψε-
8 σθε, καθὼς εἶπεν ὑμῖν. Καὶ ἐξελθῦσαι — ταχὺ, ἔφυγον ἀπὸ τῦ μνημείυ· εἶχε δὲ
9 αὐτὰς τρόμος κ ἔκςασις· κ ὑδενὶ ὑδὲν εἶπον· ἐφοβῦντο γάρ. Ἀναςὰς δὲ πρωΐ πρώ-
                                                                              τη

*(critical apparatus in small type — largely illegible)*

ac sepulturae conſtitui nefas fuiſſe. Qua propter ſi
mihi reſpondere voles haec dicito — un-
ob ſepulturam datum nemini. *Lampridius* Com-
modo 14. Vendidit etiam ſuppliciorum diverſitates
& ſepulturas.

46. *Artemid.* I. 14. ἀγαθὰ γὰρ τὰ βρίφη καὶ ἐπιλύ-
μυσα τὰς χύσας τυγχάνει.

*Sanhedrin* f. 47. 2.   A quonam tempore incipit
luctus? ex quo clauditur ſepulcrum impoſito o-
perculo, quod גולל dicitur. *Pedo Albinov.* I. 66.
Vix poſito Agrippa tumuli bene janua clauſa eſt.

1. *Demoſth.* C. Mid. ὅδη τῇ χρόνῳ ἐκείνῳ διαγινομένῳ
ἐπ' ὀκτώ. *Dionyſ. Hal.* A. V. 77. ἐπὶ δὲ τὴς κατὰ
τὰς πατέρας ἡμῶν ἡλικίας, ὁμῦ υ. διαγενομένων ἐτῶν ἀπὸ
τῆς τίτε Λαρκίε Δικταιορίας. *Plato* Apol. ἀρ' εἰσὶ θι
με πόρωθὲ ἔτη διαγινύσας, εἰ ἐκρατεῖτο τὰ ἀμφύσεια; *Plut.*
Rom. p. 32. A. σχεδὸν ἐτῶν χ. διαγενομένων. πλεῖον ἢ χίλια
ἔτη διαγίνεσθα. & . . . ἐτῶν σ. διαγενοέσθω. *Numa*
74. E. υ. δὲ νυ διαγινομένων ἐτῶν. Ageſil. p. 612. A. δ-
μοφων κ. διαγινομένων. *Lyſias* pro caede Eratoſth. μετὰ ταῦτα δὲηγόντο ἡμέραι δ. ἢ ε. *Polyaen.* VII. 31.
χρόνυ διαγινομένυ. *Ariſtides* S.S.IV. p. 322. γ. ἢ δ. ἡ-
μερῶν διαγινομένων. *Polybius* II. 19. διαγινομένων πά-
λιν ἐτῶν ι. *Herodian.* I. 10. I. χρόνυ δὲ ὐ πολλῦ δια-

γινομένυ. *Xenoph.* Cyropaed. V.   ὐ πολλῶ δὲ χρόνω
μεταξὺ διαγινομένυ. *Euſeb.* H. E. I. 10. ἐπαυτὸ δὲ
διαγινομένϕ. *Act.* XXV. 13. XXVII. 9. Verſio *Vulg.*
cum tranſiſſet ſabbatum. *Caſtalio:* exacto Sabbato.
*Alii:* cum interceſſiſſet Sabbato. *Ælian.* V. H.
III. 19. διαγινωμένων Γ. μηνῶν.

*Il. ω.* 582. Δμωῆς ἐκκαλίσασα λῦσαι κέλετ' ἄμφε ι'
ἀπειλεῖ. 588. Τὸν δ' ἐπὶ ὐν ὀμωαὶ λῦσαι καὶ χρῖσαι ι-
λαίϕ. *Od. γ.* 466. αὐτὰρ ἐπεὶ λῦσέ τε καὶ ἔχρισεν λι-
ίλαίϕ. *Plut.* de Conſol. ad Apoll. p. 119. B. τὸ μὲν
σωματίον κινῦσαι τῷ μεταλλάξαντος ταῖς γυναιξὶ παρα-
δόσθαι πρὸς τινα περιςολὴν καὶ κηδείαν.

5. *Dionyſ. Hal.* A. VI. 13. ὴ ταύτη λέγονται τῇ
ἡμέρα, δύο φωνῆναι κάλλιςΙ τι καὶ μεγίςτι μα-
κρῷ κρείντες, ἄν' υ καθ' ἡμᾶς φύσεις ἐκφῦναι, ὑπερέχομενα
γωνίων — καὶ μετὰ τὴν τροπὴν τῶν Λατίνων — ἐν τῇ
Ρωμαίων ἀγορᾷ τὸ αὐτὸ πρότερ ὀφθῆναι δύο πινεύνεσι λέγονται — μηκίετι καὶ καλλίοσι, καὶ τὴν αὐτῶ ἡλικίαν
ἴχοντες — ὡς μαρτυρῆσεσθαι πρὸς τὴν ἀγγελίαν ἐκ φᾶσιν
ἔτι λέγονθ' ὀφθῆναι. 2. *Maccab.* III. 26. *Act.* I. 10.

7. *Act.* I. 14. *Æn.* I. 30. Troas, reliquias Da-
naum atque immitis Achilli.

8. *Il. σ,* 247. ὀρθῶν δ' ἑςαότων ἀγορὴ γένετ', ὐδέ τις
ἔελα Ἕζεσθαι, πάντας γὰρ ἔχε τρόμος. & ζ. 137. κραι-
                                                                           τι-

---

Wettstein's major critical edition of the Greek New Testament
(Mark 16) (1751–52).

preference for variant readings. He was the first to proudly pronounce that the evaluation of such readings should be weighed by their quality and age rather than by the number of manuscripts supporting them. In practice, however, he felt the earlier manuscripts were contaminated by the Latin version and therefore he tended to rely upon the later Greek manuscripts.

Unfortunately, as with many pioneers in scholarly activity, Wettstein suffered harsh treatment from those who attempted to categorize him as straying from the doctrine of the inspiration of Scripture. He was accused of supporting an inferior text that contained incorrect readings. Many dismissed his often logical thinking simply because of his doctrinal views.

The 1751 edition of Wettstein's massive two-volume Greek New Testament contained a wealth of information. The prologue to the first volume contains subjects such as the description of sources he used, his textual theories, critical evaluations of others, and introductions to the rest of the work. The upper portion of each of the remaining pages contained the text itself; the middle section contained any variations he wished to note. The number of previously uncollated documents was so vast that it often took up a great deal of space. The lower part of the page included passages from classical authors and extracts from Rabbinic and Talmudic sources that he believed illuminated a particular reading either grammatically or textually.

Wettstein's textual work has not stood the test of time. His critical theory, prologue, and text have not been widely accepted or reprinted. His contribution lies primarily in his search for manuscripts and materials. Scholars later would consult his work, but his theories have faded into obscurity. Many people consider Wettstein to have closed the formative period of textual criticism. It was Griesbach who opened the modern period.

## Griesbach's New Testament—1775–1806
### (Textual criticism enters the modern age)

Wettstein had amassed a vast wealth of manuscripts and material but failed to catalog them. Earlier textual critics John A. Bengel and Richard Bentley had introduced a system for cataloging manuscripts but Wettstein ignored it. The task of organizing and introducing a managing system of recording manuscripts was left in the capable hands of Greek scholar Johann Jakob Griesbach (1745–1812), who brought textual criticism into the modern era.

A new theory to evaluate manuscripts was advanced by Griesbach. He followed critics John Bengel and John Semler[12] by advancing the idea of "families" of manuscripts. This was an attempt to classify surviving copies of New Testament Greek manuscripts by deciding which reading came from an earlier or parent manuscript. He attempted to investigate the history of the transmission of the text and then to group them into these "families." His names for the major families of manuscripts are used today: Alexandrian, Western, and Byzantine. Modern textual scholars Kurt and Barbara Aland point out that although Griesbach is given credit for these modern names, he really was following Bengel and Semler, and that his influence should not be overemphasized since his critical theories have been proven inadequate.[13]

The Alands are, perhaps, correct in their criticism, but Griesbach left an indelible impression on textual

NOVVM

# TESTAMENTVM

GRAECE.

TEXTVM
AD FIDEM CODICVM VERSIONVM ET PATRVM
RECENSVIT
ET
LECTIONIS VARIETATEM
ADJECIT
D. JO. JAC. GRIESBACH.

VOLVMEN I.
IV. EVANGELIA
COMPLECTENS.

EDITIO SECVNDA
EMENDATIOR MVLTOQVE LOCVPLETIOR.

LONDINI
APVD PETR. ELMSLY.
ET HALAE SAXONVM
APVD JO. JAC. CVRTII HAEREDES
MDCCLXXXXVI.

Griesbach's second critical edition, vol. 1, of the Greek New Testament (1796). Vol. 2 was published in 1806.

criticism nonetheless. For the first time he dared to stray from the beloved *Textus Receptus* in some places. His careful work gained wide admiration, and his text was reprinted in smaller formats on the Continent. His work stimulated others to collate manuscripts and texts for further evaluation. Soon after its publication, several other scholars published collations that greatly increased the availability of material from Greek manuscripts, early versions, and church fathers.[14]

Griesbach's contribution was to stimulate other scholars to continue the work of textual criticism and to begin the process that was ultimately to bring the downfall of Stephanus's *Textus Receptus*.

Up to and including Griesbach, no one dared to abandon the 1550 printed text of Stephanus. Any alterations were either very slight or were placed in the critical apparatus. The popularity of the Stephanus text prohibited any mass relinquishing of its text.

## The Text Debated: Lachmann (1831) to Westcott and Hort (1881)

Textual criticism was about to take a giant step forward. Advancing from the simple act of citing the Greek variant readings in the footnotes to now actually inserting them into the text announced a new age in textual criticism. The fear of abandoning the "untouchable" Greek texts of Erasmus, Stephanus, and Elzevir gave way to the freedom to print an eclectic Greek text based on new discoveries and new theories.

### Lachmann's New Testament—1831
### (The text of Erasmus abandoned in the text)

The dominance of the Greek text of Erasmus and Stephanus was about to end. German textual critic Caroli Lachmann published a small edition of the New Testament that abandoned the *Textus Receptus* in the printed text itself. The only indication of what he had done was a small section at the end of the work that listed without comment the places where he abandoned the *Textus Receptus* and the readings he changed. Undoubtedly the lack of notice of his procedure indicates his awareness of the unpopularity

ὁ ἀπὸ Ἀριμαθαίας, εὐσχήμων βουλευτής, ὃς καὶ αὐτὸς
ἦν προσδεχόμενος τὴν βασιλείαν τοῦ θεοῦ, τολμήσας
εἰσῆλθεν πρὸς Πιλάτον καὶ ᾐτήσατο τὸ σῶμα τοῦ Ἰη-
σοῦ. ⁴⁴ὁ δὲ Πιλάτος ἐθαύμασεν εἰ ἤδη τέθνηκεν, καὶ
προσκαλεσάμενος τὸν κεντυρίωνα, ἐπηρώτησεν αὐτὸν εἰ
ἤδη ἀπέθανεν, ⁴⁵καὶ γνοὺς ἀπὸ τοῦ κεντυρίωνος ἐδωρή-
σατο τὸ πτῶμα τῷ Ἰωσήφ. ⁴⁶καὶ ἀγοράσας σινδόνα,
καθελὼν αὐτὸν ἐνείλησεν τῇ σινδόνι καὶ ἔθηκεν αὐτὸν
ἐν μνημείῳ ὃ ἦν λελατομημένον ἐκ πέτρας, καὶ προσε-
κύλισεν λίθον ἐπὶ τὴν θύραν τοῦ μνημείου. ⁴⁷ἡ δὲ Μαρία ἡ Μαγδαληνὴ καὶ Μαρία ἡ Ἰωσῆτος ἐθεώρουν
ποῦ τέθειται. ¹Καὶ διαγενομένου τοῦ σαββάτου Μαρία ἡ Μαγδαληνὴ καὶ Μαρία ἡ τοῦ Ἰακώβου καὶ Σα-
λώμη ἠγόρασαν ἀρώματα, ἵνα ἐλθοῦσαι ἀλείψωσιν αὐτόν. ²καὶ λίαν πρωὶ μιᾷ σαββάτων ἔρχονται ἐπὶ τὸ
μνημεῖον ἀνατείλαντος τοῦ ἡλίου. ³καὶ ἔλεγον πρὸς ἑαυ-
τάς Τίς ἀποκυλίσει ἡμῖν τὸν λίθον ἀπὸ τῆς θύρας τοῦ
μνημείου; ⁴καὶ ἀναβλέψασαι θεωροῦσιν ὅτι ἀποκεκύ-
λισται ὁ λίθος· ἦν γὰρ μέγας σφόδρα. ⁵καὶ εἰσελθοῦ-
σαι εἰς τὸ μνημεῖον εἶδον νεανίσκον καθήμενον ἐν τοῖς
δεξιοῖς, περιβεβλημένον στολὴν λευκήν, καὶ ἐξεθαμβήθησαν. ⁶ὁ δὲ λέγει αὐταῖς Μὴ ἐκθαμβεῖσθε· Ἰησοῦν
ζητεῖτε τὸν Ναζαρηνὸν τὸν ἐσταυρωμένον· ἠγέρθη, οὐκ
ἔστιν ὧδε· ἴδε ὁ τόπος ὅπου ἔθηκαν αὐτόν. ⁷ἀλλὰ
ὑπάγετε εἴπατε τοῖς μαθηταῖς αὐτοῦ καὶ τῷ Πέτρῳ,
ὅτι προάγει ὑμᾶς εἰς τὴν Γαλιλαίαν· ἐκεῖ αὐτὸν ὄψε-
σθε, καθὼς εἶπεν ὑμῖν. ⁸καὶ ἐξελθοῦσαι ἔφυγον ἀπὸ
τοῦ μνημείου· εἶχεν γὰρ αὐτὰς τρόμος καὶ ἔκστασις·
καὶ οὐδενὶ οὐδὲν εἶπον· ἐφοβοῦντο γάρ.

⁹Ἀναστὰς δὲ πρωὶ πρώτῃ σαββάτου ἐφάνη πρῶτον
Μαρίᾳ τῇ Μαγδαληνῇ, παρ᾽ ἧς ἐκβεβλήκει ἑπτὰ δαι-
μόνια. ¹⁰ἐκείνη [δὲ] πορευθεῖσα ἀπήγγειλεν τοῖς μετ᾽ αὐτοῦ γενομένοις, πενθοῦσιν καὶ κλαίουσιν. ¹¹κἀκεῖνοι ἀκού-
σαντες ὅτι ζῇ καὶ ἐθεάθη ὑπ᾽ αὐτῆς ἠπίστησαν. ¹²μετὰ
δὲ ταῦτα δυσὶν ἐξ αὐτῶν περιπατοῦσιν ἐφανερώθη ἐν
ἑτέρᾳ μορφῇ, πορευομένοις εἰς ἀγρόν. ¹³κἀκεῖνοι ἀπελ-
θόντες ἀπήγγειλαν τοῖς λοιποῖς· οὐδὲ ἐκείνοις ἐπίστευσαν. ¹⁴ὕστερον δὲ ἀνακειμένοις αὐτοῖς τοῖς ἕνδεκα ἐφανερώθη, καὶ ὠνείδισεν τὴν ἀπιστίαν αὐτῶν καὶ σκλη-

ροκαρδίαν, ὅτι τοῖς θεασαμένοις αὐτὸν ἐγηγερμένον ἐκ
νεκρῶν οὐκ ἐπίστευσαν. ¹⁵καὶ εἶπεν αὐτοῖς Πορευθέντες
εἰς τὸν κόσμον ἅπαντα κηρύξατε τὸ εὐαγγέλιον πάσῃ
τῇ κτίσει. ¹⁶ὁ πιστεύσας καὶ βαπτισθεὶς σωθήσεται, ὁ
δὲ ἀπιστήσας κατακριθήσεται. ¹⁷σημεῖα δὲ τοῖς πιστεύ-
σασιν παρακολουθήσει ταῦτα. ἐν τῷ ὀνόματί μου δαι-
μόνια ἐκβαλοῦσιν, γλώσσαις λαλήσουσιν καιναῖς, ¹⁸ὄφεις
ἀροῦσιν· κἂν θανάσιμόν τι πίωσιν, οὐ μὴ αὐτοὺς βλά-
ψῃ· ἐπὶ ἀρρώστους χεῖρας ἐπιθήσουσιν, καὶ καλῶς
ἕξουσιν. ¹⁹ὁ μὲν οὖν κύριος Ἰησοῦς μετὰ τὸ λαλῆσαι
αὐτοῖς ἀνελήμφθη εἰς τὸν οὐρανὸν καὶ ἐκάθισεν ἐκ δε-
ξιῶν τοῦ θεοῦ· ²⁰ἐκεῖνοι δὲ ἐξελθόντες ἐκήρυξαν παν-
ταχοῦ, τοῦ κυρίου συνεργοῦντος καὶ τὸν λόγον βεβαι-
οῦντος διὰ τῶν ἐπακολουθούντων σημείων.

## ΕΥΑΓΓΕΛΙΟΝ ΚΑΤΑ ΛΟΥΚΑΝ.

¹Ἐπειδήπερ πολλοὶ ἐπεχείρησαν ἀνατάξασθαι διήγησιν
περὶ τῶν πεπληροφορημένων ἐν ἡμῖν πραγμάτων, ²κα-
θὼς παρέδοσαν ἡμῖν οἱ ἀπ᾽ ἀρχῆς αὐτόπται καὶ ὑπηρέ-
ται γενόμενοι τοῦ λόγου, ³ἔδοξε κἀμοὶ παρηκολουθηκότι
ἄνωθεν πᾶσιν ἀκριβῶς καθεξῆς σοι γράψαι, κράτιστε
Θεόφιλε, ⁴ἵνα ἐπιγνῷς περὶ ὧν κατηχήθης λόγων τὴν
ἀσφάλειαν.

⁵Ἐγένετο ἐν ταῖς ἡμέραις Ἡρῴδου τοῦ βασιλέως
τῆς Ἰουδαίας ἱερεύς τις ὀνόματι Ζαχαρίας ἐξ ἐφημε-
ρίας Ἀβιά, καὶ γυνὴ αὐτῷ ἐκ τῶν θυγατέρων Ἀαρών,
καὶ τὸ ὄνομα αὐτῆς Ἐλισάβετ. ⁶ἦσαν δὲ δίκαιοι ἀμφότεροι ἐνώπιον τοῦ θεοῦ, πορευόμενοι ἐν πάσαις ταῖς
ἐντολαῖς καὶ δικαιώμασιν τοῦ κυρίου ἄμεμπτοι. ⁷καὶ
οὐκ ἦν αὐτοῖς τέκνον, καθότι ἦν Ἐλισάβετ στεῖρα, καὶ
ἀμφότεροι προβεβηκότες ἐν ταῖς ἡμέραις αὐτῶν ἦσαν.
⁸Ἐγένετο δὲ ἐν τῷ ἱερατεύειν αὐτὸν ἐν τῇ τάξει τῆς

24. καὶ ἡ γυνὴ αὐτοῦ

E 2

---

Lachmann's Greek New Testament (Mark 16) (1831). Lachmann's Greek text was the first to abandon the *Textus Receptus* and actually place the preferred variants in the text instead of the margins.

of such an undertaking. His second edition (1842) records his full theory and rationale for his change of the text and justification of alternate readings. Few took the work seriously. Without explanations, critics wondered what text he was following. If careful analysis had been done, it would have been discovered that it was a critical text and not a printed one.

Lachmann dared to abandon the printed text, which had been that of Erasmus, and to give the Greek New Testament a form that the most ancient documents had transmitted. Since he believed it was impossible to arrive at the original text of the New Testament, his aim was to arrive at a text of about the fourth century.

## Tischendorf's New Testament—1841–72
### (Ancient manuscripts come to light)

Constantin Tischendorf, often called the "greatest textual critic in modern history," published eight editions of the Greek New Testament. His eighth edition (1869–72) was published in three volumes with a detailed textual apparatus and has never been equaled. Tischendorf's critical apparatus, patristic citations, versions, and Greek manuscripts are comprehensive and still valuable for serious students of textual criticism today.

Tischendorf thrilled the academic world with his discovery of one of the most famous Greek manuscripts, called "Sinaiticus." At the age of twenty-five, with a small stipend from the German government, he set about to decipher the famous palimpsest (a manuscript written over an erased text) *Codex Ephraemi* and other works in the Bibiotheque Nationale at Paris.[15] At the age of thirty-three, Tischendorf began an extensive journey around the world to find biblical manuscripts. While visiting St. Catharine's Monastery at Mount Sinai, he noticed leaves of parchment in a wastebasket destined for the ovens of the monastery. The leaves proved to be portions of the Septuagint in an early Greek uncial script. He retrieved forty-three leaves and convinced the monks to let him take them to Leipzig for study. [16] After several visits and much intrigue, the Sinaiticus manuscript was purchased by the czar of Russia. Sometime after the Russian revolution, it was purchased by the British Museum for $500,000.[17]

Tischendorf's primary contribution lay in his gathering of manuscript evidence and assembling it in his critical apparatus. His weakness was the heavy reliance on Sinaiticus to the exclusion of other important manuscripts.

## Westcott and Hort New Testament—1881
### (The original New Testament discovered)

A century of textual critical development opened the door for two British scholars to put a permanent mark on the text of the New Testament. B. F. Westcott and F. J. A. Hort published a two-volume work culminating a twenty-eight-year project. They put into practice the development of a text using the sources and methodologies developed by their predecessors, Lachmann, Griesbach, and Tischendorf. They did very little in collating and editing manuscripts but primarily worked in developing a text to be used by Bible students. Volume one was the text itself without a critical apparatus. Volume two was an introduction and appendix.[18]

I returned to my room. Soon I heard a faint knock on my door. It was my ignoring friends. They explained that the two men were the ones who had a stake in the collection and my friends did not want them to know they were dealing with Americans.

With all this in my mind, we went to the bank vault, collected the papyrus, and gathered in a room for our examination. The expert gazed intently at each piece with an occasional audible sound of delight or wonderment. He was careful not to reveal to us his findings, perhaps for fear an enthusiastic endorsement would increase the asking price. Several hours passed as we sat, stood, stretched, and waited for a decision, but always with an eye on that roll of ancient paper.

With the task completed, the Arabs left with the collection; and the expert, the agent, and I sat discussing the past few hours' activities. After the expert had phoned his benefactor in the U.S., to my disappointment, he said they would let us know the decision in a few days. I was disappointed because I feared they would not purchase the collection and if they did not buy it, others would soon learn of the existence of the collection.

For the next few days I waited impatiently for the phone call to confirm a buy. The call came but the buyer decided not to purchase the collection. I was never sure if they didn't really want it or if they thought they could buy it later directly from the dealers.

My worst fears materialized a few months later when a London buyer purchased the entire collection. While I didn't get the sale, the antiquities dealers gave me the choice of the papyrus for all my trouble in setting up the potential buy. While I was not able to choose the unopened six-inch complete scroll, my choice was carefully calculated and I chose those Greek fragments that had the look of New Testament. While I have not identified the papyrus texts, they have all the characteristics of New Testament pieces.

Westcott and Hort's major contribution was in their development of the history of the early transmission of the New Testament text. They believed they could arrive at the original text written by the apostles through the surviving manuscripts. They classified all manuscripts in various families. Family authority was far more important than numbers of manuscripts supporting any particular reading. The primary family according to Westcott and Hort was the neutral text represented best by Codex Vaticanus.

## The Textual Counter-Reformation: John Burgon

By the time Oxford scholar John W. Burgon (1813–88) began investigating the text of the Greek New Testament, most scholars of the time no longer accepted the Erasmus or Stephanus Greek texts as the authentic New Testament. Textual critics from Lachmann had dethroned the "received text."

Burgon steadfastly held to the view that the Holy Scripture was the infallible Word of God. As he saw it, the "traditional text" was given and preserved by God in an unbroken tradition from the Greek/Turkish (Byzantine Empire) church and passed to the Protestant church of the Reformation. He defended the "traditional text" as representing the vast number of extant Greek manuscripts. Burgon believed that during the early centuries of the Christian era, Satan attempted to attack the text of the New Testament. It was during these early years that the text today called the "critical text" (based on the Alexandrian text) was corrupted. It was God who guided the preservation of his Word through the Byzantine text type (majority of manuscripts). Modern textual critics had followed the corrupted text during those early years.

The common person occupying the pew today has no real interest in the Greek text. Only the scholars and the biblically trained can read the ancient biblical texts. Modern "people behind the plow," as Tyndale called them, are quite willing to leave textual criticism to the experts. They are asking different questions. They want to know what translation best represents God's revelation. Most are no longer satisfied with the dominance of the King James Version. It is to the story of modern translations that we now turn.

# 14

# The Bible in America

*At War and Peace*

> Their [Englishmen in pre-vernacular Bible period] free discussions about the authority of Church and state fostered concepts of constitutional government in England, which in turn were the indispensable prerequisites for the American colonial revolt. Without the vernacular Bible—and the English Bible in particular, through its impact on the reformation of English politics—there could not have been democracy, as we know it, or what today we call the "Free World."[1]

The Pilgrims landed in Plymouth, Massachusetts, in 1620 with Bible in hand and a vision of a world ordered by the dictates of the God of their beloved Scriptures. Some came with the hope of financial prosperity, others with perhaps less noble motives, but most Pilgrims came for religious reasons. When they came ashore, the new land became a sanctuary for the persecuted. As author Marion Simms states, "No nation in all history was ever founded by people so dominated by the Bible as America."[2]

## The Bible Invades the Colonies

To the new arrivals, the Bible was central to their faith and practice. This melting pot of humanity with all their differences in religion, cultural backgrounds, and national loyalties began to be molded into a union and finally into a nation. The difficulties that engulfed these hardy Pilgrims were met with dogged determination to stay the course. No amount of trouble, personal loss, or hardship would ever discourage their vision.

Refugees from the Church of England formed the first permanent settlement of Jamestown, Virginia, colonized in 1607. Their first charter assured religious worship, church establishment, and the freedom to evangelize the Native Americans.

The Puritans[3] (who began coming to America in 1628), known first and foremost for their emphasis on the Bible and their middle-class education, were eager readers of the English translations.[4] They primarily used the Geneva Bible with its commentary notes. The linking of the sacred text with the notes gave a special authority to Puritan piety. It was not long before spiritual leaders saw the danger presented by the laity reading the Bible on their own. New regulations encouraged individuals to read the Bible but forbade them from interpreting it without professional guidance. Spiritual leaders taught that Bible reading—along with the Geneva commentary notes and the accompanying sermon—could lead the pious into true spirituality.

Early Americans used the Bible for applications to all political and social issues. American historian and author Harry Stout points out that with the continued growth of Puritanism, "questions of national polity and social order increasingly received attention from the learned divines."[5] The Puritans took seriously the doctrine of the authority and infallibility of Scripture, and they applied the Bible to every area of political, religious, and social life. The clergy, however, sought a Bible without commentary that would be scholarly. That new modern translation was the King James Version of 1611. Stout writes, "Where the Geneva Bible and its marginalia served well the purpose of an embattled religious minority with thoughts fixed firmly on martyrdom and the world to come, it was less useful in fashioning binding principles of social organization and order in this world."[6] The application of such religious principles to social and religious society led to the darkest era of American religious history, known as the Salem Witch Trials, and forever identified Puritanism with this awful period.

tamœit ut Iſrael, ut nepauzaut Zif, noh na-
hohtôeu nepauz , nœche ayik wek Jehovah.

2 Kah wetu ne ketaſſœt Solomon ayimau-
ont Jehovahoh, neſahteag nequtta tahſhin-
chage iſhquanogkod, kah ne anœque kiſhkag
neſnehchag iſhquanogkod, kah ne ſohkunkog
ſhwinchag iſhquanogked.

3 Kah porch ne anaquohtag Temple wetu:
neſnechag iſhquanogkod ne ſahteag, ne a-
nœohque kiſhkag wetu, kah piogque iſquanogkod ne anohque kiſhkag, anaquohtag wetu

4 Kah wutch weetu ayim nanapompaeu
wehquayeue kenogkenegaſh.

5 Kah paſogquomogiſh kehchekomuk,
wutchamberuhkonaſh wáeenu, kehchekomuk wáeenu, naneeſwe temple kah Oracle, káh
wutchamberuhkonaſh wáeenu.

6 Wœmiyeue chamber napanna taſhiſhquanogkodte kiſhki, kah naſhaue ohtag nequtta taſhiſhquanogkodtekiſhki, kah naſhwe-
nuœk, neſauſuk taſhiſhquanogkodte kiſhki
newutche poquodchekomuk napompaikiſh
weenu weetuomut, beamſog matta woh me-
nehkeheonaoout ut ſuſſipponkomuk.

7 Kah wetu ne ayimuk, ayimun quſſuk-
quanaſh quagwaſhweetuhſhwaſh aſh na paud-
tauomuk, ne wáj matta hammer aſuh tog-
kunk, aſuh ne teagwe miſſehchuogque awoh-
teaonk nœtamœunut wetuomut , ayimuk.

8 Uſhquont wutch nanaſhaue chamber, ut
aninuhkounne wetuomut, kah naut kuhkuhq-
ſhin wiuſhinne Stairs nen naſhaue, kah wutch
naſhauwe, naſhwenuœuk.

9 Ne wuttinne ayimun wetu, kah keſteau,
kah uppuhquau wetu, naſhpe beamlaſh kah
Cedare paſœnogquaſh.

10 Neit ayim chamberſaſh paſogquamukiſh
wame wetuomut napanna taſhiſhquanogkog
neſohkunkquok, kah ukqueaſhitteauunneau
wetuomut naſhpe Cedare Timber.

11 Kah wuttinœœwaonk Jehovah peya-
onuk Solomon, nœwau.

12 Papaume yeu wetu ayiman, pómuſkaan
nukkuhkœwaonganit, kah uſſean nœſittum-
mœwongaſh, kah nanawehteauan wame nut-
annœteamœongaſh , niſh pomuſhaontaman,
neit piſh kuttinhiſh nuttinnœwaonk, *b* ne â-
nagkûp kœſh David.

13 Kah nœweeœm wunnaumonuh Iſrael,
kah matta piſh nutohquanumoh nummiſſin-
ninneumog Iſrael.

14 Neit Solómon ayim wetu kah ukkeſte-
auun.

15 Kah ayim ſuſſippunkomuk anomukkóm-
uk naſhpe Cedare pabſœnogquaſh, naneeſwe
ohkeiyeu wetu, kah ſuſſipponkomuk, kah
appuhquau anomukkommuk mehtugquaſh,
kah appuhquau ohkeiyeue wetu kœwae
plankſaſh.

16 Kah ayim neſnechag iſhquanogkod ſuſſipponkomuk, naneeſwe ohkeiyeue wetuomut, kah ſuſſippunkomuk naſhpe Cedare paſ-
ſœnogquaſh, ne wuttinne ayimun, wutch
Oracle, wutch anue wunneetupanatamwe a-
yeuonganit.

17 Kah wetu, ne, Temple anaquohtag, ne
yauunchage iſhquonogkod.

18 Kah Cedar ne anomukkommuk, kogok-
ſauſu, naſhpe wôunuhquagiſh: kah woſhwoh-
tae pethauanaſh , v a ne Cedareuœ, wahne
quſſuk nogquodtinno.

19 Kah Oracle quaquaſhwehtam ut ano-
nukkommuk na ponamunat œnoœwae wut-
Arkum Jehovah.

20 Kah Oracle, uhquae ne mo neſnehchag
iſquanogkod neſahteag, kah neeſnehchag iſquanogkod neanukiſhkag, kah neſnechag iſquanogkod neſohkunkquok: kah wutogquodtumun wanegik Gold : kah ne wuttin unk-
humun Cedaré Altar.

21 Neit Solomon ogquodtum wetu anomukkomuk naſhpe wanegik Gold: kah adnik-
heg ayim naſhpe Golde chainſaſh, ut anaquohtag Oracle, kah wutogquodtumun
Gold.

22 Kah mamuſſe wetu wutogquodtumun
gold, nó pajeh ukkeſtéauunat wame wetu :
wonk mamuſſe Altar , ne kiſhke Oracleut ,
wutogquodtumun gold.

23 Kah anóme oracleut ayeuau neſœoh
cherubimſoh, Oliváhtug, piogque iſquanogkod neſahteag.

24 Kah napanna taſhiſquánogkod paſuk
wunnuppoh Cherubim, kah napanna taſhiſ-
quanogkod onkatuk wunnuppoh Cherubim,
wutch wehqthik paſuk wunnuppoh yaen
wehqiik onkatok, piogque iſhqua nogkod.

25 Kah onkatok Cherub piogquiſhqua-
nogquſſu : naneeſwe Cherubimſog paſuk
kuhkuheg, kah paſuk ne anukkenuk.

26 Niſohkonkqſit paſuk Cherub , piog-
quiſhquanogguſſu, kah ne wonk wuttinnuſ-
ſin onkatuk Cherub.

27 Kah ponau Cherubimſoh anóme anomi- *c* Exo.
yeue weetuómut, kah *c* ſummagunáog wun  25.20.
nuppœwhunnœoh Cherubimſog. newaje paſuk wunnuppoh miſſuthk ſuſſipponkomuk ,
kah wunnuppoh onkatuk Cherub muſſinum
onkatuk ſuſſipponkomuk : kah wunnuppo-
whuſœohmiſſuhkôadtuoh ut naſhaue komuk

28 Kah hogquanau Cherubimſoh gold.

29 Kah kogokſum wame ſuſſipponkomuk
waéenu naſhpe kogokſume nunneukontunk-
ane Cherubimſog, kah palmuhtugquaſh , kah
wôhſhwohtae uppeſhauanaſh, anomukkomuk
kah poquadchit.

30 Kah ohkéiyeue wetuómut wutogquodtumun gold, anomukkommuk kah poquadchit.

31 Kah ahhut petutteamuk oracle, ayim
oliváhtugque kuppuhhœunaſh, pameetoh-
tag,

---

A leaf of the Eliot Indian Bible (1663), which was the first edition of the first
Bible published in America. It was during this period of American history
that evangelism of the American Indians began. The Algonquin Indian Bible
was translated by John Eliot in 1663, and the tribe was the first to have the
Bible in their native language.

The negative impact of the Puritans' use of the Bible soon gave way to the "Great Awakening" (1640–60) and an application of biblical principles that stressed education, establishing colleges, and political influence. During this period, the Puritans began sharing their faith in evangelism and instituted missionary programs. The churches entered a time of steady growth.

## Roman Catholics Denied Access to Bible Reading

Faithful Catholics seeking the same freedoms in America that Protestants sought found opposition to Bible reading from their own church. The Council of Trent in 1546 had declared the Latin Vulgate to be the official Bible of the Roman Catholic Church. In addition to the authority inherent in the Scripture, the Council decreed the traditions of the church as equally inspired authority. The Council also decreed "that no one shall presume in matters of faith or morals pertaining to the edification of Christian doctrine to rely on his own conceptions to turn Scripture to his own meaning, contrary to the meanings of the Holy Mother Church . . . for it belongs to her to judge the true sense and interpretation of Holy Scripture."[7]

The Catholic Church discouraged private reading and interpretation of Scripture by the Catholic immigrants who came to America.[8] The enthusiastic preaching of the Protestants was a danger to the Roman Catholic Church. The Protestant Bible in 1776 was the King James Version and was specifically forbidden to the faithful Catholics since it was not a translation of the Latin Vulgate.

> The King James Version was specifically forbidden to the faithful Catholics since it was not a translation of the Latin Vulgate.

In 1789, Mathew Carey, an Irish immigrant printer, proposed to Catholic divine John Carroll that a Catholic Bible for the American faithful should be published. He reasoned that an authorized translation would help combat the Protestant charges and give non–Latin-speaking Catholics a source for defense against Protestant accusations. Carey published a complete Douay-Rhemes Bible (revised by Bishop Challoner in 1749–50) in 1790. Bible reading was encouraged, but interpretation was still the clear charge of the Mother

Church. Clergy were permitted to interpret Scripture as long as they were always in line with the teachings of previous generations of the church. Even into the nineteenth century, the Roman Catholic Church continued to warn the laity not to get involved in personal interpretation and to especially avoid the opinions of "modern" science.

## The Bible: A Weapon in the Revolution

A small squad of Minutemen broke into the clearing, rushing for a hedge just below Church Ridge. The forest to the west of the ridge belched clouds of smoke from a barrage of musket fire from a full regiment of the British army. The smell of gunpowder hung in the air that balmy fall morning. The Minutemen trembled as the thunder of guns pounded the positions of the ragtag American army. The fear was not so much for the fierceness of the Redcoats but that they were nearly out of gun wads for their muskets. Gunpowder was plentiful but the lack of wads rendered their weapons useless. As they huddled beneath the hedge, bracing for a charge from the fully armed Redcoats, one of the enlisted men sent word to the officer in charge that there was a church just over the ridge where they could take cover. The self-appointed leader of the group motioned for three of the men to head for the church.

Shedding their backpacks, with muskets in hand and powder horns flapping, three men ran weaving and darting amidst a hail of gunfire.

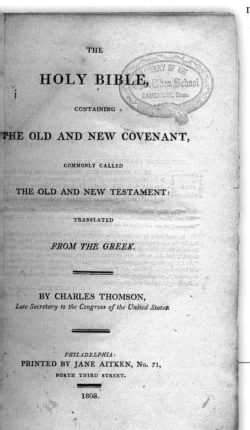

THE

HOLY BIBLE,

CONTAINING

THE OLD AND NEW COVENANT,

COMMONLY CALLED

THE OLD AND NEW TESTAMENT:

TRANSLATED

FROM THE GREEK.

BY CHARLES THOMSON,
Late Secretary to the Congress of the United States.

PHILADELPHIA:
PRINTED BY JANE AITKEN, No. 71,
NORTH THIRD STREET.

1808.

The four volume Thomson Bible, 1808. Charles Thomson, secretary of the Continental Congress 1774–89, translated his Bible from the Greek Septuagint. It was the first Bible published by a woman, Jane Aitken (Robert Aitken's daughter).

Bursting into the sanctuary, they saw a few German Bibles and some hymnbooks on a rough oak table. The young private saw immediately that the paper from the Bibles and hymnbooks could be used for making gun wads.

With Bibles and hymnbooks under their arms, they bolted back toward the hedge as bullets whistled past. Their comrades' eyes were fixed on the brave soldiers. They had a deep admiration for their courage but couldn't help wondering, "Why in the world are they toting Bibles and hymnbooks?" Even with the potentially life-threatening situation, this was not the time for a church service!

As the men cleared the hedge with a single bound, they hurriedly began passing the Bibles along the line. Each soldier ripped out a page and began tearing the pages into small pieces for gun wads. Reloading their well-worn flintlock muskets, and with a renewed sense of empowerment, the revived Americans returned fire to the surprised British unit.[9]

The Bible is a book that saves men's lives spiritually; on this day, it also saved men's lives literally. The German Bible that was so sweet to one army's taste and yet bitter to the other's was a 1776 Christopher Sauer German Bible, today called the "Gun Wad" Bible.

The American War of Independence and the Civil War brought untold destruction to hopes and dreams. In these dark hours of gloom it was the Bible that finally emerged as the light that brought unity and restored hope to a new nation. Soldiers in the field had a Bible in their own language to read and in which to place their faith.

England refused permission to the American colonies to print the sacred text on the new continent. All Bibles were imported from the mother country so that appropriate taxes and revenues could be collected. The Continental Congress sought in vain to import twenty thousand Bibles from Holland and Scotland.[10]

The successful revolution and independence from England signaled a new era for printing Bibles. In 1777, an entrepreneurial Scotsman, Robert Aitken, courageously set out to publish the *editio princeps* of the New Testament in America. The first complete Bible in small octavo size drifted onto the market in 1782. The printer's address listed on the title page reads, "Three doors above the coffee house, in Market street." The "Bible of the

A Visual History of the English Bible

20. Zwey und dreyssig jahr alt war er, da er könig ward, und regierete acht jahr zu Jerusalem;
und wandelte, daß nicht fein war: und sie begru-
ben ihn in der stadt David, aber * nicht unter der
könige gräber.        * c. 24, 25.

## Das 22 Capitel.

Ahasiä untergang: Athaliä mordthat.

UNd die zu Jerusalem * machten zum könige
Ahasja, seinen jüngsten sohn, an seine statt.
Denn die kriegsleute, die aus den Arabern mit dem
heer kamen, hatten die ersten alle erwürget, darum
ward könig Ahasja, der sohn Joram, des königs
Juda.        * 2Kön. 8, 24.

2. Zwey und vierzig jahr alt war Ahasja, da er
könig ward, und regierete ein jahr zu Jerusalem.
Seine mutter hieß * Athalja, die tochter Amri.
* 2Kön. 11, 1.

3. Und er wandelte auch in den wegen des hauses
Ahab: denn seine mutter hielt ihn dazu, daß er
gottlos war.

4. Darum thät er, das dem HERRN übel ge-
fiel, wie das haus Ahab. Denn sie waren seine
rathgeber, nach seines vaters tode, daß sie ihn ver-
derbeten.

5. Und er wandelte nach ihrem rath. Und er zog
hin mit Joram, dem sohn Ahab, dem könige Israel, in den streit gen Ramoth in Gilead, wieder
Hasael, den könig zu Syria. Aber die Syrer
schlugen Joram,

6. Daß er umkehrete sich heilen zu lassen zu Jesreel; denn er hatte wunden, die ihm geschlagen waren zu Rama, da er stritte mit Hasael, dem könige
zu Syria. Und Asarja, der sohn Joram, der könig Juda, zog hinab zu besehen Joram, den sohn
Ahab, zu Jesreel, der kranck lag.

7. Denn es war von GOtt Ahasja der unfall
zugefügt, daß er zu Joram käme, und also mit
Joram auszöge wieder Jehu, den sohn Nimsi;
* welchen der HERR gesalbet hatte, auszurot-
ten das haus Ahab.        * 1Kön. 19, 16. 2Kön. 9, 2.

8. Da nun Jehu straffe übete am hause Ahab,
fand er etliche obersten aus Juda, und die kinder
der brüder Ahasja, die Ahasja dieneten, und
erwürgete sie.

9. Und er suchte Ahasja, und gewann ihn, da er
sich verstecket hatte zu Samaria. Und er ward zu
Jehu gebracht, der tödtete ihn, und man begrub
ihn. Denn sie sprachen: Er ist Josaphats sohn,
der nach dem HERRN trachtete von gantzem
hertzen. Und es war niemand mehr aus dem hause Ahasja, der könig würde.

10. Da aber * Athalja, die mutter Ahasja, sahe,
daß ihr sohn todt war, machte sie sich auf, und
brachte um allen königlichen samen im hause Juda.
* 2Kön. 11, 1.

11. Aber Josabath, des königs schwester, nahm
Joas, den sohn Ahasja, und stahl ihn unter den
kindern des königs, die getödtet wurden, und
thät ihn mit seiner amme in eine schlaffkamer. Also verbarg ihn Josabeath, die tochter des königs
Joram, des priesters Jojada weib, (denn sie war
Ahasja schwester) vor Athalja, daß er nicht getödtet ward.

12. Und er ward mit ihnen im hause GOttes ver-
steckt sechs jahr, weil Athalja königin war im lande.

## Das 23 Capitel.

Jojada salbet Joas zum könige: Athalja wird
getödtet: Baal zerstöhret.

ABer * im siebenten jahr nahm Jojada einen
muth, und nahm die obersten über hundert,
nemlich Asarja, den sohn Jeroham, Ismael,
den sohn Johanan, Asarja, den sohn Obed,
Maeseja, den sohn Adaja, und Elisaphat, den
sohn Sichri, mit ihm zum bund.        * 2Kön. 11,4.

2. Die zogen umher in Juda, und brachten die
Leviten zu hauffe aus allen städten Juda, und die
obersten väter unter Israel, daß sie kämen gen Jerusalem.

3. Und die gantze gemeine machte einen bund im
hause GOttes mit dem könige. Und er sprach zu
ihnen: Siehe, des königs sohn soll könig seyn, wie
der HERR geredt hat über die kinder David.

4. So solt ihr nun also thun: Euer das dritte
theil, die des sabbaths antreten, soll seyn unter
den priestern und Leviten, die thorhüter sind an der
schwellen;

5. Und das dritte theil im hause des königs, und
das dritte theil am grundthor; aber alles volck soll
seyn im hofe am hause des HERRN.

6. Und daß niemand in das haus des HERRN
gehe, ohne die priester und Leviten, die da dienen,
die sollen hinein gehen, denn sie sind heiligthum;
und alles volck warte der hut des HERRN.

7. Und die Leviten sollen sich rings um den könig
her machen, ein ieglicher mit seiner wehre in der
hand. Und wer ins haus gehet, der sey des todes.
Und sie sollen bey dem könige seyn, wenn er aus
und eingehet.

8. Und die Leviten und gantz Juda thäten, wie
der priester Jojada geboten hatte, und nahm ein
ie licher seine leute, die des sabbaths antraten, mit
denen, die des sabbaths abtraten. Denn Jojada,
der

---

The Sauer Bible edition, called the "Gun Wad" Bible (1776). The story goes that soldiers of the Revolution used pages from this German Bible to make gun wads for their muskets.

Revolution," as it is called, received full congressional support as the first and only Bible ever to have such approval. The statement used by Congress and published in the Aitken Bible preliminaries reads,

> *Resolved,* That the United States in Congress assembled highly approve the pious and laudable undertaking of Mr. Aitken, as subservient to the interests of religion, as well an instance of the progress of arts in this country, and . . . they recommend this edition of the Bible to the inhabitants of the United States, and hereby authorize him to publish this recommendation in the manner he shall think proper. Cha. Thomson, Secy.[11]

Bibles printed in the colonies enabled every person to have a Bible of their own. However, money was often in short supply. So to assure that potential

Leaves from an Aitken Bible (1782). This Bible, printed in America, was the only Bible to have congressional approval.

buyers could afford the purchase, Bible printer Isaiah Thomas offered a large family Bible for sale in the local newspaper, the *Massachusetts Spy*, dated December 10, 1789. After a lengthy description of the beauty and size of this Bible the ad read:

> To make payment easy to those who wish to be encouragers of this laudable undertaking, and to be in possession of so valuable property as a Royal Quarto Bible, and who are not able to pay for one all in cash—from such the Publisher will receive one half of the sum or 21 shillings, in the following articles, viz.

In 1789, the *Massachusetts Spy* printer Isaiah Thomas advertised that those who were not able to pay cash for a royal quarto Bible could pay with corn, wheat, and other commodities.

Wheat, Rye, Indian Corn, Butter, or Pork, if delivered at his store in Worcester, or at the store of himself and Company in Boston, by the 10th day of December, 1790: the remaining sum of 21 shillings to be paid in Cash, as soon as the books are ready for delivery. This proposal is made, to accommodate all, notwithstanding the sum of 21 shillings will by no means be the portion of cash that each Bible bound, will cost the Publisher.

Christians often wonder about the faith of our nation's father, George Washington. Was he a genuine believer or a politician who used his faith for political advantage? Near the end of the Revolutionary War, Presbyterian

## Significant American Bibles

**Bay Psalm Book,** 1640. The Cambridge, Massachusetts, printing of the Bay Psalm Book was the first English-printed book in America. The colonists desired to have a Psalter more closely reflecting the Hebrew text. They were still using the Psalms published in the Great Bible in 1569. The new Psalter was begun in 1636 and involved thirty pious and learned divines, each assigned portions of the Psalms.

**Eliot Indian Bible,** 1663. John Eliot came to America in 1631, when he began to study the Algonquin American Indian language. A highly successful missionary and church planter, Eliot was able to preach in their language by 1646. The finished Bible was completed in 1663 and dedicated to King Charles II. The translation was difficult and many mistakes were made. Simms points out that the parable of "the Ten Virgins" is called "the Ten Chaste Men." In Algonquin culture chastity is a male virtue. The Indian assisting in translation substituted masculine gender for female gender.[12]

**Rhemes/Douay Bible,** 2 vols. 1790. This is the first American edition of the Rhemes New Testament published by Carey and Stewart, Philadelphia, and may be the first quarto Bible printed in America. Carey himself was most likely a Roman Catholic. While living in Ireland he took up writing against injustices, and one of those was the persecution of Irish Catholics. Taking refuge in France, he befriended Benjamin Franklin. He was later imprisoned, and when released he came to America and became one of the most respected and largest printers in his new land.

minister Dr. John Rogers suggested that the Aitken Bible be given to each member of the Continental Army. The proposal found favor with George Washington but with his army disbanding, he thought it would not be financially responsible to approve such a measure. His letter is a classic part of the history of the Bible in America and was featured in facsimile in *The Bible of the Revolution* published by the Grabhorn Press for John Howell in 1930.[13] In a letter dated June 11, 1783, George Washington writes,

> Your Proposition respecting Mr. Aitkin's Bible would have been particularly noticed by me, had it been suggested in season. But the late Resolution of Congress for discharging Part of the Army, taking off near two thirds of our Numbers, it is now too late to make the Attempt. It would have pleased me well, if Congress had been pleased to make such an important present to the brave fellows, who have done so much for the Security of their country's Rights & Establishment.[14]

One of the most famous Bibles of the Revolution is a German Bible published in Germantown, Pennsylvania, by Christopher Sauer in 1776; this was the "Gun Wad" Bible referred to earlier. Sauer was a deeply religious man. Some suggest he was a member of the German Baptist Church. Even if he was not, he certainly was in sympathy with it. Two German Bibles were in use in Sauer's day: the Berlegerg and the Luther Bible (both printed in Germany). The Berlegerg Bible was in four volumes and very expensive— out of the reach of most poor German Americans. This led Christopher Sauer to advocate the printing of Bibles in America.

The German Baptists raised money for the purpose of providing religious books and a printing press for their friends in America. The incompetence of their printer, Jacob Gaus, led to failure and the business was suspended. Christopher Sauer purchased the press and began printing books. He published an issue of 1,200 copies of the first Bible printed in America in a European language in 1743. (The Eliot Indian Bible in the Algonquin language of 1663 was the first Bible printed in America.)

On May 8, 1816, the American Bible Society was organized in New York City.[15] The society's charter called for the printing of Bibles without notes or comments in order to have a wide distribution. This newly formed society

THE
**S O U L D I E R S**
Pocket Bible :

Containing the moſt (if not all) thoſe
places contained in holy Scripture,
which doe ſhew the qualifications of his
inner man, that is a fit Souldier to fight
the Lords Battels, both before the fight,
in the fight, and after the fight ;

Which Scriptures are reduced to ſeverall heads, and fitly applyed to the
Souldiers ſeverall occaſions, and ſo may
ſupply the want of the whole Bible,
which a Souldier cannot conveniently
carry about him :

And may bee alſo uſefull for any
Chriſtian to meditate upon, now in
this miſerable time of Warre.

Imprimatur,    *Edm. Calamy.*

*Joſ.* 18. This Book of the Law ſhall not depart out
of thy mouth, but thou ſhalt meditate therein day
and night, that thou maiſt obſerve to doe according to all that is written therein, for then thou
ſhalt make thy way proſperous, and have good
ſucceſſe.

Printed at *London* by *G.B.* and *R.W.* for
*G.C.* 1 6 4 3.

The title page in F. Fry's 1862 edition of the Soldiers Pocket Bible (1643). Soldiers were encouraged to seek biblical support and comfort from the scriptural texts published in this Bible.

is responsible for the distribution of millions of Bibles. Their impact on America's religious society is unmistakable.

## The Bible Enters the War Between the States

The King James Version[16] had a tremendous impact on the men of the Civil War. In May 1861, with the War Between the States just underway, the board of the American Bible Society made it known to all distributors both in the South and North that it was their intention to supply all soldiers with copies of the Bible. President Abraham Lincoln made a proclamation in August 1861 that forbade trade with the enemy. This made it very difficult for the society to provide Bibles and New Testaments across enemy lines to the Confederate Army. During the next year, however, the society found legitimate ways through governmental agencies and with special army permission to get Bibles to the Confederates. It was reported in 1863 that the Maryland Auxiliary placed 86,424 Bibles in Confederate hands.[17]

In spite of the genuine efforts to get the Bible into the hands of all soldiers of both Union and Confederate armies, a scarcity of Bibles developed in the South. By 1863 Northern prisoners in Richmond were selling copies of Bibles to Confederates at inflated prices of twelve to fifteen dollars each, enabling them to buy food.

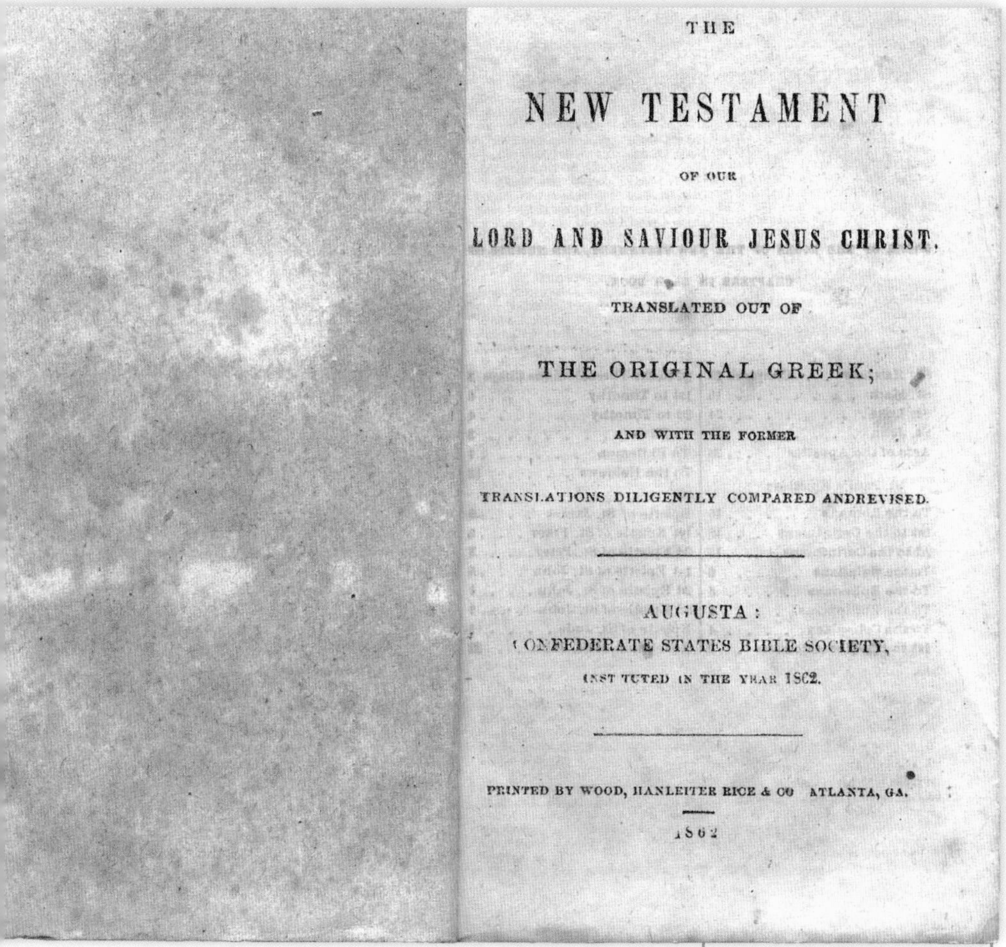

THE

NEW TESTAMENT

OF OUR

LORD AND SAVIOUR JESUS CHRIST.

TRANSLATED OUT OF

THE ORIGINAL GREEK;

AND WITH THE FORMER

TRANSLATIONS DILIGENTLY COMPARED AND REVISED.

AUGUSTA:
CONFEDERATE STATES BIBLE SOCIETY,
INSTITUTED IN THE YEAR 1862.

PRINTED BY WOOD, HANLEITER RICE & CO ATLANTA, GA.

1862

Even the "mother country" got into the commercial enterprise of selling Bibles to the former colonies. The Confederate States Bible Society attempted to import Bibles from England in 1862. England's tendency to sympathize with the South gave them courage to make 50,000 New Testaments, 10,000 Bibles, and 250,000 portions of the Bible available free of charge.[18] This was a dangerous task since it meant running the Northern blockade. Several shipments successfully reached the South. In some cases, the Union blockade intercepted the ships and the Bibles were taken as contraband. My collection has copies of all the Bibles printed during the War Between the States. One very interesting New Testament has on the flyleaf a statement identifying

A rare Confederate printing of the New Testament from the state of Georgia (1862). The Union army printed plenty of New Testaments, but the Confederate army had to depend on supplies from England.

FROM THE CARGO OF THE
Anglo Rebel Blockade Runner
MINNA,
CAPTURED DECEMBER 6th, 1863,
OFF WILMINGTON,
By the Government Dispatch Ship
CIRCASSIAN,
CAPT. W. B. EATON.

For Sale by W. H. Piper & Co.
133 WASHINGTON ST., BOSTON.

The rebel ship *Minna* attempted to smuggle these New Testaments into the South by avoiding the Northern blockade. The ship was intercepted by the Union army and the New Testaments were confiscated and sold at auction.

the "Rebel, *Minna*," a ship that attempted to run the Northern blockade, was captured, and had its shipment of Bibles confiscated and sold at public auction.

In 1862, the Confederate States Bible Society published a New Testament in Atlanta, Georgia. It was a simple copy bound in heavy brown paper covers, measuring 2⅜ × 5 inches. A crude sewing of the leaves and plain cover reveals the Confederates' attempt to print New Testaments very inexpensively. These are extremely rare today.

During the war, the American Bible Society supplied more than three million Bibles and New Testaments to soldiers of both sides. The edition of 1860 and 1861 supplied most of the total number. However, each year of the war, the American Bible Society printed New Testaments to be distributed to soldiers. In 1866 (the Jubilee year of the founding of the American Bible

# eBay—The Collector's Delight

I began buying from eBay shortly after the trading site went online. In the early days, bargains were there for the taking. In the last few years, however, the supply and demand of rare Bibles have left the bargains to survive only occasionally. The compensation for a lack of bargains has come in a better quality of selection to the market.

I began collecting Civil War New Testaments because of their connection with the common person and especially the soldier who often carried and read the Bible on his own. I soon learned that the one who gets the prize must be a tactician as well as a bidder with means. I missed a number of items because someone would wait until the last few seconds to make their final bid. My computer was a bit slow, and by the time I counter-bid, the item was gone.

I managed to learn the game just in time for the purchase of a rare 1862 Georgia Confederate New Testament. On this occasion, the price had advanced to about $325 with just a few minutes before closing. I wanted it very badly. With a minute to go, I bid $650. I was hoping the other bidder would not have time to counter my bid if he didn't go beyond $650. My scheming and plotting paid off. The other bidder had placed a bid for just $600.

To confirm my "wisdom" and "great deceptive" work, the next day I received an email offering me $2,500! Of course, I could not part with such a treasure and the manifest evidence of a successful encounter with eBay.

Civil War New Testaments (1862–66) printed during the war and immediately after the war.

Society) when the War Between the States had finished, the society printed a large run of New Testaments to replenish the supply lost during the war.

The end of the Civil War stirred the desire to read and study the Bible. A renewed hope and a vision of a free America danced in the hearts of the survivors.

# 15

# The Bible as Bestseller

*"As Wide as the Waters Be"*

The laughing and hooting hung in the still, cool air of the fifteenth-century December night. Wade, one of the local gravediggers, thought the evening's assignment rather unusual. The fact that the local priests were the leaders of the mission did nothing to relieve his uneasiness. Yet the jingle of extra shillings in his pocket was welcome, providing an opportunity to raise his spirits at the local pub before embarking on the night's labor.

The exhumation of a body seemed a most loathsome task. But he needed the extra work and, after all, that was part of his job. The seriousness of the situation brought to mind the words of Nelson, an acquaintance, who had been telling him for weeks how important the reading of Scripture was. Admittedly, Nelson's words had a ring of truth to them. "Could it be that God saves by faith alone?" Nelson suffered a lot for his faith. Just two weeks before, the priests had come to his house in search of the Bible of the common version. Having been warned, Nelson had slipped out the back with his small Bible tucked under his heavy tunic.

The priests had arrived earlier and began building a fire near the gravesite. Sobered by their previous conversations, the gravediggers began the

An engraving of the desecration of Wycliffe's bones (1428). John Wycliffe was condemned at the council of Constance (1414–16) along with Bohemian Reformer John Huss, who was burned at the stake. They ordered the grave of Wycliffe (d. 1384) opened and his bones burned. Photo: John Foxe, *Acts and Monuments* (1844), vol. 3, 96.

unsavory task. The beverages consumed at the pub kept their tongues loose and the hole grew quickly. With a thud, the shovel struck its target.

After clearing the top of the crude, wooden coffin, the lid was removed and their eyes fell on the contents. Their lighthearted, even nervous, laughter was silenced. The workmen suddenly were face-to-face with the mortality of mankind. Fear overwhelmed them, seeming to freeze time. "Move, move quickly." The priest's sudden harsh commands jolted them back to the task at hand.

Thinking they were violating the dead, they gathered the bones of the departed soul and gave them to the priests who had been stoking the hot fire. The bones were immediately thrown into the burning logs and coals. As Wade watched, his eyes transfixed on the flames, he couldn't help but wonder why it was necessary to go to all of this trouble to desecrate a man who had stirred the religious consciousness of a nation. Men and women everywhere were secretly reading God's Word. Why was this man so hated?

He glanced at the makeshift grave marker and saw in bold writing, "John de Wyclif." "His only crime was to translate the Bible into the English language," Wade mused. "It is hard to understand the intense hatred the holy fathers had for Wycliffe." The local gossip was that almost everyone was fed up with the practice of selling indulgences. The church seemed to issue indulgences just to fill their coffers, and that didn't seem right to Wade. But how could he, a simple gravedigger, challenge the teachings of the Holy Church?

The bones were quickly reduced to ashes by the raging fire attended by the priests. They ordered Wade to scoop up the ashes and throw them into the River Swift (tributary to Avon). Wade felt a bit sick at his stomach as the last handful went swirling into the rapidly running stream. His private thoughts broke his furrowed brow and tightly drawn lips into a slight smile. *How ironic*, he thought. *The River Swift took Wycliffe's ashes into the sea and ultimately into the ocean.* Little did Wade know that an unknown poet would soon immortalize his deeds in this poem:

> The Avon to the Severn runs,
> The Severn to the sea,
> And Wycliffe's dust shall spread abroad,
> Wide as the waters be.[1]

The poem is a fitting tribute to the "Morning Star of the Reformation" and his translation that one day would provide the English world with a Bible in her own language. The picture is much bigger—and the influence of Wycliffe, his translation, and Reformation theology went much wider—wider than anyone of the fourteenth century could ever imagine.

John Wycliffe's translation principle was that the language of the message did not affect the gospel; therefore, it should be translated into the most familiar language possible. The Bible in the hands of the masses was a deterrent to an authoritative church and clergy gone astray. As long as the body of Christ can read and understand the Bible, the church is in good hands. Wycliffe's concept was expressed in a Latin sermon found in an Oxford manuscript, which translated says:

> Although the common expressions may change over time, the truthful principles that are articulated from the Gospel are the same in number. Likewise, even

though the languages are different, the evangelical truths do not change. Therefore the scriptures should be written and spoken in Latin and Greek, in Gaelic, in English, and should also be articulated in all other languages. But especially, the scriptures should be written in English because a translation does not have to be true to the idioms but rather the translation should rely on the perfection of truth confirming the truths of God.[2]

By the close of the nineteenth century the struggle for the survival of the Bible in the hands of the common person was over. The new challenge beginning in the twentieth century turned to the question, "Which translation best conveys God's revelation given to the prophets and apostles?" It has been estimated that there have been over 350 English translations of the Bible over the last one hundred years. Bible translation has been undertaken by scholars, Bible commentators, preachers, committees, and individual laypeople. Translations have been characterized as literal, periphrastic, cultural, and gender specific; some Bibles include notes for spiritual development, for athletes, for women, for nurses, for fathers, and many, many others.

## Why Are Modern Translations Needed?

One needs only to read an ancient English document to observe language in flux. The famous King James Version phrase "superfluity of naughtiness" (James 1:21) means "abundance of evil." The New International Version simply says "evil." Which is the easiest to understand? It has very little to do with the meaning of the original Greek text but everything to do with how we understand it today in modern English. New translations aid in updating ever-developing language expressions.

Translations of the Bible are God's Word and, as such, they carry his truth

Modern Bible translations. There have been hundreds of English translations developed during the last one hundred years. They should be seen as a help, not a hindrance, to understanding the Bible. Photo: A. Sanchez.

## The Blessing of a Modern Translation

He faithfully carried his slim edition King James New Testament in his out-side suit pocket to church every Sunday. He returned home, placed his New Testament on the dresser, and there it safely waited until the next Sunday. His eighth-grade education didn't prevent this factory worker from rising to foreman and later to supervisor, or from being a highly respected member in the community of a small Illinois town. The lack of education did, however, hinder my dad's ability to read.

In 1966, about two years before my father passed away, someone gave him a copy of the *Good News for Modern Man* translation of the New Testament. I was deeply engaged in seminary education in Texas and visited my parents as often as our family budget allowed. On this occasion, I returned home to find that my father had been reading the *Good News for Modern Man*. My seminary training gave me an appreciation for a "literal translation" and I sometimes "poked fun" at anyone reading a paraphrase—until then.

In a discussion about my schoolwork and preparation for ministry, Dad confided in me that until he began reading this modern translation, he did not know the Bible was supposed to be read by ordinary people. He believed that only "preachers" could understand the Bible and that they were to tell the people in the pew what it meant. I was shocked! Then "my soul was strangely warmed." I gained a great appreciation that day for a translation into modern English with a vocabulary for those whose reading skills were deficient. God's Word was indeed for everyone, no matter what reading level they had achieved.

and authority. Yet, there are many questions surrounding translations: Which translation is the best? Why isn't one translation selected as the universal translation? Why continue to make more translations? If a translation contains elements of interpretation by the one translating, then who is qualified to translate the Bible? How can a translator's biases be avoided? Do translations need footnotes and study aids? How many notes should a Bible have? These questions are important to answer as you select a translation that best fits your needs.

## The Goal of Translation: The Communication of God's Word

It may seem obvious, but the Scriptures are to be understood by the reader—a revelation, not a secret code. During much of the nineteenth century it was believed that the language of the New Testament was a "Holy Ghost" language (a special language used by God for his revelation). The German scholar Adolf Deissmann, when comparing New Testament manuscripts with papyrus fragments, demonstrated without question that the language of the New Testament was the common language of the period. The New Testament was given to instruct believers on the application of Old Testament theology and to understand God's dealing with humanity after Christ's death and resurrection. The Old Testament was a formal display of God's intentions as revealed through the sacrificial system (Torah), a description of historical events of Israel's past (historical books), and a manual for worship (poetic books). Worship and obedience to prescribed laws dominated the revelation, compared with the New Testament's principles for daily living in grace.

The goal of translation is the transfer of meaning from one language to another. The primary question then is, "What is the best method and process for such transfer of meaning?" Two basic approaches attempt to answer this question. Some advocate literal, word-for-word translation, while others advocate a meaning-based thought-for-thought translation. The latter places emphasis on the importance of meaning rather than form, and it emphasizes the transfer of meaning from an ancient socio-linguistic context to a modern socio-linguistic context. As linguist Mark Strauss puts it, "*Meaning* not *form* is the goal of Bible translation. Lexical and syntactical *semantics* must always take precedence over lexical and *syntactical* forms."[3]

> The goal of translation is the transfer of meaning from one language to another.

Early translations into English paid close attention to honoring God's Word. They believed the holiness of the written Word justified equivalent English words to represent Greek and Hebrew words. The King James Version has an English word or expression for every Greek word or expression. The difficulty of this method surfaces when it is understood that Greek and Hebrew formal structures are not the same as English formal structures. Of course, all translators recognize that there are times when no formal equivalent exists and then function or meaning takes precedence. Using Matthew 5:2, Strauss compares six translations to reveal noticeable differences:[4]

The Good News for Modern Man (*Today's English Version*), 1966.

New King James Version (NKJV): Then **He opened His mouth and taught them,** saying:

Revised Standard Version/English Standard Version (RSV/ESV): And **he opened his mouth and taught them**, saying:

New American Standard Bible (NASB): And **opening His mouth He began to teach them,** saying,

New International Version/Today's New International Version (NIV/TNIV): and **he began to teach them,** saying:

Holman Christian Standard Bible (HCSB): Then **He began to teach them;**[5]

Good News Translation (GNT): and **he began to teach them.**

New Living Translation (NLT): and **he began to teach them**.

Strauss points out the awkwardness of the first three and the smoothness of the last four texts. He continues to suggest the phrase "He opened his mouth and taught them" is a Greek idiom composed of two phrases to express a single action. In English the same meaning is expressed in a single phrase. As these various translations are read, it is obvious that they all have the same meaning but the single action is clearly the easiest English expression. Some, however, argue that there is a literary quality that is lost when using the single action translation. Others feel that a formal language to express the principles of a holy God is preferred. Hopefully this chapter will help guide you in deciding for yourself which translation approach is best for you.

While the clear meaning of Matthew 5:2 is captured by the NLT, GNT, and NIV/TNIV, it may not be best in the broader sense. This phrase does not always precede a saying or teaching, so it is not a formal introduction to a "saying." In Matthew 23:1 it is a simple statement: "Then Jesus spoke to the multitudes and to His disciples, saying" (NKJV). Is the direct meaning all that is important? If only cognitive meaning is important in biblical passages, why is so much of the Bible written in poetry or apocalyptic forms?

Is there some nuance intended by the added action of "He opened His mouth"? Is there a loss in style as expressed by individual biblical authors that is important to maintain? Is it possible that the added action in 5:2 expresses a culturally significant nuance that does have meaning beyond just the statement "He began to teach them"? If so, the statement should be translated as it is in the NKJV, RSV, and NASB (and in the HCSB note). In many cases, the interpreter should determine whether or not the added phrase has a cultural significance. Yet, to the common reader, the more natural reading contains the clearest meaning.

## Translation Theory in Practice

Translation theory is not just for use among scholars—that was the thought in the early days of Bible translation. It is for the common person in the pew. *Thought-for-thought translation* has the advantage of modern linguistic theory. It recognizes that no two languages can have a direct transfer of meaning in a word-for-word translation. It also recognizes that no English translation is sacrosanct and that the development of language demands new translations to accompany the change. This theory recognizes that translators are interpreters and must make decisions on the meaning as they translate. The emphasis is placed on the receptor language and clear meaning for the English reader. Bible translator consultant Ronald Youngblood summarizes this view: "The translation shall be designed to communicate the truth of

God's revelation as effectively as possible to English readers in the language of the people. Every effort shall be made to achieve good English style."[6]

Thought-for-thought translation theory rightly places importance on the equivalence of response to the message by the modern readers as it was to the original readers. Passages in the Psalms and emotive language are handled with particular care to avoid wooden literalness that leads to factual content only, missing the intended emotional response by the reader.

Word-for-word translation has the advantage of taking seriously the source language as the base for meaning. It considers biblical metaphors and idioms, sees the original revelation as God's Word, emphasizes the importance of theology, and realizes the importance of culture to its language. Word-for-word translation considers the necessity of style for meaning, the exegetical potential of the original text, the fidelity of the original words, and the confidence in the accuracy of the transfer of meaning. It resists the temptation to let a translation become a commentary.

> Words express ideas and when words are changed, meaning is affected. To know what the Bible means requires knowledge of what the Bible says.

There are several important principles that strengthen the use of the word-for-word (formal equivalence) style of translation:[7]

### 1. Accuracy to the original text.

While accuracy is the goal of both translation methods, word-for-word theory attempts to maintain the fullness and richness of the biblical text in a readable style, maintaining various levels of meaning, theological terminology, and literary style. The fear is that a thought-for-thought translation reduces the biblical text to a form of common language below the normal educational level of its readers.

### 2. Fidelity to the words of the original.

This translation principle is uncompromising in its emphasis on preserving the words of the original text insofar as the translation process allows it.

Words express ideas and when words are changed, meaning is affected. To know what the Bible means requires knowledge of what the Bible says.

### 3. Effective diction through clarity of words, accuracy of connotations, and vividness of expression.

While many ideas expressed in Scripture are simple and easy to understand, other concepts are difficult and would not have been understood by the first readers or hearers. These concepts require the assistance of biblical scholars or linguistic specialists and should not be inserted in a translation.

### 4. Preserve ambiguity of meanings.

Often scholars who read a particular translation complain that thought-for-thought translations make interpretative decisions that should be left to the reader to decide. A case in point is 1 Thessalonians 1:3:

**NASB:** Constantly bearing in mind **your work of faith and labor of love and steadfastness of hope** in our Lord Jesus Christ . . .

**NKJV:** Remembering without ceasing **your work of faith, labor of love, and patience of hope** in our Lord Jesus Christ in the sight of our God and Father . . .

**NIV:** We continually remember before our God and Father **your work produced by faith, your labor prompted by love, and your endurance inspired by hope** in our Lord Jesus Christ.

**NLT:** As we pray to our God and Father about you, we think of **your faithful work, your loving deeds, and the enduring hope you have** because of our Lord Jesus Christ.

**HCSB:** We recall, in the presence of our God and Father, **your work of faith, labor of love, and endurance of hope** in our Lord Jesus Christ . . .

The NASB, NKJV, and HCSB leave the interpretation of the phrase to the reader whereas the NIV and NLT make the interpretative decision for the reader.

### 5. Preserve the full exegetical potential of the original text.

A person reading the translation, and especially those from the pulpit, should not be deprived of the precision of meaning the original text allowed.

### 6. Transparency to the original world of the Bible.

A good translation removes the barriers to the reader's ability to become immersed in the culture of the biblical world. These barriers are clouded when the biblical languages stray too far from a literal meaning.

### 7. Respect for the styles of the biblical writers.

The Bible's reputation for incorporating poetic style, metaphors, simile, paradoxes, figures of speech, literary beauty, flowing rhythm, and unqualified dignity is a part of the revelation. Meaning in the Bible must consider the styles of writers. Thought-for-thought translations are in danger of emphasizing the translator's style rather than the distinctive style of the biblical author. Note the following example from Psalm 1:1:

**NKJV:** Blessed is the man who walks not in the counsel of the ungodly, nor stands in the path of sinners, nor sits in the seat of the scornful.

**NASB:** How blessed is the man who does not walk in the counsel of the wicked, nor stand in the path of sinners, nor sit in the seat of scoffers!

**NLT:** Oh, the joys of those who do not follow the advice of the wicked, or stand around with sinners, or join in with mockers.

**HCSB:** How happy is the man who does not follow the advice of the wicked, or take the path

The Cotton Patch Version, 1968. A modern version that presents a text with a Southern accent rich in humor. This version attempted to translate not only the words but the events. Cities and regions of the South were often substituted for Middle East names.

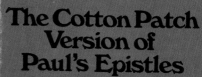

The Cotton Patch Version of Paul's Epistles

*A colloquial modern translation with a Southern accent, vigorous and fervent for the gospel, unsparing in earthiness, rich in humor.*

**Clarence Jordan**

of sinners, or join a group of mockers! (A more literal rendering is provided in the HCSB's footnotes.)

This passage is highly metaphorical. It is not literal—but the impression of the passage in using metaphors carries an impact that the NASB and NKJV maintain, while the HCSB combines both the metaphor and the ease of reading. The NLT weakens the effect altogether. A translation that emphasizes transference of meaning and ignores the linguistic use of metaphoric languages loses an important force intended by the original writer. Beauty, rhythm, and dignity of style heighten the reader's response to the message when themes such as love, worship, war, destruction, and revenge are presented.

> Bible students seeking sound exegesis, cultural clarity, and theological accuracy will never be completely satisfied with a single English translation . . . nor should they.

Bible students seeking sound exegesis, cultural clarity, and theological accuracy will never be completely satisfied with a single English translation—no matter how careful the word-for-word or thought-for-thought translation—nor should they. No English word study, no diagramming of a sentence, no comparing of verses can be a substitute for an immersion in the original languages. The scholar must study the original documents in their original languages, cultural setting, theological worldview, and biblical contexts. That does not mean nonscholars can't understand the Bible. It does mean they must pay careful attention to the translations they use.

The average Bible teacher or theologian may prefer the word-for-word translation. The man or woman in the pew will most likely prefer the thought-for-thought translation. Exegesis—the critical analysis of a text—is the task of the translator, while hermeneutics—the interpretation of a biblical passage—is the task of the Bible teacher. It is in the practice of hermeneutics where consideration for culturally relevant material, context, and application to the modern audience will be made.

The King James Version of 1611 is a prime example of expressing period English in a formal sense. The King James Version followed, as its basic translation, the Bishops' Bible (1602 edition) that primarily expresses the

English of the Tyndale and Coverdale Bibles of the early sixteenth century, seventy-five years earlier. By the time of the King James Version, the English of Tyndale's period was already out-of-date.

Unlike Wycliffe's or Tyndale's day, believers today have a plethora of translations available for reading, studying, and memorizing. The question is not, "Do we have a Bible in our language?" but, "Of all the Bibles we have, which one is best?" Many complain that the multiplication of translations creates more questions than it solves problems. I can't help but recall the words of the late Dr. Edward Goodrick, my colleague and mentor, who said many times, "If you compare six modern translations, you will have the meaning of the original text." The "many translations" now available should be viewed as a blessing rather than a curse.

## The Greek Text of the New Testament

Another important issue in choosing a modern New Testament translation is to consider which Greek New Testament was used by the translators. The King James Versions used the Byzantine (*Textus Receptus*[8]) text while most modern translations favor the Nestle-Aland text (critical text). Since translations have different purposes, they are useful for different reasons. It is difficult to settle on one Bible that meets all the requirements of a translation:

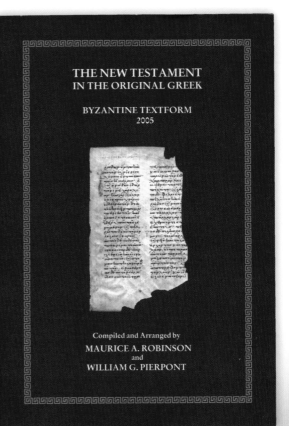

THE NEW TESTAMENT
IN THE ORIGINAL GREEK

BYZANTINE TEXTFORM
2005

Compiled and Arranged by
MAURICE A. ROBINSON
and
WILLIAM G. PIERPONT

A modern edition of the Greek New Testament. This is one of several Greek New Testaments that attempts to arrive at the original first century New Testament. It pictures the author's leaf of a twelfth century manuscript of a portion of Luke's Gospel.

## The Legacy of a Collector

Most Bible collectors have special interests. Since there are thousands of Bibles and editions of Bibles, no collector can collect them all. My specialty became English Bibles, Greek New Testaments, and Latin Bibles and later, as my collection became complete, various editions of the early American and soldiers' Bibles and New Testaments. Vincent Savarino was more of an eclectic collector. Anything that appealed to him or he could afford, he bought. Vincent had a great desire to produce facsimiles of papyri. He decided to copy a whole book of the New Testament in the same manner as the original manuscripts. Using a hand-carved stylus and a method for making straight lines like the early copyists, plus a carbon-based ink to match materials of the first century, he produced the scroll of Philemon on actual papyrus and the book of Mark. His prototype was from the fourth-century finds at Nag Hammadi, the earliest known book (codex).

Vincent's finished copy of Mark was a wonderful treasure. He recorded his method, his procedures, and the number of hours it took to complete the project. I read with utter amazement his journal's description of the ordeal. I returned the journal to Vincent at his request when I purchased the scroll and codex he had so laboriously copied. To my knowledge, these are the only facsimiles of their kind ever done.

Vince died at a premature age a few years ago, but to collectors, he has left a marvelous legacy of hundreds of hours and painstaking effort to produce an exact facsimile of the book of Philemon and the Gospel of Mark as they may have appeared in the first century.

representing the original languages, having the best notes, containing the best modern English expression, and being best for inductive study.

Modern textual criticism has identified three major families of manuscripts. Most surviving manuscripts can be classified within one of these families.[9] Before a modern English translation can be selected, one must determine the translators' basic textual critical theory and the family of manuscripts in which they place most confidence. Their English translation will be based on the Greek text they prefer. While these Greek texts are only slightly different, there are some variants that make exegetical distinctions.

It must also be noted that, in some instances, translators mix the text based upon evidence pointing to superior internal readings.

Translations using the Nestle-Aland Greek text that consider readings from all the families place the heaviest emphasis on the Alexandrian family in most cases. Nevertheless, translations can be classified along the lines presented in the following chart. Three basic "families" used by the English translations represent the three Greek manuscript families called Alexandrian," "Byzantine," and "Western." They are as follows:

| Greek Families | *Alexandrian Family* | *Byzantine Family* | *Western Family* |
|---|---|---|---|
| **Representative Manuscripts** | Codex Sinaiticus A Codex Vaticanus B | Codex Alexandrinus A Codex Ephraemi C (mixed) | Codex Beza D Codex Claromontanus D2 |
| **Popular Names** | Critical text (Eclectic Text) | *Textus Receptus* (Traditional Text) | Latin Text (Catholic Text) |
| **English Translations** | English Revised Version 1881–85 | Tyndale New Testament 1526 King James Version 1611 | Wycliffe New Testament 1382–88(92?) Rhemes New Testament 1582 |
| | American Standard Version 1901 | King James Version (Paragraph Bible) 1873 | Challoner New Testament 1749 |
| | Revised Standard Version 1946–52 | New King James Version 1982 (Majority Text noted) | Knox Version 1955 |
| | Phillips New Testament 1958 | 21st Century King James Version 1994 | Jerusalem Bible 1966 |
| | New English Bible 1970 | | New American Bible 1970 |
| | New American Standard Bible 1971 | | ( JB and NAB followed Nestle-Aland's 25th edition but often departed to reflect Latin readings.) |
| | Good News Bible 1976 | | |
| | New International Version 1978 | | |
| | New Living Translation 1996 (Revised 2004) | | |
| | English Standard Version 2001 | | |
| | Holman Christian Standard Bible 2003 | | |

This chart is representative of major translations only. Not all of the versions translate directly from one family. In some cases they are eclectic, based on individual manuscript variants and the value placed on specific readings.

A few illustrations of typical differences between the Byzantine and Alexandrian text types are as follows (**boldface** indicates words that are missing or different from the other texts):

| Text | Alexandrian reading as translated in ASV | Byzantine reading as translated in NKJV | Western reading as translated in Knox/ Jerusalem Bible[10] |
|---|---|---|---|
| Matthew 5:44 | Love your enemies, and pray for those who persecute you. | Love your enemies, **bless those who curse you, do good to those who hate you,** and pray for those who **spitefully use you and** persecute you. | Love your enemies, **do good to those who hate you,** pray for those who persecute **and insult you.** |
| Matthew 9:13 | I did not come to call the righteous, but sinners. | For I did not come to call the righteous, but sinners, **to repentance.** | I did not come to call the **virtuous,** but sinners. |
| Matthew 24:36 | Not even the angels of heaven, **nor the son,** but the father alone. | Not even the angels of heaven, but **My** Father only. | Neither the angels of heaven, **nor the Son,** no one but the Father only. |
| Luke 1:28 | The Lord is with you. | The Lord is with you; **blessed are you among women.** | The Lord is with thee; **blessed art thou among women.** |
| Galatians 3:1 | Who has bewitched you? | Who has bewitched you **that you should not obey the truth?** | Who is it that has cast a spell on you, **that you should refuse your loyalty to the truth?** |
| 1 Timothy 4:12 | In speech, conduct, love, faith and purity. | In word, in conduct, in love, **in spirit,** in faith, in purity. | The way you speak and behave, and in your love, your faith and your purity. |
| 1 John 1:7 | The blood of Jesus his Son cleanses us from all sin. | The blood of Jesus **Christ** His Son cleanses us from all sin. | The blood of his Son Jesus **Christ** washes us clean from all sin. |

The families of manuscripts are the basis for the Western (Catholic) Church, Eastern Orthodox Church, and Egyptian Coptic Church. The Byzantine family is found in the area of modern Turkey (Asia Minor or Byzantium kingdom) and Greece where the church from the apostle Paul's time grew to greatness. Native Greek speakers copied the text from the first century. The move of the capital from Rome to Constantinople in AD 381 released the Western Church from the tight control of the emperor. The Western Church and the Greek Church each developed their texts along slightly different lines. In the meantime, the church in Alexandria, Egypt (Coptic), under the influence of Origin and Tertullian, developed yet another family of manuscripts. Some textual variants can, quite possibly, be traced to theological issues and the developments of the various doctrinal traditions.[11]

# 16

# The People Triumph

*The Bible for All Seasons*

A fter nine months of twelve-hour days spent in intensive language study, listening to countless language tapes, many conversations with native speakers, and many written and reading assignments, I soon realized I had only begun to learn the Ethiopian language. Three years later, after daily teaching in a Bible school with Amharic as the medium of instruction, hundreds of down country conferences, and many shopping excursions, I understood that a language couldn't be learned without a thorough induction into the culture of the people speaking the language.

Once I had lived in that culture for a period of time, I began to understand figures of speech, "common expressions," strange word order, and often, unacceptable language usage. It has been said a true bilingual must learn the languages before he or she reaches the age of twelve. While there may be exceptions, language and culture are intricately related and they are learned intimately from childhood.

In third world cultures or in the culture of a modern industrialized nation, a translation must meet the needs of the culture and understand common word expressions. I have heard young people complain about the inability of the King James Version and the New American Standard Bible to meet their needs. The Bible is meant to be understood by all, whether young or old, man or woman, living in Africa or a Western nation.

## Criteria for Judging a Translation

Once readers have settled on an underlying Greek text, they must begin to evaluate the many English versions based upon sound translation and linguistic principles. The highly respected linguist Eugene A. Nida lists three important areas to consider, and I have added two others:[1]

1. Is it efficient in translation? The reading is best that translates without expanding the text by redundant explanation.
2. Does it comprehend the original intent? The original intent of the author is best claimed when the reading is both accurate to the original language and it is comprehensible to the reader in the receptor language.
3. Is there equivalence of response? The response the reader has to the translation must be equivalent to the response of the original hearer.
4. Does it achieve good English style in the various literary genres, metaphors, and figures of speech? The finished product must be suitable for public reading and worship.
5. Does it allow for interpretive ambiguities, theological difficulties, accuracy of meaning, and cultural peculiarities?

While the average Bible reader may have difficulty in answering these questions as they peruse the local bookstore shelves, it will be necessary to have your questions and translation philosophy ready for the professional bookstore operator to help guide you in your selection. Most modern versions explain their

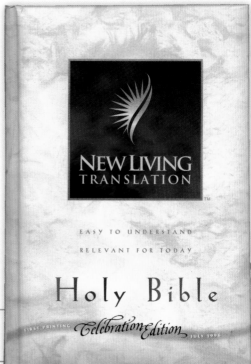

The New Living Translation, 1996. It was designed to make a fresh, vital, and living translation understood even by children.

translation theory in the introduction. It is always prudent to seek that information before making your selection.

## Literary Styles in Translation

While it may not be obvious, artistic and literary style must always be considered during translation. In modern English, a variety of writing styles are used to express thought. One style is used in news reporting, quite another in legal descriptions such as contracts, and yet another in romantic novels. The question asked by a translation is, "Which style is best to communicate God's Word?" The problem with "formal equivalent" language translations is that they often are so tied to the "minimal transference" that the connotation is one of an innate authority based simply on its formal language. To many, the New American Standard Bible and the New King James Version contain just such authoritative language. This reduces the Bible to a formal religious book seen as authoritative simply through the words as divine oracles from God instead of it being a dynamic word for handling life's problems.

> Artistic and literary style must always be considered during translation.

Literary styles in the Bible vary depending upon whether one is reading poetic literature, the prophets, or the historical books. The New Testament adds gospel, didactic, and apocalyptic genres. Since the Scriptures are a revelation and not a hidden or secret message, they were delivered in the common tongue of the period. Tyndale and Wycliffe were convinced the Scripture must be translated into the common language of the people. It was not until the King James Version that literary excellence played a major role in the finished product of the Bible. This is not to say that earlier sixteenth-century English versions did not pay attention to style, but the emphasis on a Bible conforming to Elizabethan English with all its refinements came with the King James Version.

No language has a vocabulary for the infinite varieties of ideas and descriptions of interpersonal relationships. Instead, qualifiers and comparisons are used to further define the subject being discussed. Look around the room in which you are sitting and describe what you see. How do you define the hues of colors of the various objects or the relationship of items to each other? Now if a friend enters the room and begins a conversation in which he is animated about a topic, then you quickly realize that all kinds of qualifying and descriptive language is being used in his animated nonverbal language. So in addition to the difficulty of describing visual observations, the difficulty in interpreting meaning from animated gestures is another complicating factor.

> No language has a vocabulary for the infinite varieties of ideas and descriptions of interpersonal relationships.

The Bible in its written form does not express voice intonation, hand gestures, or facial expressions. This is a part of the need for interpretation of the literature of the Scriptures. In translating the Bible, "functional equivalents" are imperative if one wants to get the intended meaning of the author. Meaning is not just expressed by lexical meanings but also by sensing the emotional impact and determining the motivation to act. To seek only lexical meanings by "formal equivalents" actually will distort some passages that deal with the emotional impact of love, worship, appreciation, duty, regret, hope, fear, and joy. On the other hand, in didactic literature, where the facts and intellect are engaged and exact meanings of terms and syntax is sought, "formal equivalent" may be desired.

One reason the King James Version has had such a lasting effect on Bible readers is that its beautiful literary style is so powerful in the poetic literature. It is also true that many view the King James Version language as somewhat more inspiring and worshipful. Note the style when comparing "formal equivalents" style with "functional equivalent" in Isaiah 35:1–2:

The Holman Christian Standard Bible, 2004 and The New King James Version, 1979.

A Visual History of the English Bible

**KJV:** The wilderness and the solitary place shall be glad for them; and the desert shall rejoice, and blossom as a rose. It shall blossom abundantly, and rejoice even with joy and singing: the glory of Lebanon shall be given unto it, the excellency of Carmel and Sharon, they shall see the glory of the LORD, and the excellency of our God.

**NKJV:** The wilderness and the wasteland shall be glad for them, and the desert shall rejoice and blossom as the rose; It shall blossom abundantly and rejoice, even with joy and singing. The glory of Lebanon shall be given to it, the excellence of Carmel and Sharon. They shall see the glory of the LORD, the excellency of our God.

**NASB:** The wilderness and the desert will be glad, and the Arabah will rejoice and blossom; like the crocus it will blossom profusely and rejoice with rejoicing and shout of joy. The glory of Lebanon will be given to it, the majesty of Carmel and Sharon. They will see the glory of the LORD, the majesty of our God.

**NLT:** Even the wilderness and desert will be glad in those days. The wasteland will rejoice and blossom with spring crocuses. Yes, there will be an abundance of flowers and singing and joy! The deserts will become as green as the mountains of Lebanon, as lovely as Mount Carmel or the Plain of Sharon. There the LORD will display his glory, the splendor of our God.

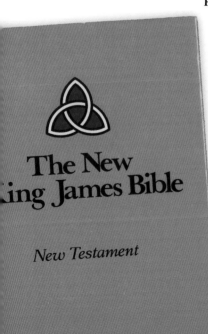

**HCSB:** The wilderness and the dry land will be glad; the desert will rejoice and blossom like a rose. It will blossom abundantly and will also rejoice with joy and singing. The glory of Lebanon will be given to it, the splendor of Carmel and Sharon. They will see the glory of the LORD, the splendor of our God.

The NASB ("formal equivalent") is clearly awkward in style, while the KJV (although archaic) and NKJV have a cadence and beauty that is smooth and pleasing. The NLT, as a "functional equivalent," is clear and is in a modern literary style that is still adequate. The HCSB ("optimal equivalent") has successfully combined the meaning and literary beauty into a pleasant translation.

Literary style in "formal equivalence" depends heavily on direct transfer of vocabulary from the biblical language to modern language. "Functional equivalence" depends more heavily on language qualifiers to express a meaning that is functionally equivalent to the biblical language. It must be recognized that no language has direct transfer of lexical meaning to another language. A word often has cultural implications or connotations that can be observed only when the language and culture are thoroughly understood. The expression "gay clothing" in James 2:3 is translated from the Greek word *lampros* and means "bright, splendorous, elegant, or gorgeous" attire. Modern translations, even the NKJV, recognize that "gay" has contemporary connotations that preclude its use in James 2:3 and have used the term "fine clothing."

> The intention of modern translations is to express the message of God to his subjects in a clear, perceptive, and accurate fashion.

When it comes to style, "functional equivalence" is more important in poetic and apocalyptic literature than historical narrative. In literature such as epistolary and many forms of historical narrative, a "formal equivalence" has more validity. It must be kept in mind that "functional equivalence" is not the antithesis of "formal equivalence"; "functional equivalence" simply aims to translate from one language to another with a thorough understanding and appreciation for the source language and culture to find the expressions in the receptor language that accurately convey the meaning, emotional impact, and motivation to action intended by the original author. This certainly calls for more than a direct lexical transfer.

The King James Version, which was produced in the "golden age of the English language," should not be held up as the only accurate translation of the "Word of God." Even so, as J. B. Phillips observes, "Most people refuse to believe that the majesty and dignified simplicity of the Authorized Version [KJV], however lovely in themselves, are no more a part of the original message than the scarlet and blue and gold illumination on a medieval manuscript."[2]

The intention of modern translations is to express the message of God to his subjects in a clear, perceptive, and accurate fashion. All modern translations must be judged on this basis. Christians should view the Bible as both God's revelation and a piece of literature. It should be suitable for public worship as well as critical analysis.

## Biblical Words in Translations

Any student will be reminded that the issue of translation theory has not been resolved to everyone's satisfaction. Many today believe word-for-word, literal translations are the only way to achieve an accurate translation. Wycliffe Bible Translators says, "The more educated one becomes the more literal a translation he/she demands." Words represent ideas and concepts, but meaning requires the use of words in their syntactical relationships as expressed by a human being. A text without an author has no meaning. An author's communication includes his thoughts, intentions, and inferences. Biblical meaning is found only when the reader discovers the impact of the author's intention. The reader must understand the author's language, his assumptions, his cultural background, and his life's experiences.

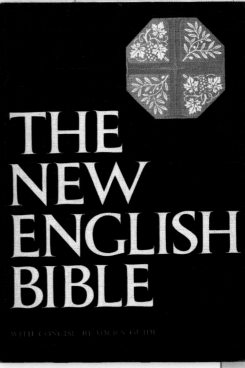

The New English Bible, 1972.

This inevitability brings us to the question of the exegesis or meanings of "words." Should we spend energy studying "words," and if so, what about "words" expressing figures of speech? The following comparison in Luke 12:20 points out some of the differences between the use of "words" in word-for-word and thought-for-thought translations. The literal translation of the Greek text will aid in seeing how English word order must be considered by the translator.

## The Big One That Got Away

Brian and I had been Bible-collecting telephone "mates" for several years. We had not met, but we kept in touch through the common bond of phoning each other to exchange stories of our purchases. Occasionally, we would try to "con" each other out of something the other desperately wanted. One morning as I was busy in my office, I received a phone call from Brian. He was at the stage in life where he was going to sell his collection, or at least some of it. He inquired as to my interest, knowing of course I would be anxious to purchase some or all of his collection. He invited me to London to see his collection and to discuss its disposition. As was normal for me, my funds were limited, but my appetite was unquenchable.

I unhesitatingly determined a mutually agreeable date and "set sail" for London. His home in the northern London suburb of Loughton, Essex, was a quaint English home I found absolutely fascinating; his wife was most hospitable. They warmly invited me to stay with them while discussing and examining Brian's wonderful collection. For the next several days, I reveled in a world of rare Bibles and inhaled the sweet aroma of musty books that only a bibliophile could appreciate.

I recorded the Bibles he was ready to part with and placed an appraisal price I felt was fair. I certainly did not want to take advantage of his need to sell nor my inability to pay premium prices. At the end of the visit, we had agreed on the price for more than a hundred volumes. The total price was out of my price range, so I hoped I could get some buyers at home to purchase some of the volumes I already had to help finance the rest. A great plan, I thought.

**Greek Text:** He said but to him the God: foolish man, in this the night the *soul* of you they demand from you;

**NKJV:** But God said to him, "You fool! This night your *soul* will be required of you."

**NASB:** But God said to him, "You fool! This very night your *soul* is required of you."

**TNIV:** But God said to him, "You fool! This very night your *life* will be demanded from you."

**NLT:** But God said to him, "You fool! You will die this very night."

**HCSB:** But God said to him, "You fool! This very night your *life* is demanded of you."

Brian's collection contained a beautiful copy of the 1611 first edition, first issue King James Version that had come from the Cambridge Library, a very rare copy of the Bassandyne Bible (1579), and an exquisite copy of the two-volume first edition of the Dore Bible. I simply couldn't leave without them. My mental calculator began to fumble through the numbers and, while not adding up to the acceptable number, I quickly announced I would take the three now and would send a check in British sterling for them when I got back to the States. Then I would begin to raise the funds for the others.

Back at home I began wheeling and dealing for the money to buy the rest. I had verbal commitments for some; I had the possibility to borrow for others. My enthusiasm had clouded reality. I informed Brian that I would take all of his collection. Brian wrapped up the Bibles, placed them in storage, and awaited the check and instructions from me to send them.

Over the next several weeks, commitments to help me purchase Brian's Bibles fell through and the money I sent for the three volumes I brought home depleted my bank account and borrowing power. With great disappointment and embarrassment, I called Brian and told him I could not fulfill the deal. He graciously acknowledged my plight and assured me he would hold them for a while to see if I could get the funds later.

Several months later Brian called to inform me that he had sold the collection to a local library where he was put in charge of the rare book collection. What seemed "the big one that got away" turned out to be a blessing for Brian; and I did, after all, get the three most important volumes for my collection.

Each of the translations can be understood, and the meaning in each is quite clear. However, the NKJV and NASB maintain the metaphor of "soul," which certainly means "life" in this context. The question for the translator is, "Do we retain the metaphor or spell out the meaning of the metaphor?" If translating for societies that have no biblical heritage, the metaphor may be confusing. If translating into a modern society, retaining the metaphor has merit.

Just as modern English uses figures of speech, so did biblical languages. Languages are replete with lexical meanings that are not literal but figurative. This can compound the decisions for translators. In Luke 13:32, Herod is called a "fox." Jesus is called a "door" in John 10:9. Neither of these terms is intended to be literal. The terms used to describe Jesus's and Herod's persons are intended to reveal something about them. The translators normally transfer the idiom in a literal, straightforward way. "Door," however, is translated as "gate" in the NLT, but the figure is translated literally. In neither case is there an attempt to translate its figurative significance such as, "Jesus is the way of access to God," or "Herod is cunning and sly."

> Translators as interpreters always struggle with how much of a figure of speech should be introduced into a version as opposed to leaving it for the reader to interpret.

Translators as interpreters always struggle with how much of a figure of speech should be introduced into a version as opposed to leaving it for the reader to interpret. There frequently is a concern that figures of speech reflect their corresponding literal significance. Many biblical figures arise directly from their culture, worldview, and behavioral patterns of the time. Figures can only be understood when one thoroughly understands the biblical background. Some figures of speech may elude modern interpreters. Did New Testament people understand "door" as "a way of access" or did they see it as "a barrier to entrance"? Modern translators must ask the question, "How did the original writer and readers understand the nature of the figure used?" One certainly would not want to pour twenty-first-century understanding of figures into the biblical context.

"Words, words." How we love to use figurative words to make a point, for humor, or to insult someone with their clever use. For Bible translators, however, words pose great challenges if using "etymology" to determine meaning. Etymology is the use of the history of a word to determine its meaning in a contemporary context. Not only is it a questionable way of determining meaning, it is often misleading. Words and meanings change over a period of time. The word "naughty" in the sixteenth century (James 1:21 KJV) meant "vicious in moral character" or "wicked." Earlier in the twentieth century "naughty" had the connotation of "lewd or licentious behavior." To look at a questionable picture in a magazine, one might say it was "naughty." "Naughty" today generally means "lacking in taste" or "disobedient." In 1 Timothy 2:12 Paul uses the term *authentein*, translated "have authority." This term is used only once in the New Testament, and it is the word from which we get the English word *autocratic*. Some interpreters suggest this lends support to the idea that women are not to teach men so as not to be "autocrats" or "domineering."

If there is no other way of determining meaning, etymology—even though questionable—may assist interpretation. "Inspired" in 2 Timothy 3:16 is used only once in all ancient Greek literature. It is a combination of two words: "God" and "breathed." It is fairly safe to conclude that Paul coined the term intending it to mean that God himself in some way authored the Scriptures.

Words are important to meaning, but their definitions must be determined by context, not by etymology or by searching for the same word in many other contexts. It is tempting when doing a "word study" to search the Bible for word usage throughout, determine the meaning as it is used, and then pour all of that meaning back into the study at hand. Such a study will only reveal the range of a particular word's meaning. Instead, all meaning must be determined by context.

Let's look at some of the major translations to compare them for practical use.

**Comparison and Evaluation of Modern Versions[3]**

| Version (Date) | Translation type | Greek Text New Testament | Accuracy to Greek | Beauty of style | Clarity of reading | Weakness | Strength |
|---|---|---|---|---|---|---|---|
| KJV 1611 Revised 1769 | Literal "Formal" | Byzantine *Textus Receptus* | Excellent | Excellent | Good | Archaic language | Beauty; true to original |
| ASV 1901 | Literal "Formal" Revised ERV | Westcott-Hort/*Textus Receptus*[4] | Excellent | Poor | Good | Readability, style | True to original |
| RSV 1952 | Formal | Eclectic | Good | Fair | Good | Considered liberal, often wooden | True to original text |
| NASB 1971 | Literal "Formal" Revised ASV | Critical Nestle 23rd | Excellent | Fair | Good | Literary style | True to original |

*Continued*

| Version (Date) | Translation type | Greek Text New Testament | Accuracy to Greek | Beauty of style | Clarity of reading | Weakness | Strength |
|---|---|---|---|---|---|---|---|
| GNT 1976 | Free style "Dynamic" | Critical United Bible Society | Fair | Fair | Good | Free at expense of accuracy | Ease of reading style |
| NIV 1978 | Free style "Functional" New translation | Critical Eclectic | Good | Good | Excellent | Sometimes inaccurate | Modern linguistic style |
| NKJV 1982 | Literal "Formal" Revised KJV | Byzantine Text | Excellent | Good | Good | Revision of KJV | Improved KJV revision |
| RNEB 1989 | Free | Eclectic R. Tasker 1961 Greek New Testament | Fair | Fair | Fair | Excess liberty with text | Attempts to render idiom |
| NRSV 1990 | Literal/free "Formal" Revision of the RSV | Critical United Bible Society 3rd | Deficient/ fair | Fair | Good | Theology; liberal bias | Can be faithful to original |
| The Message 1993 (2002) | Functional | "Original languages" | Does not attempt to be true to Greek | Good | Excellent | Often quite loose with the translation | Response oriented; seeks to be more relevant than accurate |
| KJ21 1994 | Literal "Formal" KJV updated | Byzantine *Textus Receptus* | Excellent | Excellent | Good | Very little contribution | Updated English of KJV |
| NLT 1996 (2004) | Free style "Functional" New translation | Critical Nestle-Aland 27th | Good/ excellent | Good | Excellent | Leads to some inconsistency | Reading ease omits vulgarities of Living Bible |
| ESV 2001 | "Essentially literal" "Formal" Revision of RSV | Nestle-Aland 27th UBS | Conservative, excellent | Good | Good | Some inconsistencies | More literal than the NIV, more idiomatic than the NASB |

*Continued*

| Version (Date) | Translation type | Greek Text New Testament | Accuracy to Greek | Beauty of style | Clarity of reading | Weakness | Strength |
|---|---|---|---|---|---|---|---|
| HCSB 2004 | "Optimal equiva-lence"[5] | Critical Nestle-Aland 27th | Excellent | Good | Good/ excellent | Occasional inaccuracies | Modern style; accurate |
| TNIV 2005 | Free style "Functional" NIV revised | Critical Eclectic | Good | Good | Excellent | Considered a work in progress and will continue revision | Modern language; more exegetical than NIV |
| NET 2005 | Literal "Formal" New translation | Critical Nestle-Aland 27th | Excellent | Good | Excellent | Artificial in places | Notes explain choices; accurate |

Years of study, improved tools, better language skills, and more scholars have presumably brought better scholarship to the problems confronted by a study of the Scriptures. For these reasons, new translations are needed. What Bible readers want today is a translation of God's Word that is faithfully accurate to the original languages, artistically beautiful, genuinely dignified, easily readable, and crystal clear.

# Conclusion

The use of the Bible by peasant, priest, landowner, and tradesman has not come easily throughout the ages. Priests and scholars attempted to take the role of "interpreters" under the false assumption that the layperson was incapable of understanding God's Word properly. The Scriptures became a tool for hierarchal authority to control the masses through doctrines of purgatory, excommunication, and physical torture. As a result, the Bible became a forbidden book.

It is my hope that *A Visual History of the English Bible* has enabled you to enter into that struggle, feel the tension, and smell the flames of persecution. We can see why it is so important that the Scriptures given by God himself are translated into modern languages. After all, the person in the pew is capable of determining the will of God, complying with his demands for spiritual integrity, and obeying his commands to go and spread the message to the world.

From the time of its delivery, the New Testament was readable by the literate and understood by the illiterate. In the fourth century, Jerome translated the Old Latin version into the modern Latin of the empire. It became the official—and the Roman Catholic Church's authorized—version. As a result, the language of the Bible was fixed and did not change. Yet the language of the people developed over the course of centuries. The natural corollary was that eventually the common person was not only unable to understand the Scriptures but was forbidden to read them.

Relief was soon to come. The Reformation brought the centrality of Scripture back into Christianity. With men like Wycliffe and Tyndale the world was soon to see what people totally dedicated to the will of God could accomplish. Twenty-first-century believers can sleep tonight, for they have his Word at their fingertips. Whatever translation you decide to use, be sure it is one you can read with understanding, memorize with ease, and obey with faith.

## Postscript

The Bible has overcome all challenges to become the world's bestseller. Destruction of ancient manuscripts by fire, floods, and deliberate textual attacks challenged its endurance. In the period of the Reformation, men and women were tortured and put to death for simply owning a portion of a Bible. Scriptures were deliberately burned. Critical thinking of the Enlightenment sought to destroy the credibility and authenticity of the Scriptures.

Modern interpretation principles challenged the message of the revealed Word of God. And yet, all attempts at preventing common people on the street from having the sacred text in their own language, in their own possession, have failed. God's Word has triumphed.

Future generations will continue to face challenges to the message from God to humankind, but if history means anything, those threats will come to nothing. The Bible is not a "forbidden book," but a book that forbids scholarly or priestly self-indulgent control. It is a window into the heart and mind of "that Great God and Savior, Jesus Christ." Amen and Amen!

# Acknowledgments

No book could be produced without the influence and efforts of many gifted men and women. This book is no exception. The journey to the production of this book began nearly thirty years ago when I stretched our budget to make my first Bible purchase. The rare book business is filled with many wonderful people who, while making a living from their craft, have gone out of their way to assist me in research, collecting, and allowing financial plans so that I could purchase works that seemed out of the reach of an ordinary seminary professor. The Bibles illustrated in this book are the fruits of these influences. Although it is impossible to include everyone along this journey, I am pleased to recognize:

### In Collecting

The late Dr. Ed Goodrick, who first stirred my interest in Bible collecting.

Dr. Al Baylis, who assisted me in producing my contribution to Bible collecting when we published an exact facsimile of the Wycliffe New Testament.

Allen Latty, who helped finance many volumes in the early days of collecting.

Charles Ryrie, who was a constant encouragement and who provided advice for the purchase of important works.

The late Les Walker, rare book dealer in Wales, who provided many important Bibles and books about the Bible and textual criticism.

The late Alan G. Thomas, rare Bible dealer extraordinaire, whose kindness enabled me to buy many very rare volumes on special terms.

Dr. David C. Lachman, for his help in providing some of my most important works.

F. J. "Rusty" Maisel, who has been a source of encouragement for more than a decade.

International Society of Bible Collectors, for encouraging Bible collecting and providing a venue to share "war stories."

Carol Brake, my beloved wife who has wholeheartedly embraced my "gentle madness."

My children: Donnie, Debbie, and Michael, who also sacrificed and thought it was "cool" for dad to collect archaic Bibles when he could have bought a new one for less money.

Last but not least, Dr. John Hellstern, whose creative eye gave a special touch to many of the photos. His tireless and creative work in displaying our collections in various venues over the years has always been an encouragement to us. And to his wife, Jean Hellstern, whose encouragement and sacrifice is equal to Carol's.

## In Book Preparation

Carol, for her continual encouragement and helpful suggestions during editing.

Sanford Communications, Inc., for their work on my behalf and for editing the manuscript in preparation for publication: David Sanford, Elizabeth Jones, Rebekah Clark, and Elizabeth Honeycutt. Also thanks to co-literary agent Tim Beals of Credo Communications.

Rusty Maisel, Bob Bahner, and Michael Brake for many of the photographs used in this book.

Steve Stogsdill for the artwork on the chart "From Ancient Manuscripts to Modern Translations" and Sharon Van Loozenoord for her design of the chart.

Marian O'Connor, Kristen Hepner Badriaki, and LaVonne Kampen for scanning photos and general office assistance.

Angela Sanchez for her photographing of some of the pictures.

Dr. Dan Lockwood, president, Multnomah Bible College and Seminary, for encouraging the writing of this book.

Baker Books, and especially Chad Allen, for their vision for a book of this nature.

Tim Beals for his editorial assistance with developmental and copyediting.

Paul Brinkerhoff, my project editor, and the Baker editorial and design teams.

# A Visual Glossary

**Act of Supremacy.** This royal act of 1534 rejected Roman papal authority and decreed Henry VIII Supreme Head of the Church of England.

**Aelfric** (955–1020; Eynsham, Oxfordshire, England; Benedictine monk). He translated parts of the Old Testament into Anglo-Saxon but primarily translated biblical concepts.

**Aidan** (636; Lindisfarne, British Isles; bishop). Celtic evangelist and missionary to England.

**Aland, Kurt and Barbara** (1915–94; Barbara's dates unknown; linguists). Kurt, editor Nestle-Aland Greek New Testament; both authored *The Text of the New Testament*.

**Albrecht of Brandenburg** (1490–1545; Brandenburg, Germany; archbishop). He appointed Tetzel to sell indulgences. Luther, incensed by the practice, rebelled and nailed the ninety-five theses to the Wittenberg church door.

**Aldhelm** (640–709; Sherborne, Dorset, England; poet and first bishop of Sherborne). He translated the first-known biblical text into Old English.

**Aldred** (tenth century; Northumberland, England; scribe). He introduced the practice of glossing in the translation of the Lindisfarne Gospels.

**Anglicans.** The official Church of England made possible by the Act of Succession. They were supporters of the Bishops' Bible against the Geneva Bible and later embraced the King James Version.

**Arbuthnot, Alexander** (d. 1585; Edinburgh, Scotland; printer). In 1575 he petitioned the General Assembly to permit him to print English Bibles. His request was granted and as Scotland's first publisher, he and Thomas Bassandyne printed the first Bible in Scotland in 1579.

**Arundel, Thomas** (1353–1414; Cambridge, England; archbishop of Canterbury). He was an avid opponent of Wycliffe, but attributed Wycliffe's translation to Wycliffe and authored restrictions to Bible translations in the *Constitutions* of 1407–08.

**Authorized Version.** The King James Version is known more popularly in the British Isles as the Authorized Version.

**Bale, John** (1495–1563; Ossory, England; bishop). The fall of his protector, Cromwell, sent Bale fleeing England. He became a translator of the Geneva Bible. He was able to return when King Edward VI came to the throne.

**Bancroft, Richard** (1544–1610; Cambridge, England; archbishop of Canterbury). Bancroft opposed the views of the Puritans, but supported the new version of 1611 for which he became a translator.

**Barker, Christopher** (1529–99; London, England; queen's printer). Barker printed the first Geneva Bible in England in 1575, fifteen years after it was translated. In 1578 it was printed in black letter—a feature rejected by the original translators.

**Barker, Robert** (d. 1645; London, England; king's printer). In 1600, Robert, son of Christopher, published his first Bible, a black letter Geneva Bible. He printed Bibles for many years and after his death the license was assigned to other printers.

**Bassandyne, Thomas** (d. 1577; Edinburgh, Scotland; publisher). As Scotland's first publisher, he and Alexander Arbuthnot printed the first Bible in Scotland in 1579.

**Bede, Venerable** (672–735; Yarrow, North England; priest and historian). He continued the work of Aldhelm and wrote *Ecclesiastical History*.

**Bengel, John A.** (1687–1752; Stuttgart and Tübingen, Germany; theologian and textual critic). While a student at Tübingen, Bengel became perplexed by the various readings in the Greek New Testament. He gathered all the editions and manuscripts known and in 1734 published a critical apparatus that became the starting point for modern textual criticism.

**Beza, Theodore** (1519–1605; Geneva, Switzerland; Reformed theologian). Beza assisted in the translation of the Geneva Bible and printed the Greek New Testament in 1565, which became the standard for the King James Version in 1611.

**black letter.** Gothic-style printing with thick square type.

**Blayney, Benjamin** (1728–1801; Oxford, England; Hebrew scholar). Employed by Clarendon Press to revise the King James Bible in 1768; completed it in 1769. His became the standard Oxford edition.

**Bodley, John** (sixteenth century; London, England; printer). Bodley was one of the exiles to Geneva who participated in the translation of the Geneva Bible. He was the father of Thomas and the exclusive printer of the Geneva Bible in 1562, a right granted by Queen Elizabeth I.

**Bodley, Thomas** (1545–1613; Oxford, England; layman). He was the founder of the Bodleian Library at Oxford University.

**Bois, John** (1561–1644; Suffolk, England; translator). Bois revised the King James Version in 1629 and again in 1638.

**Boleyn, Anne** (1507–36; London, England; roy-

alty). Anne was the wife of Henry VIII and mother of Elizabeth I. She was executed for high treason. She was a strong supporter of the Bible in English.

**Bonner, Edmund** (1500–69; London, England; bishop). Appointed bishop of London by Queen Mary, Bonner played a major role in the execution of Protestants.

**Broughton, Hugh** (1549–1612; Shropshire, England; rabbinical scholar). Broughton vigorously opposed the newly translated King James Version. His attacks were probably precipitated by the committee's snubbing him as a translator.

**Burgon, John W.** (1813–88; Chichester, England; textual critic). Burgon vigorously attacked the English Revised Version and the Greek New Testament of Westcott and Hort. His argument was theological, in that he believed God would not preserve his Word in an eclectic text in a few older, and perhaps corrupted, manuscripts, but in the text of the *Textus Receptus*, represented by the vast majority of surviving manuscripts.

**Caedmon** (ca. 680; Northumbria, England; poet/herdsman). He translated Anglo-Saxon poems and Bible texts.

**Calvin, John** (1509–64; Geneva, Switzerland; Reformed theologian). He wrote the introduction to and assisted in the translation of the Geneva Bible. One of the most influential theologians of the Reformation.

**Cardwell, Edward** (1787–1861; Oxford, England; scholar). A controversy began over the claim by Curtis of Islington that all modern translations departed from the 1611 edition. Cardwell, from Oxford printing interests, and Turton, from Cambridge, set to printing an exact reprint of the 1611 edition. It resulted in a general acceptance that it was impossible to return to the 1611 and that the 1769 was superior to the 1611.

**Caxton, William** (1422–91; London, England; printer). He was the first to bring printing to England and was responsible for printing several editions of the *Golden Legend*.

**Challoner, Richard** (1691–1781; Douay, France; bishop). He revised the Douay-Rhemes Roman Catholic version in 1749–50.

**Chaucer, Geoffrey** (1340–1400; Oxford, England; English poet). His writings—such as *The Canterbury Tales* and others—were of the same period as Wycliffe.

**Cochlaeus, John** (1479–1552; Cologne, Germany; scholar). He is believed to be the one who discovered Tyndale's work at Cologne and spread it to Tyndale's enemies.

**Colet, John**
(1466–1519; London/Oxford, England; scriptural preacher). He was well known for his lectures on the apostle Paul's epistles.

**collocate.** This is the process of comparing a manuscript or individual readings with a standard.

**Coverdale, Miles**
(1488–1569; Yorkshire, England; pastor). He was the primary translator of the Coverdale Bible and the Great Bible. He may have assisted in the Geneva Bible project as well. Elizabeth Macheson was Coverdale's wife.

**Cranmer, Thomas**
(1489–1556; Cambridge, England; archbishop of Canterbury). He penned the introduction to the 1540 Great Bible, which became known as Cranmer's Bible. He declared Henry's marriage to Boleyn void.

**Crespin, Jean** (sixteenth century; Geneva, Switzerland; printer). A quality printer known for printing Bibles in many languages, including a 1570 English Geneva Bible.

**Cromwell, Thomas**
(1485–1540; London, England; Vicar General). Cromwell was the most powerful

ecclesiastical figure appointed by Henry VIII. His support for the English Bible helped get it recognized.

**Darnley, Henry Stuart** (1545–67; London, England; royalty). Darnley was the husband of Mary Stuart and they were the parents of King James I.

**de Cisneros, Francisco Ximenes** (1436–1517; Castile, Spain; cardinal). He was the champion of reform in the Roman Catholic Church and was known mostly for his printing of the Complutensian Polyglot Bible, a massive multivolume Bible in several languages.

**de Voragine, Jacobus** (1230–98; Genoa, Italy; archbishop and writer). He was the author of the famous *Golden Legend.*

**de Worde, Wynken (Wynkyn)** (d. 1534; London, England; printer). He issued several editions of the *Golden Legend* in English, brought printing into the modern age, and was the first to use Latin letter in type.

**duodecimo (12mo).** See "folio."

**Edward VI** (1537–53; Hampton Court, London, England; king of England 1547–53). Under Protestant Edward VI no new English translations were made. He was the son of Henry VIII and Jane Seymour.

**Eliot, John** (1604–90; Massachusetts, USA; teacher and translator). He translated the first Bible in America in 1663 in the American Indian language of Algonquin.

**Elizabeth I** (1533–1603; Hampton Court, London, England; queen of England 1558–1603). She was the daughter of Henry VIII and Anne Boleyn, succeeded Mary, restored Protestantism to England, and is considered to be one of the greatest rulers in English history.

**Elstrack, Renold** (1590–1630; London, England; engraver). He was the engraver for the map for the first edition King James Version (1611).

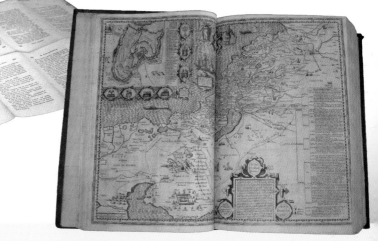

**Elzevir "brothers," Abraham and Bonaventure** (seventeenth century; Leyden, Holland; printers). Although often referred to as brothers, these cousins printed many seventeenth-century Greek New Testaments; the most famous was the 1633 edition that claimed to be the received text (*Textus Receptus*).

> **Erasmus, Desiderius** (1466–1536; Rotterdam, Netherlands; humanist). Compiled the first published Greek New Testament in 1516.

> **Eyre, George** (eighteenth and nineteenth century; London, England; printer). Although a minor player as a printer to the queen, Eyre and his partner William Spottiswoode printed several editions of the Bible.

**Fell, John** (1625–86; Oxford, England; bishop). In order to prevent theologians from tampering with the text, he published the first Greek New Testament in England in 1675.

**Fichet, Guillaume** (1433–80; Sorbonne, France; printer). He established the first printing press in France. He was known for giving credit to Gutenberg as the printer of the first Bible.

**first edition.** The first time a book or Bible is published it is called a "first edition."

**first issue.** The first edition of the King James Version was issued twice, once in 1611, known as the first edition, first issue. It was published again in 1613, which is called the first edition, second issue. Some scholars believe the 1613 edition should be called a second edition.

**folio (F°).** Before 1800, the number of folds the printer's sheet was divided into determined the size of Bibles. A large page folded once would be a folio. It would have two leaves printed on front and back making for four printed pages. When the sheet was folded twice, a quarto (4to), four pages front and back (eight pages); when folded to eight leaves (sixteen pages), octavo (8vo); when folded to twelve leaves (twenty-four pages), duodecimo (12mo); and when folded to sixteen leaves (thirty-two pages), a sextodecimo (16mo).

**formal equivalent.** The method of translating the Bible that seeks to render a word-for-word equivalence from one language to another in order to retain a literal meaning of the text.

> **Foxe, John** (1516–87; Lincolnshire, England; English martyrologist).

He wrote the important *Acts and Monuments*, the basis for much of our knowledge of the persecutions of Christians. He may have participated in the translation of the Geneva Bible.

**Fredrick the Wise** (1463–1525; Saxony, Germany; elector). He was the founder of the University of Wittenberg and appointed Luther and Melanchthon as professors.

**Froben, Johann** (1460–1527; Basel, Germany; printer). Froben was the first printer to print the Greek New Testament (Erasmus text 1516).

**Fry, Francis** (1803–86; Bristol, England; English bibliographer). Fry gathered as many editions of the Great Bible and the King James Version as were available and collated them.

**Fulke, William** (1538–89; London, England; Puritan divine). Fulke is most known for his anti-Catholic tirade against the Roman Catholic Rhemes New Testament, known as his counterblast against Gregory Martin, translator of the Rhemes New Testament.

**functional (dynamic) equivalent.** The method of translating that seeks to emphasize the transfer of meaning from one language to another with words having the same force of meaning in today's language that they had in an ancient culture.

**Fust, Johann** (ca. 1400–66; Mainz, Germany; printer and goldsmith).

He gained possession of Gutenberg's printing presses when Gutenberg defaulted on a loan from Fust.

**Geneva Bible translators** (1557–60; Geneva, Switzerland; translators). The major translators are William Williams, Anthony Gilby, Christopher Goodman, Thomas Wood, and Thomas Cole.

**Gilby, Anthony** (d. 1585; Lincolnshire, England; Puritan divine). One of the exiles in Geneva who participated in the translation of the Geneva Bible.

**glossing.**

Glossing is the work of translating by inserting the equivalent meaning above, below, or in the margin of the text. The end result is an interlinear translation.

**Gothic type.** These square-cut letters have added flourishes and are also known as black letter type.

**Grafton, Richard** (d. 1572; London, England; printer). Grafton was a merchant who became an avid supporter of the Reformation. He and Edward Whitchurch printed the Matthew's Bible and several editions of the Great Bible (1539–41).

**Griesbach, Johann Jakob** (1745–1812; Halle, Germany; textual critic). His valuable work led the way to abandoning the *Textus Receptus*, which had been the standard since 1516.

**Gutenberg, Johann** (1396–1468; Mainz, Germany; printer). He invented printing with moveable type and is credited with having printed the first Bible.

**Haydock, Thomas** (1772–1859; Manchester, England; studied for priesthood). He revised the notes of Challoner in 1811. Haydock's large folio family Bibles became very popular in Ireland, England, and America.

**Henry VII** (1457–1509; London, England; first Tudor king). Henry VII reigned from 1485 to 1509. He married Elizabeth of York and fathered eight children, one of whom was Henry VIII.

**Henry VIII** (1491–1547; Hampton Court, London, England; king of England 1509–1547). Henry separated England from the Roman Church to establish the Anglican Church as the official state church. His cruel treatment of those who opposed him is well documented.

**Hereford, Nicholas** (b. ca. 1345, d. ca. 1417/1420; Hereford, England; scholar and translator). He is credited with translating portions of the Wycliffe Bible.

**Holbein, Hans** (1497–1543; Augsburg, Germany; printer). He was one of the world's greatest painters of portraits. His greatest accomplishments were his detailed engraving of the title page of the Great Bible and many sixteenth-century portraits of important figures.

**Huss, John** (1369–1415; Bohemia; Reformer). Huss's views were similar to those of the more well-known Reformers Wycliffe and Luther. He is also important for his recognition of John Wycliffe as the translator of the Wycliffe Bible.

**illuminated manuscript.** A manuscript that is decorated with colored initials, pictures, or borders.

**incunabula (singular, incunabulum).** A Bible printed before 1501, in the "cradle of printing," is known as an incunabulum Bible.

**James I, of England and Scotland** (1566–1625; Hampton Court, London, England; king of Scotland 1567–1603, king of England 1603–1625). He was the son of Mary Stuart, queen of Scots, and Lord Darnley. He is most famous for granting permission to Puritans and Anglicans to translate the 1611 King James Version.

**Jerome (Hieronymus)** (340–420; Rome, Italy; Latin translator). He translated the Bible from Greek and Hebrew into Latin, which became the standard Roman Catholic Bible.

**Joye, George** (d. 1553; Strasburg, Germany; English scholar). Joye attempted to revise Tyndale's New Testament without his permission and drew his ire.

**Jugge, Richard** (1531–77; Cambridge, England; printer). Jugge published several of Tyndale's New Testaments beginning in 1552 (1553 and 1566).

**Junius, Franciscus** (1545–1602; France; Huguenot). In 1594 Junius inserted detailed notes into Revelation. In many editions they replaced Tomson's notes in the Geneva Bibles.

**Kethe, William** (d. 1608; Scotland; Reformer). He spent time with the exiles in Geneva, Switzerland, translating the Geneva Bible and returned to England in 1561.

**Knightly, Richard** (1533–1615; Northamptonshire, England; patron of Puritans). Sir Richard was knighted in 1566 by the Earl of Leicester and was present in his official capacity as Sheriff of Northampton at the execution of Mary Queen of Scots.

**Knighton, Henry** (d. ca. 1396; Leicester, England; writer). He is the earliest person to mention Wycliffe as translator of the Bible in his *Chronicon*.

**Knox, John** (1513–72; Haddington, Scotland; ordained priest). He preached the doctrines of the Reformation and worked to translate the Geneva Bible. He fled Scotland when Queen Mary ascended the throne (1553).

**Koberger, Anton** (1440–1513; Nuremberg, Germany; printer). He was the first to establish a printing press in Germany and was the printer of the famous *Nuremberg*

*Chronicles* and many incunabula Bibles.

**Lachmann, Caroli (Karl)** (1793–1851; Leipzig, Germany; textual critic). The founder of modern textual criticism. Lachmann published the first Greek New Testament to abandon the traditional *Textus Receptus.*

**Latin letter.** A printing type formed after the style of manuscripts in the Latin language.

**Lollards** (Poor Preachers) (fourteenth and fifteenth century; Oxford, England; preachers). They were well known for the spread of pre-Reformation theology, and they ultimately influenced Luther through the work of John Huss.

**Luther, Martin** (1483–1546; Wittenberg, Germany; Reformer). He translated the New Testament into the German language in 1522 and the whole Bible in 1534. Mother and father were Hans and Margarethe Luder.

**Martin, Gregory** (d. 1582; Maxfield, Sussex, England; translator). Gregory translated the Roman Catholic Douay-Rhemes Bible from the Latin Vulgate.

**Mary Stuart** (1542–87; Linlithgow Palace, Scotland; queen of Scotland 1561–67). She is the mother of James I, king of England and Scotland. She was executed by Queen Elizabeth I without much opposition from her son, King James IV of Scotland.

**Mary Tudor** (1516–58; Hampton Court, London, England; queen of England 1553–58). She was the daughter of Henry VIII and Catherine of Aragon. She reversed the Protestant emphasis in the kingdom

and made Roman Catholicism the favored Christianity. She is forever known as "Bloody Mary."

**Matthew, Thomas.** See Rogers, John.

**Melanchthon, Philipp** (1497–1560; Wittenberg, Germany; Reformation scholar). He was a highly qualified scholar who defended Luther's theology and was a central figure in the development of Reformation theology.

**Mill, John** (1645–1707; Oxford, England; textual critic). Two weeks before his death, Mill completed the Greek New Testament with full apparatus of Greek manuscripts, early versions, and the church fathers.

**miniature.** A small colored figure (person or scene) inserted in a manuscript, usually at the beginning of chapters or divisions.

**More, Thomas** (1478–1535; London, England; Lord Chancellor of England). More was Tyndale's archenemy; he especially resisted Tyndale's English translation.

**Munster, Sebastian** (1489–1552; Heidelberg, Germany; Hebraist). Munster was one of Germany's greatest Hebrew scholars who translated the first German edition of the Hebrew Scriptures into Latin. The Latin version became a major text for Coverdale in his translation work.

**Nicholson (Nycholson), James** (d. ca. 1420; Hereford, England; Lollard scholar). He was a Lollard writer and may have translated some of the Wycliffe Bible (1384).

**octavo (8vo).** See "folio."

**Old English letter.** This is another name for black letter or Gothic letter.

**optimal equivalent.** The term used to apply a mediating method of transferring meaning from one language to another by using principles applied to both the formal equivalent and functional equivalent methods.

**Packington, Augustine** (sixteenth century; London, England; businessman). He purchased Tyndale New Testaments as they entered England from Germany and sold them to men waiting to burn them. When it was reported to Tyndale he encouraged it so he could have the funds for later editions.

**Paris, F. S. (Thomas)** (eighteenth century; Cambridge, England; scholar). He made a serious attempt to revise the King James Version in 1762 by standardizing spelling and punctuation, and correcting printer's errors.

**Parker, Matthew** (1504–75; Cambridge, England; archbishop of Canterbury). He was the chaplain to Queen Anne Boleyn (1535) and the

primary translator of the Bishops' Bible of 1568.

**Poyntz, Thomas** (sixteenth century; Antwerp, Belgium; layman). Tyndale found safe haven while staying with Poyntz in Antwerp until Tyndale was betrayed by Henry Phillips, who pretended to be interested in his translation work. From there Tyndale was arrested and imprisoned.

**Puritans.** As a conservative branch of the Church of England, they sought scriptural justification for life and worship. They were very influential in the sixteenth century.

**Purvey, John** (1354–1428; Oxford, England; Lollard leader). He revised the Wycliffe Bible (1388).

**quarto (4to).** See "folio."

**Quentel, Peter** (sixteenth century; Cologne, Germany; printer). He was the first to print a portion of the Tyndale New Testament in 1525.

**Rainolds, John** (1549–1607; Oxford, England; translator and author). The Puritan Rainolds called for a new translation at Hampton Court in 1604. He worked with the Oxford group to translate the Old Testament. He died before it was published.

**Regnault, Fraunces** (sixteenth century; Paris, France; printer). He was the printer of the Great Bible and Coverdale's diglot third edition, November 1539.

**revision.** The work of translators seeking to reexamine a version in order to amend its texts is called a revision.

**Rogers, John** (1505–55; Birmingham, England; rector [clergyman] of Holy Trinity Church, translator). He was associated with the "outlaw" Tyndale, and so he used the pseudonym "Thomas Matthew" (probably after the biblical personalities) for translating the Matthew's Bible. Rogers was the first martyr under Bloody Mary.

**Rolle, Richard** (1295–1349; Hanpole, England; hermit and mystic). He translated the Latin Vulgate into the Anglo-Norman language. Wycliffe's only guidelines for translating were the glosses developed by Rolle. This may account for Wycliffe's wooden literal translation and the tendency to follow the Latin word order.

**rubrication.** To print or write the heading of a paragraph or chapter in a manuscript or printed book in red (has come to include blue).

**Sauer, Christopher** (1693–1784; Germantown, Pennsylvania; printer). Sauer established the first German printing press in America and published three German Bible editions: 1743, 1763, and 1776. Legend has it that the pages of the 1776 edition were used for gun wadding for militia muskets.

**Schoeffer, Peter** (1425–1502; Mainz, Germany; printer). He joined Fust (his father-in-law) in printing the *Mainz Psalter* from Gutenberg's press (1457).

**Scrivener, F. H. A.** (1813–91; London, England; biblical scholar). He produced the most accurate and critical edition of the King James Version, called the Paragraph Bible. His critical analysis of previous versions is still valuable today.

**sextodecimo (16mo).** See "folio."

**Seymour, Jane** (d. 1538; wife of Henry VIII). Jane bore Henry a son, Edward, in 1537 and died twelve days after giving birth.

**Spottiswoode, William** (eighteenth and nineteenth century; London, England; printer). Spottiswoode and Eyre were printers to Queen Victoria.

**Stephanus, Robert** (1503–59; Paris, France; printer). He was most known for his printing of Greek New Testaments between 1546 and 1551. His 1550 and 1551 editions, more than any other Greek New Testaments, influenced the English Bible.

**Taverner, Richard** (1505–75; Cambridge, England; translator and scholar). He is the author of the Taverner Bible of 1539, which is considered a very good translation but had little effect on later translations.

**Tetzel, Johann** (1465–1519; Leipzig, Germany; Dominican monk). He began preaching and selling indulgences in 1501. It was the practice to which Luther took exception.

**Tischendorf, Constantin** (1815–74; Leipzig, Germany; textual critic). He discovered *Codex Sinaiticus* in 1844 and published eight editions of the Greek New Testament. His most famous and important edition was the eighth edition (1865–72).

**Tomson, Laurence** (1539–1608; London, England; scholar). In 1576 Tomson revised the Geneva New Testament based a great deal on Beza's Latin edition. From this date editions are known as just "Geneva" or, with revision, "Geneva-Tomson."

**translation.** The work of a linguist to render the meaning of a word or text from one language into another without loss of the intended meaning of the original author.

**Trevisa, John** (1342–1402; Oxford, England; medieval scholar). He may have assisted in the Wycliffe Bible translation. He was one of the Lollards.

**Tunstall, Cuthbert** (1474–1559; Duresme [Durham], England; bishop of London). He opposed the work of Tyndale but later endorsed the 1541 edition of the Great Bible (slight revision of Tyndale's New Testament).

**Turton, Thomas** (1753–1800; Cambridge, England; physician). He represented Cambridge in the controversy over the superiority of the 1769 Blayney edition of the King James Version to the 1611 edition. Along with Cardwell, he produced an exact copy of the 1611 in 1633. It revealed to all the impossibility of going back to the 1611. See also Cardwell, Edward.

**Tyndale, William (Guillaume Hytchins)** (1494–1536; Glouchestershire, England; scholar and translator). He translated the first New Testament from the Greek language into English. He was betrayed by a trusted friend and sent to the flames of martyrdom.

**Ulfilas** (311–381; Asia Minor; apostle to the Goths). He translated the Bible into Gothic (pre-Old English version).

**Ussher, James** (1581–1656; Dublin, Ireland; archbishop of Armagh). He wrote the *Annals of the Old and New Testament*, the basis for the chronology of the King James Version beginning in 1701.

**Van Meteren, Jacobus** (sixteenth century; Antwerp, Belgium; printer). He printed the first complete Bible in the English language in 1535, the Coverdale Bible. From this time on, all surviving Coverdale Bibles were printed in England.

**version.** The resulting work of a translation from one language to another is considered a version.

**Walsh, John** (sixteenth century; Little Sodbury, England; homeowner). While tutoring the Walsh family children, Tyndale spent time at their manor, where he may have begun translating the New Testament.

**Walton, Brian** (1600–61; Chester, England; bishop). Walton was the editor of the important six-volume London Polyglot Bible (1655–57) that included nine languages.

**Ward, Samuel** (d. 1645; Cambridge, England; scholar). Ward was responsible for the 1629 revised edition of

the King James Version and, with John Bois, revised it again in 1638.

**Westcott, Brooke Foss, and Hort, Fenton John Anthony** (1825–1901, 1828–92; Birmingham and Cambridge, England; textual critics). Their greatest work was *The New Testament in the Original Greek*. It is the standard approach for modern Greek textual critics, although their methods are not followed precisely today.

**Wettstein, Jacob** (1693–1754; Basel, Switzerland; textual critic). His two volumes of sound textual critical principles were somewhat overlooked because of his theory that many Greek manuscripts were contaminated by Latin versions (1751–52).

**Whitchurch, Edward** (d. 1581; London, England; Protestant publisher). His initials EW appear below the prophet's page "*Esaye*" along with RG (Richard Grafton) in the Matthew's Bible that he and Grafton published. The initials of William Tyndale (WT), King Henry (HR for Henricus Rex), and John Rogers (JR) appear as large flourished letters. *See* Grafton, Richard.

**Whittingham, William** (1524–79; Chester, England; dean of Durham). He was the primary translator of the Geneva New Testament (1557) and the Geneva Bible (1560).

**woodcut.** An ink print from a design

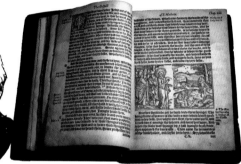

cut in wood, usually a scene or portrait.

**Wycliffe, John** (1320–84; Yorkshire, England; scholar and translator). He is responsible for the translation of the first English Bible. He is often referred to as "The Morningstar of the Reformation."

**Zell, Ulrich** (fifteenth century; Cologne, Germany; writer). In his work in the *Cologne Chronicle* (1499) he called attention to Gutenberg and Fust as the first to print the Bible.

# Notes

## Chapter 1 Ancient Bibles

1. Yigael Yadin, *The Message of the Scrolls* (New York: Simon and Schuster, 1957), 15–26. Yadin tells the story from his father's private journal found after his death.

2. Pliny, *Natural History*, bk. 33, par. 20–24.

3. Bruce M. Metzger, *Manuscripts of the Greek Bible: An Introduction to Greek Palaeography* (New York: Oxford University Press, 1981), 26.

4. Ibid., 45.

5. H. F. D. Sparks, "Jerome as Biblical Scholar," in *The Cambridge History of the Bible*, vol. 1, *From the Beginnings to Jerome*, ed. P. R. Ackroyd and C. F. Evans (Cambridge: Cambridge University Press, 1970), 519. The term *vulgate* means "common." It refers to a translation as a version using the common language of the day. Jerome's Bible translation is called the Latin Vulgate even though the term *vulgate* did not come into use until the thirteenth century.

6. Robert G. Calkins, *Illuminated Books of the Middle Ages* (Ithaca, NY: Cornell University Press, 1983), 63. This colophon in modern English dates from the mid-tenth century and was written by Aldred. This manuscript is from the British Library (MS Cotton Nero D. IV).

7. Geoffrey Shepherd, "English Versions of the Scripture before Wyclif," in *The Cambridge History of the Bible*, vol. 2 *The West from the Fathers to the Reformation*, ed. G. W. H. Lampe, (Cambridge: Cambridge University Press, 1969), 364.

8. Ibid., 364–65.

9. Ibid., 367.

10. Robert McCrum, William Cran, and Robert MacNeil, *The Story of English* (New York: Elisabeth Sifton Books, 1986), 102.

11. Wikipedia contributors, "Number of words in English," *Wikipedia, The Free Encyclopedia*, http://en.wikipedia.org/wiki/Number_of_Words_in_English (accessed September 10, 2006).

12. McCrum, Cran, and MacNeil, *Story of English*, 56–60.

13. Joseph Bosworth, *The Gothic and Anglo-Saxon Gospels* (London: John Russell Smith, Soho Square, 1865), ii–iii.

14. Modern translation provided by Paul Cavill, *A Treasury of Anglo-Saxon England* (Grand Rapids: Zondervan, 2001), 71. Original language quoted in Bruce Mitchell and Fred Robinson, *A Guide to Old English*, 5th ed. (Oxford: Blackwell, 1992), 222.

15. Shepherd, "English Versions," 375.

16. David Daniell, *The Bible in English: Its History and Influence* (New Haven: Yale University Press, 2003), 23.

17. McCrum, Cran, and MacNeil, *Story of English*, 69.

18. Norman L. Geisler and William E. Nix, *A General Introduction to the Bible* (Chicago: Moody, 1986), 545.

19. Shepherd, "English Versions," 375.

20. Ibid., 378.

21. McCrum, Cran, and MacNeil, *Story of English*, 78. Although the French language greatly influenced English, English as a widely spoken vernacular remained resilient. The Hundred Years' War between England and France (1337–1453) was a major reason for the English to speak their own language rather than French.

22. David C. Fowler, *The Bible in Middle English Literature* (Seattle: University of Washington Press, 1984), 59. The first Christmas song appeared about 1350. "Hand by hand we shall us take, And joy and bliss shall we make, For the devil of hell man hath forsaken, And God's Son is made our mate."

23. Ibid., 3–52. Fowler discusses in great detail the development of drama during the Middle Ages.

24. Daniell, *Bible in English*, 41.

## Chapter 2 He Dared to Act

1. While the story is fictitious, there is evidence that Wycliffe was discouraged near the end of his life. His body showed the effects of strokes and his movement was being threatened; nevertheless he optimistically looked to the future. Recent scholarship suggests Purvey had no connection with Wycliffe until his last days.

2. Alfred W. Pollard, *Records of the English Bible* (Oxford: Oxford University Press, 1911), 80–81. The text of the first article of the *Constitutions* reads: "The Holy Scripture not to be translated into the vulgar tongue, nor a translation to be expounded, until it shall have been examined, under pain of excommunication and the stigma of heresy. Moreover, it is a perilous thing . . . to translate the text of Holy Scripture from one idiom into another, inasmuch as in the translations themselves it is no easy matter to keep the same meaning in all cases, like as the Blessed Jerome, albeit inspired, confesses that he often went astray in this respect. We therefore enact and ordain that no one henceforth on his own authority translate any text of Holy Scripture into the English language . . . by way of book, pamphlet, or tract . . . either already recently composed in the time of the said John Wyclif or since then. Or that may in future be composed, in part or in whole, publicly or privily, under pain of the greater excommunication, until

the translation itself shall have been approved by the diocesan. . . ."

3. John Wyclif, *Speculum Secularium Dominorum, Opera Minora*, trans. and ed. John Loserth (London: Wyclif Society, 1913), 74.

4. Bodleian Library, *Wyclif and His Followers* (Oxford: Bodleian Library, 1983), 9.

5. Modern scholarship acknowledges that John Wycliffe did not translate the entire Bible that bears his name. More than likely several were involved in the work. It is not, as one might conclude from many works on the Wycliffite Bible, that it was a work of a host of translators as in later translations. It is better understood that other Lollards assisted in the Old Testament translation with Wycliffe doing some if not most of the New Testament. Direct evidence for a Wycliffe translation does not exist. In the twenty years following Wycliffe's death, many, if not most, of his English works were destroyed. Only his works taken to Bohemia by his Hussite followers survived. Modern scholarship tends to understand the lack of evidence as a support for his role in much of the translation and Lollard influence as minor.

6. "Lollardy," *Dictionary of the Christian Church*, ed. F. L. Cross (London: Oxford University Press, 1929), 19. Lollards, or "Poor Preachers" as they were known, were responsible for the spread of Wycliffe's teachings. Their teaching and influence in the fifteenth century extended beyond the spread of the Bible. They emphasized the authority of Scripture and the need for a personal relationship with Christ, and they attacked the church on such issues as celibacy, transubstantiation, indulgences, and others.

7. John Lewis, *The History of the Life and Sufferings of . . . John Wycliffe* (London: Robert Knaplock, St. Paul's Churchyard, 1723), 36.

8. Christopher de Hamel, *The Book: A History of the Bible* (London: Phaidon, 2001), 170. De Hamel's statement regarding Wycliffe's participation in the translation is a voice of sound reason: "There is quite good evidence that he was credited with the translation in the late Middle Ages, but we must balance two historical trends. One is the medieval passion for dogmatically linking texts with the names of famous authors. The other is the modern mania for downgrading the personal achievements of popular heroes of the past."

9. David Fowler, in his book *The Life and Times of John Trevisa, Medieval Scholar* (Seattle: University of Washington Press, 1995), argues for John Trevisa as one of the translators of the early versions of the Wycliffite Bible. Fowler cites the first mention of Trevisa as a translator by William Caxton who noted that Trevisa, at the request of Thomas Lord Barkley, translated the Bible. Other evidences are deduced from the timetable of Trevisa's work unaccounted for in the 1370s. Seeking to answer the objection that Trevisa was not a follower of Wycliffe, Fowler attempts to show that Trevisa, although not a Wycliffite, did embrace many of his reformed ideas (pp. 213–34). Fowler could have added to his evidence "To the Reader" in the 1611 King James Version where the writers attribute a translation of the Bible to Trevisa: "John Trevisa translated them [Scriptures] into English and many English Bibles in written hand are yet to be seen with diverse, translated as it is very probable, in that age" (p. 5). Although not altogether convincing, Fowler's argument does make the case for others involved in the translation of the Wycliffe Bible, and possibly even Trevisa did some of it.

10. De Hamel, *Book*, 170–73. Christopher de Hamel has inserted photographs of the Wycliffe pages with these peculiarities.

11. Daniell, *Bible in English*, 83.

12. De Hamel, *Book*, 173. De Hamel suggests that the colophon naming Nicholas as the translator is an actual autograph and not a later addition by a scribe.

13. Fowler, *Life and Times of John Trevisa*, 213–34. Fowler goes to great lengths to demonstrate that John Trevisa was involved in the translation of the Old Testament but does not conclude he did the New Testament.

14. De Hamel, *Book*, 172.

15. Daniell, *Bible in English*, 73. Daniell denies Wycliffe's direct involvement when he writes, "It seems unlikely that Wycliffe himself, pen in hand, translated any of his Bible. But that the manuscripts were the work of men close to him, influenced by him, inspired by his teaching and preaching, there can be no doubt."

16. Jose Rawson Lumby, ed., *Chronicon Henri Knighton monachi Leycestrensis*, vol. 1 (London: Master of Rolls, 1889), quoted in Margaret Deanesly, *The Lollard Bible* (Cambridge: Cambridge University Press, 1920), 239.

17. Michael Wilks, *Wyclif: Political Ideas and Practice* (Oxford: Oxbow Books, 2000), 154.

18. Archbishop Arundel quoted in Henry Hargreaves, "The Wycliffite Versions," in *The Cambridge History of the Bible:* vol. 2, *The West from the Fathers to the Reformation*, ed. G. W. H. Lampe (Cambridge: Cambridge University Press, 1969), 388.

19. Ibid.

20. Conrad Lindberg, ed., "Ms. Bodley 959 Genesis-Baruch 3:20," in *The Earlier Version of the Wycliffite Bible*, vol. 5 (Stockholm: Almqvist and Wiksell, 1969), 92.

21. Josiah Forshall and Frederic Madden, eds., *The Holy Bible, Containing the Old and New Testaments, with Apocryphal Books, in the Earliest English Versions Made from the Latin Vulgate by John Wycliffe and His Followers*, vol. 1 (Oxford: Oxford University Press, 1850), xvi.

22. To reduce confusion the earlier version identified by Forshall and Madden will be referred to as "Wycliffe's Version" and the later edition "Purvey's Revision."

23. F. F. Bruce, "John Wycliffe and the English Bible," *Churchman* 98, no. 4 (1984): 300. Bruce mentions Robert Gosecteste (thirteenth century) as an exception and notes that Greek was taught in Oxford in 1320–21.

24. Deanesly, *Lollard Bible*, 145.

25. Ibid., 234.

26. Hargreaves, "Wycliffite Versions," 410.

27. Anne Hudson, *Lollards and Their Books* (London: Hambledon Press, 1985), 43–84. Hudson, a well-acknowledged Wycliffe and Lollard scholar, has argued that Purvey was not the most important leader of the Lollards after Wycliffe's death. Her lengthy discussion in which she argues against the conclusions of most of the accepted Wycliffe studies reduces Purvey to a minor role in the Lollard movement and certainly not a candidate for the translation of the revised edition of the Bible. One gets the feeling from her detailed polemic that she is seeking evidence to deny Purvey any significant place in history. While the study certainly raises new questions and challenges past conclusions, it is not the last word on Lollard studies. Nevertheless, her research must be consulted if any sense of this very important

period can be made. A lot of room exists for further study on the authorship of the Wycliffite Bible.

28. De Hamel, *Book*, 173.

29. Wilks, *Wyclif*, 90.

30. John Foxe, *Acts and Monuments*, vol. 5 (London: Seeley, Burnside, and Seeley, 1848), 117. Foxe attributes a quote to Tyndale in the company of a learned man: "I defy the Pope and all his laws; if God spare my life, ere many years I will cause a boy that driveth the plough shall know more of the Scripture than thou dost."

31. Forshall and Madden, *Earliest English Versions*, vol. 1, xx.

32. Thomas M. C. Lawler, Germain Marc'hadour, Richard C. Marius, eds., *Complete Works of St. Thomas More, Dialogues*, vol. 6 (New Haven: Yale University Press, 1984), 314.

33. J. Usserii, *Auctarium Historiae Dogmaticae*, 424, quoted in Forshall and Madden, *Earliest English Versions*, vol. 1, xxi.

34. Forshall and Madden, *Earliest English Versions*, vol. 1, xxi.

35. John Lewis, *A Complete History of the Several Translations of the Holy Bible* (London: H. Woodfall, 1739), 17.

36. The prologue is fully printed in modern English in Forshall and Madden, *Earliest English Versions*, vol. 1, 1–60.

37. Deanesly, *Lollard Bible*, 377.

38. De Hamel, *Book*, 176.

39. Deanesly, *Lollard Bible*, 266. Deanesly argues forcibly in her appendix 1 for Purvey as the author of the prologue. See pp. 2, 376–81.

40. Forshall and Madden, *Earliest English Versions*, vol. 1, xxv. Hudson, *Lollards and Their Books*, 104. Hudson dismisses the handwriting as Purvey's by following S. L. Fristedt who considered it irrelevant.

41. It is not possible here to develop the argument in detail. See Forshall and Madden, *Earliest English Versions*, vol. 1, lix–lxi.

42. Deanesly, *Lollard Bible*, 379. Deanesly argues effectively for Purvey's authorship of the prologue stating many more evidences (see pp. 376–82 for detailed evidence).

43. Ibid., 18. Translations in the vernacular were not generally prohibited in Europe. However, translations used to popularize the reading of the Bible among the people were prohibited immediately.

44. Foxe, *Acts and Monuments*, vol. 3 (1844), 245. John Foxe (1516–87) is a major source for the history of the church for the periods from John Huss (priest and martyr) and John Wycliffe (thirteenth century) to 1559 (early beginning of Queen Elizabeth's reign). His life was greatly affected by Catholic Queen "Bloody" Mary's brutal reign of terror (1553–58). His *Acts and Monuments* was published in 1563 at the request of Lady Jane Grey. It was immediately attacked for its inaccuracy by the Roman Catholic Church. In 1570 he issued a corrected edition, which is a bit more conservative. While he had access to documents of the period about which he writes, he may have been easily persuaded by the stories he heard about the evil deeds of the Roman Catholic Church. He has been accused of deliberately falsifying records. However, he often appeals to living witnesses who reported the stories so the reader can verify his information. It is a tremendously important work, but caution must be used as some of the accounts simply cannot be verified.

45. It should not be concluded that the issues addressed in this chapter are easily resolved. The issue of authorship, how the manuscripts were constructed, translated, and copied is a very complicated process, and the final answers may await further research. The full discussions and argumentation of the issues cannot be completed in this brief study.

## Chapter 3 The Man of the Millennium

1. Bodleian Library, *Wyclif and His Followers*, 392.

2. Ibid., 171.

3. R. L. P. Milburn, "The 'People's Bible': Artists and Commentators," in *The Cambridge History of the Bible*: vol. 2, *The West from the Fathers to the Reformation* ed. G. W. H. Lampe, (Cambridge: Cambridge University Press, 1969), 292–93.

4. G. S. Wegener, *6000 Years of the Bible* (London: Hodder and Stoughton, 1958), 192.

5. Ibid., 193.

6. Don Cleveland Norman, *The 500th Anniversary Pictorial Census of the Gutenberg Bible* (Chicago: Coverdale Press, 1961), 10. A missal is the Roman Catholic handbook with all the readings and songs to celebrate the mass for an entire year.

7. Ibid., 11.

8. Ibid., 14.

9. Paul W. Schmidtchen, "Mostly about Books," *Hobbies: The Magazine for Collectors* (April 1962).

10. Ruth Pritchard, "Roll Over Gutenberg," *Alaska Airlines Magazine* (February 1987), 32–33. Dr. Pritchard goes into great detail in describing the scientific experiment by Tom Cahill and Dick Schwab included in the following account.

11. A rubricator was an artist who colored—normally in red—the initial words of a printed manuscript.

12. Robert Dearden Jr., *The Guiding Light on the Great Highway* (Philadelphia: John Winston, 1929), 51.

13. Alfred W. Pollard, *Last Words on the History of the Title-Page* (New York: Burt Franklin, 1981), 8.

14. Harry Thomas Frank, Charles William Swain, and Courtlandt Canby, *The Bible through the Ages* (Cleveland: World Publishing, 1967), 59.

15. Ibid., 62.

16. Ibid., 172.

17. David Sandler Berkowitz, *In Remembrance of Creation* (Waltham, MA: Brandeis University Press, 1968), 115.

## Chapter 4 He Dared to Take a Stand

1. Graham Tomlin, *Luther and His World* (Downers Grove, IL: InterVarsity, 2002), 21–22.

2. Martin Luther was haunted all of his life by his father's unwillingness to accept Luther's choice of occupation. His father had put the question in his head that maybe this was Satan's will, not God's.

3. By the time Luther arrived at Erfurt, scholars were questioning the scholasticism of Thomas Aquinas and Duns Scotus and had accepted the basic nominalism as taught by William of Ockham. The basic distinction between the two involved a complex philosophical system of the existence of universal concepts. Luther soon began embracing humanism that emphasized the classics and Scriptures in their original languages.

4. The Latin word *iustitia dei* can mean either "justice" or "righteousness" of God.

5. Tomlin, *Luther and His World*, 66. The powerful banking Augsburg family, Fuggers, advanced Albrecht some twenty-nine thousand gulden to Rome. The payback came from the sale of indulgences.

6. It was common practice to have disputations at the church hall over various controversies on All Saints' Day (November 1). The posting of the ninety-five theses on the day before All Saints' Day was normal practice. Of course, Luther would not post the theses himself but more likely sent one of his students from the university to do it.

7. Tomlin, *Luther and His World*, 73.

8. Martin Luther, quoted in Tomlin, *Luther and His World*, 109. Often included in this famous statement are the words, "Here I stand, God help me." These words are not recorded in the documents, but first surfaced a year later and have become a part of folklore.

## Chapter 5 The Fire of Devotion

1. William Tyndale, *The Obedience of a Christian Man* (repr., London: Religious Tract Society, 1999), 265. In his "The Four Senses of the Scriptures," Tyndale defends literal interpretation: "Thou shalt understand, therefore, that the scripture hath but one sense, which is the literal sense." He also felt strongly that Scripture knowledge alone was like babble if it did not have a use in life. He says, "It is not enough therefore to read and talk of it only, but we must also desire God day and night instantly to open our eyes and to make us understand and feel wherefore the scripture was given, that we may apply the medicine of the scripture, every man to his own sores, unless that we intend to be idle disputers, and brawlers about vain words, ever gnawing upon the bitter bark without and never attaining unto the sweet pith within, and persecuting one another for defending of lewd imaginations and fantasies of our own invention." David Daniell, ed., *Tyndale's Old Testament* (New Haven: Yale University Press, 1989), 7.

2. Foxe, *Acts and Monuments*, vol. 5, 117.

3. William Tyndale was also known by his Latin name, Guillaume Hytchins. In fact, his 1534 edition of the New Testament is known as the GH edition.

4. William Tyndale, "Practice of Prelates," in *Expositions and Notes on Sundry Portions of the Holy Scriptures together with the Practice of Prelates*, ed. H. Walker (1849; repr., Cambridge: Cambridge University Press, 1968), 291.

5. David Daniell, *William Tyndale* (New Haven: Yale University Press, 1994), 34. Daniell reminds us that Colet did not know Greek.

6. Tyndale approached Cuthbert Tunstall, bishop to London, to authorize his translation of the New Testament. Tunstall refused to grant permission because of his fear of the winds of reformation and his fear of being associated with Lutheranism. However, he did not persecute Tyndale. Cardinal Wolsey, a corrupt and deceitful priest, persecuted reformers with great pleasure.

7. J. F. Mozley, *Coverdale and His Bibles* (1953; repr., Cambridge: Lutterworth Press, 2005). Existing records indicate that Tyndale was in Hamburg in May 1524 and in April 1525. Did he remain in Hamburg for the entire time and translate the New Testament? Was it printed in Hamburg during his stay? Or, did he go to Wittenberg, as many scholars believe? Demus notes that there were no known printers in Hamburg even though it was a successful commercial town. It was only after Tyndale's death that printing was established in Hamburg. Mozley lists detailed arguments for Tyndale's Wittenberg visit.

8. Foxe, *Acts and Monuments*, vol. 5, 119.

9. Luther scholar Andras Mikesy has done extensive comparisons of Tyndale's New Testament and Luther's New Testament and concluded that Tyndale's New Testament was definitely independent. Unpublished study, 2006.

10. F. F. Bruce, *The English Bible* (Oxford: Oxford University Press, 1970), 31.

11. Daniell, *Bible in English*, 145. Daniell doubts the authenticity of the often-repeated story. His argument centers on his skepticism that Tyndale would never have sanctioned the burning of Scripture. Rather, he suggests, the transaction was with the pirate printer of Tyndale's New Testaments, Christopher Van Endhoven. One really cannot know either way for sure.

12. Ibid., 133.

13. David Daniell, ed., *Tyndale's New Testament* (New Haven: Yale University Press, 1989), 16. The figure "not to play boo peep" is Tyndale's way of saying Joye's practice was claiming Tyndale's work as his own. He used other rather crude figures to say the same thing.

14. This is the revision known as the "GH edition," most probably referring to Tyndale's earlier name Guillaume Hytchins.

15. Foxe, *Acts and Monuments*, vol. 5, 121–22.

16. Daniell, *Bible in English*, 150. Daniell describes a visit by Thomas Cromwell's emissary, Stephen Vaughan, offering Tyndale safe conduct in 1531. The skeptical Tyndale—fearing a trap—refused.

17. Bruce, *English Bible*, 52.

18. Before 1800, the number of folds the printer's sheet could be divided into measured the size of Bibles. A large page folded once would be a folio. It would have two leaves printed on front and back making for four printed pages. When the sheet was folded twice, a quarto (4to), four pages front and back (eight pages); when folded to eight leaves (sixteen pages), octavo (8vo); when folded to twelve leaves (twenty-four pages), duodecimo (12mo); and when folded to sixteen leaves (thirty-two pages), a sextodecimo (16mo).

19. Foxe, *Acts and Monuments*, vol. 5, 129.

### Chapter 6 A Political Pastor Struggles in Exile

1. Miles Coverdale, *Dedications and Prologues to the Translation of the Bible* (1535; repr., Cambridge: Cambridge University Press, 1846), 19.

2. John Hooker of Exeter, quoted in Mozley, *Coverdale and His Bibles*, 16.

3. Coverdale's attention to literary style produced a Psalter that became the standard into the seventeenth century. While his translations gave way to improved editions, the Psalter endured.

4. W. J. Heaton, *The Bible of the Reformation* (London: Francis Griffiths, 1910), 166.

5. Coverdale, *Dedications and Prologues*, title page.

6. See Mozley, *Coverdale and His Bibles*, 78–109, for a more detailed discussion of Coverdale's text.

7. Foxe, *Acts and Monuments*, vol. 5, 566–67.

8. Mozley, *Coverdale and His Bibles*, 122.

9. Coverdale even had a part in the translation of the Geneva Bible.

### Chapter 7 A Royal Court Intrigue

1. Mozley, *Coverdale and His Bibles*, 157.

2. Rogers's translation was primarily from Tyndale and Coverdale, although it claims originality and unquestionably made specific improvements in many Old Testament passages. It is still

considered one of the finest translations of the period. His notes were borrowed from the French works of Lafevre and Olivetan and, perhaps, a few from Luther. His contribution was more for his inclusion of notes in the Bible. See Daniell, *Bible in English*, 197.

3. Pollard, *Records of the English Bible*, 215.

4. Foxe, *Acts and Monuments*, vol. 6, 611.

5. The Great Bible got its name from the enormity of its size: 16½ × 11 inches.

6. Bruce, *English Bible*, 69.

7. Pollard, *Records of the English Bible*, 234.

8. Mozley, *Coverdale and His Bibles*, 206.

9. Sebastian Munster (1489–1552), a German scholar, produced the Hebrew Bible and published it with the Latin text and notes in 1534.

10. Erasmus's Latin text varies only slightly from the Vulgate.

11. Pollard, *Records of the English Bible*, 261–62. The third and fourth of the Injunctions issued by Cromwell as vicar-general were, "Item, that ye shall provide on this side of the feast . . . next coming, one book of the whole Bible of the largest volume in English, and the same set up in some convenient place within the said church that you have cure of whereas your parishioners may most commodiously resort to the same, and read it." This was printed under the date of 1536, but as Pollard says, it was probably two years later.

12. Foxe, *Acts and Monuments*, vol. 5, 451.

## Chapter 8 Theology Influences Bible Versions

1. This was the only English Bible printed during the reign of Queen Mary (1553–58). Mary actually translated the Gospel of John in Erasmus's paraphrases when she was Princess Mary in 1548.

2. Actually a 1528 Latin Bible, translated by Sanctes Pagninus, first included verse divisions, but it was an entirely different system and it did not influence any later Bibles.

3. A. S. Herbert, *Historical Catalogue of Printed Editions of the English Bible 1525–1961* (London: British and Foreign Bible Society; New York: American Bible Society, 1968), 61.

4. I have chosen to use the original sixteenth-century language spellings.

5. Charles C. Butterworth, *The Literary Lineage of the King James Bible, 1340–1611* (Phila-

delphia: University of Pennsylvania Press, 1941), 163.

6. It is nearly impossible to trace many of Shakespeare's sources for his quotations since the sixteenth-century Bibles were often very similar in translation. While some quotations and illusions can be traced to the Bishops' Bible, clearly the most quotes identifiable are from the Geneva Bible. Naseeb Shaheen, *Biblical References in Shakespeare's Plays* (Newark: University of Delaware Press, 1999), 38–39.

7. It is a mistake to call the Geneva Bible just the Bible of the Puritans. The Puritans may have preferred the Geneva, but so did many Anglicans. It was a favorite until the Anglican Bible was printed in 1611.

8. Lancelot Andrewes, *Sermons* (London: George Miller for Richard Badger, 1629), 238. Andrewes was a translator of the King James Version. In his sermon on February 26, 1623, before King James himself, he quotes directly from the Geneva Bible.

9. *The Geneva Bible*, introduction by Lloyd E. Berry (Madison, WI: University of Wisconsin Press, 1969), 10–11.

10. Pollard, *Records of the English Bible*, 285.

11. Herbert, *Historical Catalogue of Printed Editions*, 81–82. As Herbert notes, the first Geneva Bible printed in England was a small octavo in 1575. Barker printed a folio from the newly purchased license in 1576.

12. David Ewert, *From Ancient Tablets to Modern Translations* (Grand Rapids: Zondervan, 1983), 195.

13. Lewis Lupton, *A History of the Geneva Bible* vol. 5 (London: The Olive Tree, 1973), 110.

14. Various passages reveal the negative Geneva attitude toward royal authority. The note at Romans 13:5 reads, "For no private man can condemn what God hath appointed without the breach of his conscience and here he speaketh of evil magistrates so that Antichrist and his can not wrest this place to establish their tyranny over the conscience."

15. John Eadie, *The English Bible*, vol. 2 (London: Macmillan, 1876), 28.

16. Charles C. Ryrie, "The Notes of the Geneva Bible, 1560," in *Fine Books and Book Collecting*, ed. Christopher de Hamel and Richard A.

Linenthal (Leamington Spa, Warwickshire: James Hall, 1981), 56.

17. J. R. Dore, *Old Bibles: An Account of the Early Versions of the English Bible* (London: Eyre and Spottiswoode, 1888), 203.

18. Herbert, *Historical Catalogue of Printed Editions*, 89.

19. Ibid., 116.

20. Italics functioned as a way to mark out words needed for making the meaning clear, but without interrupting the flow of the text.

21. Lord Regent, quoted in William T. Dobson, *History of the Bassandyne Bible* (Edinburgh: William Blackwood and Sons, 1877), 96.

22. Theodore Fry, *A Brief Memoir of Francis Fry of Bristol* (London, 1887), 19–20.

23. Recently, a complete copy was discovered in Germany including the title leaf.

24. Fry, *Brief Memoir of Francis Fry of Bristol*, 70–71. Theodore Fry counts 1,300 Bibles and New Testaments in Francis's collection. These include 28 editions of Tyndale, 16 editions of the Great Bible, 75 editions of the Geneva Bible, and innumerable King James Versions.

25. Dobson, *Bassandyne*, 113.

26. Ibid., 121.

## Chapter 9 The Clergy's Version

1. Eadie, *English Bible*, vol. 2, 61–62.

2. Pollard, *Records of the English Bible*, 290. It is suggested that Bishop Cox first proposed a new translation.

3. David Price and Charles C. Ryrie, *Let It Go Among Our People* (Cambridge: Lutterworth Press, 2004), 102.

4. Bruce, *English Bible*, 94.

5. The term "Johann Comma" refers to a portion of 1 John 5:7 and 5:8 that are not in the oldest Greek manuscripts. It is also known as the "three witness" reading.

6. Herbert, *Historical Catalog of Printed Editions*, 56.

7. Dore, *Old Bibles*, 282.

8. Herbert, *Historical Catalogue of Printed Editions*, 247.

## Chapter 10 The Catholic Church Responds

1. H. W. Robinson, ed., *The Bible in Its Ancient and English Versions* (Oxford: Clarendon Press, 1940), 193.

2. Gregory Martin, "A Discovery of the Manifold Corruptions of the Holy Scriptures by the Heretics of our Days" (Rhemes, 1582), reprinted in William Fulke, *A Defence of the Sincere and True Translations of the Holy Scriptures into the English Tongue* (1583; reprint, Cambridge: Cambridge University Press, 1843), 2.

3. Fulke, *Defence of the Sincere and True Translations*, 2.

4. Ibid., 588.

5. Pollard, *Records of the English Bible*, 37. Pollard writes, "Fulke's folio . . . was regarded for over forty years as a standard work on the Protestant side, and probably every reviser of the New Testament for the edition of 1611 possessed it."

6. Antonia Fraser, *Mary Queen of Scots* (New York: Delacorte, 1969), 531–32.

7. The phrase comes from the title of the book by Nicholas Basbanes, *A Gentle Madness* (New York: Henry Holt and Company, 1995).

8. Sidney K. Ohlhausen, "Douay-Rhemes: A Story of Faith," *Catholic Heritage*, May–June 1999, 21.

9. Ibid., 21.

10. T. H. Darlow and H. F. Moule, *Historical Catalog of the Printed Editions of Holy Scripture in the Library of the British and Foreign Bible Society*, vol. 2 (London: The British and Foreign Bible Society, 1903–11), 936.

11. Ibid., 958.

## Chapter 11 A Royal Translation

1. Benson Bobrick, *Wide as the Waters* (New York: Simon & Schuster, 2001), 199.

2. As a Scotsman, James embraced the reformed principles of the Geneva Bible but did not approve of its view on kingship and authority. His decision to support a new translation was based as much on politics and his power base as king as it was on a desire to abandon the Geneva Bible. Puritans expected his support for the Geneva Bible rather than a new translation.

3. Alister E. McGrath, *In the Beginning: The Story of the King James Bible and How It Changed*

a Nation, a Language, and a Culture (New York: Doubleday, 2001), 140. In Scotland, James had to answer to a council, but in England he was monarch. His desire for sole power over the kingdom was stronger than his theological convictions. In fact, James hated the Presbyterian Church in Scotland for their failure to give proper place to bishops. Andrew Melville had openly declared his public support of James, but privately he proclaimed Christ the true King of Scotland. His accusation that James was "God's silly vassal" did not endear him to James. James did not have the slightest intention of supporting the Presbyterian agenda.

4. The Puritans wanted to purify the Church of England from the practices of Elizabeth's popish leanings. They hoped James would help them get rid of many unwanted practices.

5. McGrath, In the Beginning, 150. The Puritan petition known as the "Millenary Petition," containing misgivings from more than a thousand members of the Church of England, was presented to the Hampton Court. These petitions charged the Church with popish tendencies.

6. This was an interesting development since the 1579 Bassandyne Bible was dedicated to James of Scotland.

7. Geddes MacGregor, The Bible in the Making (London: John Murray, 1961), 111.

8. Records differ in number, perhaps due to untimely deaths of certain translators.

9. William Barlow, The Summe and Substance of the Conference Which It Pleased His Excellent Majestie to Have With the Lords, Bishops, and Other of His Clergie (Gainesville, FL: Facsimiles and Reprints, 1965), 46. This is the closest statement we have to an official authorizing of the KJV.

10. Robinson, Bible in Its Ancient and English Versions, 201. Samuel Ward, an English delegate to the Synod of Dort in 1618 and one of the King James translators encouraged the translators not to depart from the ancient translation unless the original languages demanded it: "In the first place caution was given that an entirely new version was not to be furnished, but an old version, long received by the Church, to be purged from all blemishes and faults; to this end there was to be no departure from the ancient translation, unless the truth of the original text or emphasis

demanded." It was clear that the original languages were carefully consulted.

11. Butterworth, Literary Lineage of the King James Bible, 9–21; and McGrath, In The Beginning, 253–76. It is quite clear that the English translation of the King James Version was not the common everyday English usage. Butterworth and McGrath demonstrate from Shakespeare and contemporary writings that the KJV translators' insistence on using the Bishops' Bible as the basic translation, changing it only when the Greek or Hebrew demanded it, guaranteed a language of the early to mid-sixteenth century.

12. David Norton, Textual History of the King James Bible (Cambridge: Cambridge University Press, 2005), 62.

13. Shaheen, Biblical References in Shakespeare's Plays, 39–41.

14. Olga S. Opfell, The King James Bible Translators (Jefferson, NC, and London: McFarland, 1982), 111.

15. Norton, A Textual History of the King James Bible, 63.

16. Bod 1602 is a complete 1602 Bishops' Bible with translators' annotations.

17. McGrath, In the Beginning, 214. In the 1530s Barker's constant financial woes caused him to fight to reduce the wages of his proofreaders. Unhappy with the lack of their boss's support of decent wages, they may have been motivated to sabotage the reading.

18. It must be noted that the 1881 Revised Version accepted the "he" reading as correct whereas most scholars acknowledge that the "she" reading is the correct one, based primarily on the fact that all succeeding printings had the "she" reading.

19. The New Testament title page of the 1611 "He" Bible omits the phrase, while the 1611/13 "She" Bible includes it.

20. Norton's Textual History of the King James Bible has given us a valuable discussion on these issues.

21. Francis Fry, one of the most famous Bible biographers of the nineteenth century, has done the most thorough work by comparing a hundred copies of the 1611 edition. Details of his important study can be found in his book A Description of the Great Bible (London: Willes and Sotheran, 1865).

22. A careful comparison of the folios reveals differences on many, many pages. These were possibly the results of the pages being reprinted. After the printer carefully collated the pages he had left over from the previous stock, he then needed to reprint missing pages. These were reset and corrected or edited in the new galley. This helps explain some of the differences, but probably not all of them.

23. Fry, *Description of the Great Bible*, 24.

24. It should be remembered that one of the principles of translation governing the KJV translators was to use the 1602 Bishops' Bible except when other versions or the original languages demanded changes. This Bible had the same woodcut as many of the 1611 King James Bibles.

25. Norton, *Textual History of the King James Bible*, 63. Norton suggests an accident in the printing office may have destroyed the Boel title.

26. I recently purchased a 1611 "He" Bible in which one complete signature (Qq) of six leaves had been omitted. These were not pages someone would remove to sell or treasure. They may have been overlooked when binding.

27. Pollard, *Records of the English Bible*, 68–70.

28. Norton, *Textual History of the King James Bible*, 65. Norton insists the 1613 edition should not be considered a second issue but a genuine second edition. While his arguments are well taken, for our purposes, we will continue to use the common designation of first edition second issue for the 1613 edition.

29. Fry, *Description of the Great Bible*, 24.

30. McGrath, *In the Beginning*, 279. Broughton's reputation as a prima donna had preceded him and may explain why he was not invited to be a translator.

31. I have a copy of the Geneva printed in 1776 with Cranmer's Prologue from the Great Bible of 1540. Most books focus on the 1644 date as the last edition without knowing of the 1776 and another 1778 edition.

32. McGrath, *In the Beginning*, 219.

33. Pollard, *Records of the English Bible*, 60. Pollard states that there is no evidence that it was "authorized" in the sense of royal approval. The word *appointed* that appears on the title page is much weaker than the term *authorized*. Had it

been "authorized" by the king, it certainly would have used the stronger term.

34. Herbert, *Historical Catalog of the Printed Editions*. Herbert is the short name referring to the standard Bible bibliographer of the twentieth century.

35. McGrath, *In the Beginning*, 287–89. Complaints about the misprints and inaccuracies in the KJV around 1645 led to demands for a revision of the KJV. The influence of the Puritans grew during the end of the reign of Charles I. The Geneva Bible, however, still did not gain popular support. It was in the restoration of Charles II's reign (1660) that the KJV became the "pillar of the Restoration society." All demand for a revision of the KJV ceased.

## Chapter 12 The King's Bible Revised

1. This change in the text is claimed by some to have been inserted for theological reasons by the Puritans. However, here it is inserted under the "Royal License." Other renderings can be found in F. H. A. Scrivener, *The Authorized Edition of the English Bible* (Cambridge: Cambridge University Press, 1884).

2. Italics were inserted in the text to draw attention to the fact that additional English words were necessary to accurately express the concept from the original language.

3. Lord" is the KJV spelling of the Hebrew term *Yahweh*; *Adonai* is rendered "Lord." The Hebrew text reads "Adonai," making the translation "Lord" the correct one.

4. Norton, *Textual History of the King James Bible*, 107.

5. Thomas Curtis, *The Existing Monopoly: An Inadequate Protection of the Authorized Version of the Scripture* (London: Thomas Curtis, 1833), quoted in Scrivener, *Authorized Edition of the English Bible*, 35.

6. *The Holy Bible, an Exact Reprint Page for Page of the Authorized Version* (London: Oxford University Press, 1833), 1.

7. Scrivener, *Authorized Edition of the English Bible*, 36–37.

8. I must mention that a serious attempt to publish a KJV with the language updated but without creating a new revision has been completed. The 21st Century King James Version published in 1994 by 21st Century King James

Publishers (a division of Duel Enterprises, Inc., Gary, SD) has made a unique contribution to the modern debate. They have seriously attempted to update the language of the 1611 KJV and avoided the common criticisms of various detractors. The result is an easy-to-read KJV without the loss of any potential doctrinal content. They maintained the use of "thee," "thou," "hath," "art," "cometh" and "hast" since the editors believe these are still understood today and do have some advantages over modern usage because of the parallel usage with the Greek text of the New Testament.

9. According to market share statistics supplied by Evangelical Christian Publishers Association (ECPA), as of October 2007, the translations currently being purchased are as follows:

> New International Version (25.61%)
>
> New King James Version (15.72%)
>
> King James Version (15.32%)
>
> English Standard Version (10.13%)
>
> New Living Translation (9.32%)
>
> Holman Christian Standard Bible (2.51%)
>
> *The Message* (2.1%)
>
> New American Standard Bible (1.8%)

These figures do not include sales from Wal-Mart, Barnes and Noble, and Amazon.com.

10. Norton, *Textual History of the King James Bible*, 136–41.

11. James G. Carleton, *The Part of Rhemes in the Making of the English Bible* (Oxford: Clarendon Press, 1902), 32. Carleton has conclusively demonstrated words from the Rhemes (R) survived in the KJV. The Rhemes published in 1582 was the last translation prior to the KJV and was referred to frequently in the "Translators to the Readers." Carleton observes, "One cannot but be struck by the large number of words which have come into the Authorized Version from the Vulgate through the medium of the Rhemish New Testament." Example: in the Rhemes, Matthew 8:30 reads, "But your very hairs of the head are all numbered." KJV states, "But the very hairs of your head are all numbered." The other versions used by the KJV translators are clearly different.

12. Dearden, *Guiding Light on the Great Highway*, 231.

## Chapter 13 The Source for English Translations

1. While the legendary account has been told many times, Daniel B. Wallace points out that no statement has been found to support the story. Private correspondence from Daniel B. Wallace, 2008.

2. Bruce M. Metzger, *The Text of the New Testament* (New York: Oxford University Press, 1968), 97.

3. Samuel Prideaux Tregelles, *The Printed Text of the Greek New Testament* (London: Samuel Bagster and Sons, 1854), 9–15.

4. Desiderius Erasmus, *In Annotationes Novi Testamenti Prefatio* (Basel: Johann Froben, 1516), 385.

5. On the term "Johann Comma," see note 5 of chapter 9.

6. This Greek manuscript now is housed in the Trinity College Library in Dublin, Ireland. Many believe that a Franciscan friar, Roy, translated it back into Greek from the Vulgate for the occasion in 1520.

7. Tregelles, *Printed Text of the Greek New Testament*, 26–28.

8. Although this was the first printed Greek New Testament to have verse divisions and the same divisions used by the Geneva New Testament and the King James Version, it was Pagninus in 1528 who was the first to use verse divisions in the whole Bible. However, Pagninus's divisions had no impact, nor were they the same as Stephanus's.

9. Metzger, *Text of the New Testament*, 105.

10. The Rhemes New Testament reads "her."

11. Tregelles, *Printed Text of the Greek New Testament*, 39.

12. Semler was the first to use the term *recension* for groups of New Testament witnesses, which today is equivalent to "families" of manuscripts.

13. Kurt Aland and Barbara Aland, *The Text of the New Testament* (Grand Rapids: Eerdmans, 1987), 9.

14. Metzger, *Text of the New Testament*, 121.

15. Ibid., 126.

16. The accuracy of this story has been questioned in recent years because of new evidence that has come to light.

17. Ibid., 43–45. The complete story is told by Metzger. An alternate story has surfaced in which Tischendorf is accused of stealing the Sinaiticus from St. Catharine's.

18. Brooke Foss Westcott and Fenton John Anthony Hort, *The New Testament in the Original Greek*, 2 vols. (New York and London: Macmillan, 1881).

## Chapter 14 The Bible in America

1. Bobrick, *Wide as the Waters*, 269.

2. P. Marion Simms, *The Bible in America* (New York: Wilson-Erickson, 1936), 14.

3. Adam Nicolson, *God's Secretaries* (New York: HarperCollins, 2003), 122–23. Originally *Puritan* was a pejorative word making fun of those embracing Puritan virtues. Nicolson quotes a London lawyer, John Manningham, who wrote in 1602, "A Puritan is such one as loves God with all his soul, but hates his neighbor with all his heart."

4. Ibid. Literacy in all social classes had been increasing from the mid-sixteenth century. The growing literacy among all populations was the "seed-bed" in which Puritanism flourished. The people were thirsty for reading God's Word. The Bible provided the head of every home, "direction for his apparel, his speech, his diet, his company, his disports, his labour, his buying and selling, yea and for his very sleep."

5. Harry S. Stout, "Word and Order in Colonial New England," in *The Bible in America: Essays in Cultural History*, ed. Nathan O. Hatch and Mark A. Noll (New York: Oxford University Press, 1982), 25.

6. Ibid., 26.

7. Gerald P. Fogarty, "The Quest for a Catholic Vernacular Bible in America," in *The Bible in America*, ed. Hatch and Noll, 163.

8. Ibid., 164–65. Fogarty, a Roman Catholic, draws attention to Lyman Beecher's stereotyping of the Roman Catholic teaching that Catholics were forbidden to read and interpret Scripture. His point is that this teaching was exaggerated.

9. This story is a dramatization to illustrate the legend of the Sauer Bible. The story has a suspicious origin that the Bible got its name as the "Gun Wad" Bible from minutemen using pages for their muskets. As with so many legends, it is impossible to know for sure its origin.

10. Harold R. Willoughby, *Soldiers' Bibles through Three Centuries* (Chicago: University of Chicago Press, 1944), 17.

11. United States in Congress, quoted in ibid., 18.

12. Simms, *Bible in America*, 192.

13. Robert R. Dearden Jr. and Douglas S. Watson, *An Original Leaf from the Bible of the Revolution* (San Francisco: John Howell, 1930), 20–21.

14. Deardon and Watson, *Original Leaf*, 27–28.

15. Ibid., 23.

16. The Bible in America during the War of Independence and the Civil War was almost exclusively the King James Version.

17. Simms, *Bible in America*, 27.

18. Ibid., 29.

## Chapter 15 The Bible as Bestseller

1. Unknown poet, quoted in Bobrick, *Wide as the Waters*, 73.

2. John Wycliffe, quoted in Hudson, *Lollards and Their Books*, 153. Oxford Bodleian MS Laud Misc. 200 folio 201. Translated from the Latin by the fourth-year high school Latin class at Coram Deo Academy, Flower Mound, Texas, under the supervision of Advanced Latin Instructor Daniel R. Fredrick, PhD.

3. Mark L. Strauss, "Form, Function, and the 'Literal Meaning' Fallacy in Bible Translation" (paper presented to Society of Biblical Literature, November 2003), 4.

4. Ibid., 5.

5. Holman Christian Standard Bible notes in the margin that the literal translation is "Then opening his mouth . . ."

6. Ronald Youngblood, "Translation versus Transliteration: The Triumph of Clarity over Opacity" (paper presented to Society of Biblical Literature, November 2003), 7.

7. Leland Ryken, *The Word of God in English* (Wheaton: Crossway, 2002), 287–93. Ryken's book has compelling arguments for the word-for-word theory of translation. I have adopted some of his arguments here.

8. While the Byzantine text is not exactly the same as the *Textus Receptus*, for our purposes we will consider them nearly interchangeable.

9. "Textual criticism" is a science that classifies and evaluates readings in surviving manuscripts,

and we are unable to do it justice in this short chapter. It must be noted, however, that some manuscripts do not fit in one of these three families and quite a number are mixed readings. Nevertheless, for our purposes we will use the three major families: Byzantine, Western, and Alexandrian.

10. The Jerusalem Bible is the Roman Catholic Bible using the original languages of Hebrew (Old Testament) and Greek (New Testament). This is the Western text as it is translated from the Greek in the Jerusalem Bible.

11. Bart D. Ehrman, *The Orthodox Corruption of Scripture* (Oxford: Oxford University Press, 1993), and Eldon Jay Epp, *The Theological Tendency of Codex Bezae Cantabrigiensis in Acts* (Eugene, OR: Wipf and Stock, 2001). In recent studies, Ehrman suggests that the ancient manuscripts were altered intentionally along theological lines or followed a particular theological view. While I do not agree with his conclusions, he has provided a valuable study.

## Chapter 16 The People Triumph

1. Eugene A. Nida, *Science of Translating* (Leiden: E. J. Brill, 1964), 182–83.

2. J. B. Phillips, *The Gospels Translated into Modern English* (New York: Macmillan, 1957), vi.

3. Bible translation names included are listed as follows:

King James Version (KJV)

American Standard Version (ASV)

Revised Standard Version (RSV)

New American Standard Bible (NASB)

Good News Translation (GNT)

New International Version (NIV)

New King James Version (NKJV)

21st Century King James Version (KJ21)

New Living Translation (NLT)

Holman Christian Standard Bible (HCSB)

Today's New International Version (TNIV)

New English Translation (NET)

New Revised Standard Version (NRSV)

*The Message* (Message)

Revised New English Bible (RNEB)

English Standard Version (ESV)

4. During the production of the English Revised Version in 1881, Westcott and Hort were working on their book *The New Testament in the Original Greek*. As members of the translation committee, their work was heavily relied upon. When variant readings surfaced, the committee voted on the text to be used. The committee membership was heavily weighted with men in agreement with Westcott and Hort's heavy dependence upon manuscripts Vaticanus and Sinaiticus (mss supporting the critical text). In most cases the *Textus Receptus* was outvoted. The ASV 1901 was the text of ERV with certain American vocabulary words substituted for British ones.

5. In the introduction to the Holman Christian Standard Bible, the term "optimal equivalence" is used as an attempt to create a translation using the best of "dynamic equivalent" and "formal equivalent" principles.

# Selected Bibliography

Achtemeier, Paul J. "Omne Verbum Sonat: The New Testament and the Oral Environment of Late Western Antiquity." *Journal of Biblical Literature* (1990): 109.

Aland, Kurt and Barbara Aland. *The Text of the New Testament.* Grand Rapids: Eerdmans, 1987.

Allen, Ward S. *Translating the New Testament Epistles 1604–1611.* Ann Arbor: University Microfilms, 1977.

———. *Translating for King James.* Kingsport, TN: Vanderbilt University Press, 1969.

Allen, Ward S., and Edward C. Jacobs. *The Coming of the King James Gospels.* Fayetteville: The University of Arkansas Press, 1995.

Anderson, Christopher. *The Annals of the English Bible.* 2 vols. London: William Pickering, 1845.

Andrewes, Lancelot. *Sermons.* London: George Miller for Richard Badger, 1629.

Baber, Henry. *An Historical Account of the Saxon and English Versions of the Scriptures, Previously to the Opening of the XVth Century.* London: Paternoster Row, 1810.

Barker, Kenneth. *New International Version.* Grand Rapids: Zondervan Bible Publishers, 1985.

Barlow, William. *The Summe and Substance.* Gainesville, FL: Facsimiles and Reprints, 1965.

Barr, James. *The Semantics of Biblical Language.* Oxford: Oxford University Press, 1961.

Basbane, Nicholas A. *A Gentle Madness.* New York: Henry Holt and Company, 1995.

Berkowitz, David Sandler. *In Remembrance of Creation.* Waltham, MA: Brandeis University Press, 1968.

Blakie, James. *The English Bible and Its Story.* London: Seeley, Service, & Co. Ltd., 1928.

Bobrick, Benson. *Wide as the Waters.* New York: Simon & Schuster, 2001.

Bodleian Library. *Wyclif and His Followers.* Oxford: Bodleian Library, 1983.

Bosworth, Joseph. *The Gothic and Anglo-Saxon Gospels.* London: John Russell Smith, Soho Square, 1865.

Brake, Donald L., Sr. *The New Testament in English Translated by John Wycliffe.* Portland, OR: International Bible Publications, 1986.

Bruce, F. F. "John Wycliffe and the English Bible." *Churchman* 98, no. 4 (1984): 294–306.

———. *The English Bible.* Oxford: Oxford University Press, 1970.

Butterworth, Charles C. *The Literary Lineage of the King James Bible, 1340–1611.* Philadelphia: University of Pennsylvania Press, 1941.

Calkins, Robert G. *Illuminated Books of the Middle Ages.* Ithaca, NY: Cornell University Press, 1983.

*The Cambridge History of the Bible.* vol.1, *From the Beginnings to Jerome,* edited by P. R. Ackroyd and C. F. Evans. vol. 2, *The West from the Fathers to the Reformation,* edited by G. W. H. Lampe. vol. 3, *The West from the Reformation to the Present Day,* edited by S. L. Greenslade. Cambridge: Cambridge University Press, 1963–70.

Cammack, Melvin M. *John Wyclif and the English Bible.* New York: American Tract Society, 1938.

Carleton, James G. *The Part of Rhemes in the Making of the English Bible.* Oxford: Clarendon Press, 1902.

Cavill, Paul. *A Treasury of Anglo-Saxon England.* Grand Rapids: Zondervan, 2001.

Comfort, Philip W. *The Complete Guide to Bible Versions.* Wheaton: Tyndale House, 1996.

Cotton, Henry. *Editions of the Bible and Parts thereof in English, from the Year MDV to MDCCL.* Oxford: At the University Press, 1852.

Coverdale, Miles. *The Bible: that is, the holy Scrypture of the Olde and New Testament.* Cologne or Marburg: E. Cervicornus & J. Soter, 1535: "Apocrypha."

———. *Dedications and Prologues to the Translation of the Bible.* 1535. Reprint, The Parker Society. Cambridge: Cambridge University Press, 1846.

Cross, F. L., ed. *Dictionary of the Christian Church.* London: Oxford University Press, 1929: "Lollardy."

Dahmus, Joseph H. *The Prosecution of John Wyclif.* New Haven: Yale University Press, 1952.

Daniell, David. *The Bible in English: Its History and Influence.* New Haven: Yale University Press, 2003.

———, ed. *Tyndale's New Testament.* New Haven: Yale University Press, 1989.

———, ed. *Tyndale's Old Testament.* New Haven: Yale University Press, 1989.

———. *William Tyndale.* New Haven: Yale University Press, 1994.

Darlow, T. H., and H. F. Moule. *Historical Catalogue of the Printed Editions of Holy Scripture in the Library of the British and Foreign Bible Society.* 4 vols. London: British and Foreign Bible Society; New York: American Bible Society, 1903–11.

de Hamel, Christopher. *The Book: A History of the Bible.* London: Phaidon, 2001.

de Waard, Jan, and Eugene A. Nida. *From One Language to Another.* Nashville: Thomas Nelson, 1986.

Deanesly, Margaret. *The Lollard Bible.* Cambridge: Cambridge University Press, 1920.

Dearden, Robert, Jr. *The Guiding Light on the Great Highway.* Philadelphia: John Winston, 1929.

Demaus, Robert. *William Tindale: A Biography.* Revised by Richard Lovett. London: The Religious Tract Society, n.d., ca. 1920.

Desiderius, Erasmus. *In Annotationes Novi Testamenti Prefatio.* Basel: Johann Froben, 1516.

Dobson, William T. *History of the Bassandyne Bible.* Edinburgh: William Blackwood and Sons, 1887.

Dore, J. R. *Old Bibles: An Account of the Early Versions of the English Bible.* London: Eyre and Spottiswoode, 1888.

Duffy, Eamon. *The Stripping of the Altars.* New Haven and London: Yale University Press, 1992.

Eadie, John. *The English Bible.* 2 vols. London: Macmillan, 1876.

Edgar, Andrew. *The Bibles of England: A Plain Account for Plain People of the Principal Versions of the Bible in English.* London: Paisley, and Paternoster Row, 1889.

Ehrman, Bart D. *The Orthodox Corruption of Scripture.* Oxford: Oxford University Press, 1993.

Epp, Eldon Jay. *The Theological Tendency of Codex Bezae Cantabrigiensis in Acts.* Eugene, OR: Wipf and Stock, 2001.

Evans, G. R. *John Wyclif: Myth and Reality.* Downers Grove, IL: InterVarsity, 2005.

Ewert, David. *From Ancient Tablets to Modern Translations.* Grand Rapids: Zondervan, 1983.

Farrar, Clarissa P., and Austin P. Evans. *Bibliography of English Translations from Medieval Sources.* New York: Columbia University Press, 1946.

Fogarty, Gerald P. "The Quest for a Catholic Vernacular Bible in America." In *The Bible in America: Essays in Cultural History*, edited by Nathan O. Hatch and Mark A. Noll. New York: Oxford University Press, 1982.

Forshall, Josiah, and Frederic Madden, eds. *The Holy Bible, Containing the Old and New Testaments, with the Apocryphal Books, in the Earliest English Versions Made from the Latin Vulgate by John Wycliffe and His Followers.* 4 vols. London: Oxford University Press, 1850.

Fowler, David C. *The Bible in Middle English Literature.* Seattle: University of Washington Press, 1984.

———. *The Life and Times of John Trevisa, Medieval Scholar.* Seattle: University of Washington Press, 1995.

Foxe, John. *Acts and Monuments.* 1563. Reprint, London: Seeley, Burnside, and Seeley, 1843–49.

Frank, Harry Thomas, Charles William Swain, and Courtlandt Canby. *The Bible through the Ages.* Cleveland: World Publishing, 1967.

Fraser, Antonia. *Mary Queen of Scots.* New York: Delacorte, 1969.

Fry, Francis. *A Description of the Great Bible, 1539, and the six editions of Cranmer's Bible, 1540 and 1541, printed by Grafton and Whitchurch: also of the editions, in large folio, of the authorized version of the Holy Scriptures, printed in the years 1611, 1613, 1617, 1634, 1640.* London: Willes and Sotheran, 1865.

———. *The Bible by Coverdale 1535.* London: Willis & Sotheran, 1867.

Fulke, William. *A Defence of the Sincere and True Translations of the Holy Scriptures into the English Tongue.* London: Henrie Bynneman, 1583. Reprint, The Parker Society. Cambridge: Cambridge University Press, 1843.

Gairdner, James. *Lollardy and the Reformation in England.* 4 vols. London: Macmillan, 1908.

Geisler, Norman L., and William E. Nix. *A General Introduction to the Bible.* Chicago: Moody, 1986.

Greenslade, S. L. *The Work of William Tindale.* London and Glasgow: Blackie & Son, 1938.

Heaton, W. J. *The Bible of the Reformation.* London: Francis Griffiths, 1910.

———. *Our Own English Bible.* London: Francis Griffiths, 1913.

———. *The Puritan Bible.* London: Francis Griffiths, 1913.

Herbert, A. S. *A Historical Catalog of the Printed Editions of the English Bible 1525–1961*. London: The British and Foreign Bible Society; New York: The American Bible Society, 1968.

Hills, Margaret T. *The English Bible in America*. New York: American Bible Society and The New York Public Library, 1962.

Hirsch, E. D., Jr. *Validity in Interpretation*. New Haven: Yale University Press, 1967.

Hoare, H. W. *The Evolution of the English Bible*. New York: E. P. Dutton, 1901.

Holt, Emily Sarah. *John de Wycliffe and What He Did for England*. London: John F. Shaw, n.d., ca. 1900.

Hotchkiss, Valerie R., and Charles C. Ryrie. *Formatting the Word of God*. Dallas: Bridwell Library, 1998.

Hudson, Anne. *Lollards and Their Books*. London and Ronceverte: Hambledon Press, 1985.

————. "The Premature Reformation." *The Tyndale Society Journal* 31 (August 2006): 9–20.

————. *The Premature Reformation*. Oxford: Clarendon Press, 1988.

Hudson, Anne, ed. *Selections from English Wycliffite Writings*. Cambridge: Cambridge University Press, 1978.

Kenyon, Frederic G. *Handbook to the Textual Criticism of the New Testament*. Grand Rapids: Eerdmans, 1912.

Knighton, Henry. *Chronicon*. London, 1889. Quoted in Margaret Deanesly, *The Lollard Bible*. Cambridge: Cambridge University Press, 1920.

Kubo, Sakae, and Walter F. Sprecht. *So Many Versions?* Grand Rapids: Zondervan, 1983.

Lawler, Thomas M. C., Germain Marc'hadour, and Richard C. Marius, eds. *Complete Works of St. Thomas More, Dialogues*. New Haven: Yale University Press, 1984.

Lechler, Professor. *John Wycliffe and His English Precursors*. London: The Religious Tract Society, 1904.

Levi, Peter. *The English Bible 1534–1859*. Grand Rapids: Eerdmans, 1974.

Lewis, Jack P. *The English Bible from KJV to NIV*. Grand Rapids: Baker, 1981.

Lewis, John. *A Complete History of the Several Translations of the Bible and New Testament into English*. London: Joseph Pote, 1739.

————. *The History of the Life and Sufferings of ... John Wycliffe*. London: Robert Knaplock, St. Paul's Churchyard, 1723.

Lightfoot, Neil R. *How We Got the Bible*. 3rd ed. Grand Rapids: Baker, 2003.

Lindberg, Conrad, ed. "Ms. Bodley 959 Genesis-Baruch 3:20." In *Earlier Version of the Wycliffite Bible*. Vol. 5. Stockholm: Almqvist and Wiksell, 1969.

Long, Lynne. *Translating the Bible*. Burlington, VT: Ashgate, 2001.

Lupton, Lewis. *A History of the Geneva Bible*. 24 vols. London: The Olive Tree, 1966–81.

MacGregor, Geddes. *The Bible in the Making*. London: John Murray, 1961.

Maier, John, and Vincent Tollers, eds. *The Bible in Its Literary Milieu*. Grand Rapids: Eerdmans, 1979.

Malless, Stanley, and Jeffrey McQuain. *Coined by God*. New York: W. W. Norton, 2003.

McClure, Alexander W. *The Translators Revived*. New York: Charles Scribner, 1853. Reprint, Worthington, PA: Maranatha Publications, n.d., ca. 1973.

McCrum, Robert, William Cran, and Robert MacNeil. *The Story of English*. New York: Elisabeth Sifton Books, 1986.

McFarlane, K. B. *John Wycliffe and the Beginnings of English Nonconformity.* London: The English Universities Press, 1952.

McGrath, Alister E. *In the Beginning: The Story of the King James Bible and How It Changed a Nation, a Language, and a Culture.* New York: Doubleday, 2001.

Metzger, Bruce M. *Manuscripts of the Greek Bible: An Introduction to Greek Palaeography.* New York: Oxford University Press, 1981.

———. *The Text of the New Testament.* New York: Oxford University Press, 1968.

Michaelis, John David. *Introduction to the New Testament.* 5 vols. London: F. C. & J. Rivington, 1823.

Mombert, J. L. *English Versions of the Bible.* London: Samuel Bagster and Sons Limited, 1907.

Moynahan, Brian. *God's Bestseller.* New York: St. Martin's Press, 2003.

Mozley, J. F. *Coverdale and His Bibles.* Cambridge: Lutterworth Press, 1953. Reprint, 2005.

———. *William Tyndale.* London: Society for Promoting Christian Knowledge, 1937.

Muir, William. *Our Grand Old Bible.* London: Morgan and Scott Ltd., 1911.

Munster, Sebastian. *Hebraical Biblia Latina.* Basileae: Michaelis Isinginii & Henrici Petri, 1535.

Nestle, Eberhard. *Introduction to the Textual Criticism of the Greek New Testament.* London: Williams and Norgate, 1901.

Nicolson, Adam. *God's Secretaries.* New York: HarperCollins, 2003.

Nida, Eugene A. *Toward a Science of Translating.* Leiden: E. J. Brill, 1964.

Norman, Don Cleveland. *The 500th Anniversary Pictorial Census of the Gutenberg Bible.* Chicago: Coverdale Press, 1961.

Norton, David A. *A History of the English Bible as Literature.* Cambridge: Cambridge University Press, 2000.

———. *A Textual History of the King James Bible.* Cambridge: Cambridge University Press, 2005.

Ogle, Arthur. *The Tragedy of the Lollards' Tower.* Oxford: Pen-in-Hand Publishing, 1949.

Ohlhausen, Sidney K. "Douay-Rhemes: A Story of Faith." *Catholic Heritage* (May–June 1999): 21–23.

Opfel, Olga S. *The King James Bible Translators.* Jefferson, NC, & London: McFarland, 1982.

O'Sullivan, Orlaith, ed. *The Bible as Book: The Reformation.* London: The British Library and Oak Knoll Press, 2000.

Paine, Gustavus. *The Learned Men.* New York: Thomas Y. Crowell, 1959.

Parker, G. H. W. *The Morning Star.* Great Britain: Paternoster, 1965.

Partridge, A. C. *English Biblical Translation.* London: Andre Deutsch, 1975.

Pelikan, Jaroslav. *The Reformation of the Bible.* New Haven: Yale University Press; Dallas: Bridwell Library, 1996.

Pilgrim, A. Christian. *The Forbidden Book.* Shippensburg, PA: Lollard House, 1992.

Pollard, Alfred W. *Last Words on the History of the Title-Page.* New York: Burt Franklin, 1981.

———. *Records of the English Bible.* London: Oxford University Press, 1911.

Pollard, A. W., and G. R. Redgrave. *A Short-title Catalog of Books Printed in England, Scotland, and Ireland. 1475–1640.* New York: Bernard Quaritch Ltd., 1926.

Poole, Reginald Lane. *Wycliffe and Movements for Reform.* London: Longmans, Green, and Co., 1889.

Pope, Hugh. *English Versions of the Bible.* London: B. Herder Book Co., 1952.

Price, David, and Charles C. Ryrie. *Let It Go among Our People*. Cambridge: Lutterworth Press, 2004.

Pritchard, Ruth. "Roll Over Gutenberg." *Alaska Airlines* magazine, February 1987.

Reader's Digest Staff. *The Bible through the Ages*. Pleasantville, NY: Reader's Digest Association, 1996.

Robinson, H. W. *The Bible in Its Ancient and English Versions*. Oxford: Clarendon Press, 1940.

Rogerson, John. *The Oxford Illustrated History of the Bible*. Oxford: University Press, 2001.

Rumball-Petre, Edwin A. R. *Rare Bibles*. New York: Philips C. Duschnes, 1938.

Ryken, Leland. *Choosing a Bible*. Wheaton: Crossway, 2005.

———. *The Word of God in English*. Wheaton: Crossway, 2002.

Schmidtchen, Paul W. "Mostly about Books." *Hobbies: The Magazine for Collectors*, April 1962.

Scorgie, Glen G., Mark L. Strauss, and Steven M. Vothe. *The Challenge of Bible Translation*. Grand Rapids: Zondervan, 2003.

Scrivener, F. H. A. *The Authorized Edition of the English Bible*. Cambridge: Cambridge University Press, 1884.

Shaheen, Naseeb. *Biblical References in Shakespeare's Plays*. Newark: University of Delaware Press, 1999.

Sharpe, John, and Kimberly Van Kampen. *The Bible as Book: The Manuscript Tradition*. London: The British Library and Oak Knoll Press, 1998.

Simms, P. Marion. *The Bible in America*. New York: Wilson-Erickson, 1936.

Stacey, John. *Wyclif and Reform*. London: Lutterworth Press, 1964.

Stein, Robert. "Is Our Reading the Same as the Original Audience's Hearing It? A Study in the Gospel of Mark." *Journal of the Evangelical Theological Society* 46, no. 1 (March 2003): 63–78.

———. "The Benefits of an Author Oriented Approach to Hermeneutics." *Journal of the Evangelical Theological Society* 44, no. 3 (September 2001): 451–66.

Stevens, Henry. *The Bibles in the Caxton Exhibition, 1877*. London: Henry Stevens IV Trafalgar Square, 1878.

Stevenson, Joseph. *The Truth about John Wyclif: His Life Writings and Opinions*. London: Burns and Oates, 1885.

Stout, Harry S. "Word and Order in Colonial New England." In *The Bible in America*, edited by Nathan O. Hatch and Mark A. Noll. New York: Oxford University Press, 1982.

Strauss, Mark L. "Form, Function, and the 'Literal Meaning' Fallacy in Bible Translation." Paper presented to the Society of Biblical Literature, November 2003.

Sullivan, Edward. *The Book of Kells*. London: Bracken Books, 1988.

Thomas, Robert L. *How to Choose a Bible Version*. Great Britain: Christian Focus Publications, 2000.

Tomlin, Graham. *Luther and His World*. Downers Grove, IL: InterVarsity, 2002.

Tregelles, Samuel Prideaux. *The Printed Text of the Greek New Testament*. London: Samuel Bagster and Sons, 1854.

Trevelyan, George Macaulay. *England in the Age of Wycliffe*. London: Longmans, Green, 1904.

Tyndale, William. "The Practice of Prelates." In *Expositions and Notes on the Holy Scriptures together with the Practice of Prelates*. Edited by H. Walker. Cambridge: The University Press, 1849.

———. *The Obedience of a Christian Man*. Reprint, London: Religious Tract Society, 1999.

Vaughan, Robert. *John de Wycliffe*. London: Seeleys, 1853.

———. *The Life and Opinions of John de Wycliffe*. 2 vols. London: Holdsworth and Ball, 1831.

———. *Tracts and Treatises of John de Wycliffe*. London: Blackburn and Pardon, Hatton Garden, 1845.

Wegener, G. S. *6000 Years of the Bible*. London: Hodder and Stoughton, 1958.

Wegner, Paul D. *The Journey from Texts to Translations*. Grand Rapids: Baker, 1999.

Westcott, Brooke Foss, *A General View of the History of the English Bible*. London: Macmillan, 1872.

Westcott, Brooke Foss and Fenton John Anthony Hort. *The New Testament in the Original Greek*. Cambridge and London: Macmillan, 1881.

Wilks, Michael. *Wyclif: Political Ideas and Practice*. Oxford: Oxbow Books, 2000.

Williams, C. H. *William Tyndale*. London: Thomas Nelson, 1969.

Willoughby, Harold R. *Soldiers' Bibles Through Three Centuries*. Chicago: University of Chicago Press, 1944.

Wood, Douglas C. *The Evangelical Doctor: John Wycliffe and the Lollards*. Herts, England: Evangelical Press, 1984.

Wordsworth, Charles. *Shakespeare's Knowledge and Use of the Bible*. London: Eden, Remington & Co., 1891.

Workman, Hebert B. *John Wyclif: A Study of the English Medieval Church*. 2 vols. Oxford: Clarendon Press, 1926.

Wosh, Peter J. *Spreading the Word*. Ithaca, NY: Cornell University Press, 1994.

Wray, J. Jackson. *John Wycliffe a Quincentenary Tribute*. London: James Nisbet, 1884.

Wycliff, John. *Speculum Secularium Dominorum, Opera Minora*. Edited by John Loserth. London: Wycliff Society, 1913.

Youngblood, Ronald. "Translation versus Transliteration: The Triumph of Clarity over Opacity." Paper presented to the Society of Biblical Literature, November 2003.

# Scripture Index

5:9 210
5:44 280
8:20 173
9:13 280
9:34 219
10:18 216
12:23 208
12:45 173
13:21 219
14:32 216
16:16 212
23:1 272
23:24 216
23:27 173
24:36 280
26:36 189, 193, 198, 206, 211

**Mark**

6:53 216
8:24 173
15:41 207

**Luke**

1:28 280
2 151
2:22 233
4:8 151
7:47 209, 211
10:31 152
12:20 289
13:32 291
14:26 211
19:9 212

**John**

6:67 211
10:9 292
14:6 208
15:20 212
16:2 151, 153
20:25 206

**Acts**

6:3 208
7:28 213
7:35 219
7:45 212
9:5–6 230, 231
10:6 153
13:48 152
20:36 155, 197

**Romans**

4:12 212
6:13 207
9:15 152
11:29 152

**1 Corinthians**

4:9 216
5:2 213
6:9 209, 211
12:28 207

**Galatians**

3:1 280

**Ephesians**

4:27 192

**1 Thessalonians**

1:3 274

**1 Timothy**

2:9 216
2:12 292
4:12 280
4:16 207

**2 Timothy**

3:16 293
4:16 206

**Titus**

1:2 152

**Hebrews**

1:3 132
11:21 153

**James**

1:21 292
2:3 288

**1 Peter**

3:2 210

**1 John**

1:7 280
2:5 133
5:7 230, 231, 235
5:7–8 225
5:12 208

**Jude**

16 211

**Revelation**

3:5 192
13:16 213
21:1 211
22:16–21 230
22:23 176

# General Index

Bill, John 169, 191

bindery industry 115

Bishops' Bible 23, 160, 162–66, 167, 169, 174, 202, 276, 325n6(2), 327n11

black letters 145, 147, 304

Blankstone edition (Tyndale NT) 103, 110

Blayney, Benjamin 212, 213, 214, 305

block printing 69–70

Bloody Mary. See Mary Tudor

Bodleian Library 52, 64–65, 150, 238

Bodley, John 144, 150, 305

Bodley, Thomas 150, 305

Boel, Cornelis 194, 195, 197

Bois, John 207, 208, 305

Boleyn, Anne 116, 119–20, 134, 162, 305

Bonner, Edmund 134, 138, 139, 305

Book of Kells 33

"Breeches" Bible 23, 154–55, 210

Brelegerg Bible 259

Bristow, Richard 172

Broerss, Joost 153, 155, 160

Broughton, Hugh 202, 305, 328n30

Bruce, F. F. 132

Buck, John 207

Buck, Thomas 207, 208

"Bugge" Bible 210

Burgon, John W. 248, 305

Butterworth, Charles 149, 327n11

Byblos 29

Byzantine text 242, 277, 279, 280, 330n8(2), 331n9

Caedmon 39, 305

Caesar, Julius 37, 38

Cahill, Tom 74

Calvinism 152, 164

Calvin, John 146, 149, 151, 233, 305

Cambridge Paragraph Bible 214, 215–16, 219

Cambridge University 215

canon 53, 99, 118

Cardwell, Edward 214, 305–6

Carey, Mathew 252, 258

Carleton, James G., 329n11(1)

Carroll, John 252

Catherine of Aragon 144

Caxton, William 80, 306

chained Bibles 34

Challoner, Richard 177, 306

Charles I 328n35

Charles II 328n35

Charles V 105

Chaucer, Geoffrey 49, 51, 306

Church of England 162, 183, 250, 327n4

Civil War (American) 254, 260–64

Civil War New Testaments 262–64

Cochlaeus, John 98, 306

codex 226

   *Aleppo* 26, 28

   *Argenteus* 38

   *Cairensis* 26, 28

   *Ephraemi* 245

   *Reuchlinianus* 230

Cole, Thomas 144

Cole, William 148

Colet, John 96, 306

collocate 306

colophon 77

Common Book of Prayer 118

Complutensian Polyglot 228, 231, 234

Confederate States Bible Society 261–62

*Constance Missal* 73

Constantinople 31, 57, 92, 227, 281

*Constitutions* 47, 80, 96–97, 100, 108, 320n2

Cotton Patch Version 275

Council of Constance (1414–1416) 266

Council of Trent 53, 172, 181, 252

Counter-Reformation 122, 133

Coverdale Bible 99, 113–23, 126, 134, 162, 190

Coverdale Diglot 121, 166–67

Coverdale, Miles 53, 111–23, 126, 130, 133–34, 144, 166–67, 306

Coxe, R. 164

Cranmer's Bible 137, 178–79

Cranmer, Thomas 134, 135, 137, 144, 164, 168, 306

Cremer, Henry 75

Crespin, Jean 146, 233, 306

"critical text" 248, 277, 279

Cromwell, Thomas 102, 105, 110, 115, 116, 127–28, 130–32, 133, 135, 137, 144, 168, 306–7, 325n11(1)

culture 275, 276, 283

Curcellaeus, Stephanus 238

Curtis, Thomas 214

Cuthbert, Bishop 137

Cyprian 53

Daniell, David 40, 102, 321n15, 324n5(1), 324n11, 324n16

Daniel, Roger 208

Darnley, Henry Stuart 307
Davies, R. 164
Dead Sea Scrolls 26–27
Deanesly, Margaret 62, 63, 322n42
de Cisneros, Fransisco Ximenes 93, 227–28, 307
de Hamel, Christopher 54–55, 59, 62, 320n8, 321n12
Deissmann, Adolf 270
de Voragine, Jacobus 80, 307
de Worde, Wynken 80, 81, 307
Diet of Worms 89–90
Donne, John 202
Dore, J. R. 154
Douay-Rhemes Bible 172–73, 180, 252
Dudley, John 144
Duns Scotus, John 323n3(1)
duodecimo 324n18
dynamic equivalents. *See* functional equivalents

Eastern Orthodox Church 281
eBay, and Bible collecting 263
Edelstein Bible 77
*editio princes. See* first edition
Edward VI 307
Egyptian Coptic Church 281
Ehrman, Bart D., 331n11
Eliot Indian Bible 251, 258, 259
Eliot, John 251, 258, 307
Elizabeth I 148–49, 150, 155, 161–63, 165, 174, 175, 183, 184–85, 307
Elstrack, Renold 199, 200, 307
Elzevir brothers 235–37, 239, 243, 308
English Reformation 50, 96, 143, 184
English Revised Version (1881) 204, 331n4
English Standard Version 271, 294, 329n9(1)
Enlightenment 79, 298
equivalence of response (translation) 284
Erasmus, Desiderius 93, 95, 96, 225–26, 230, 237, 243, 244, 248, 308
Erasmus Greek New Testament 83, 86, 167, 226, 227–28, 229, 231, 235
Erasmus's English Paraphrase of the New Testament 168
errors, by copyists 226–27
Estienne. *See* Stephanus, Robert
etymology 292–93
Ewart, David 151
exegesis 276
Eyre, George 215, 308

families, of texts 279–81, 329n12, 331n9
Fawkes, Guy 187
Fell, John 238–39, 308
Fichet, Guillaume 73, 308
figures of speech 283, 284, 289–92
first edition 200–201, 254, 308
first issue 308
folio 308, 324n18
fonts 76
"Forgotten Sins" Bible 211
formal equivalents 271, 273–76, 285, 286–88, 308, 331n5
Forshall, Josiah 57, 59–60, 63
Fowler, David, 321n9, 321n13
Foxe, John 63, 95, 97, 106, 107, 144, 308–9, 322n30, 322n44
France 133–34
Francis I, King of France 133
Frankin, Benjamin 258
Frederick the Wise 89, 309
freedom of the press 180
Fristedt, S. L. 322n40
Froben, Johann 93, 228, 309
Fry, Francis 158–59, 197, 201, 260, 309, 324n24, 327n21
Fry, Theodore 324n24
Fuggers, 323n5
*Fulke's Counterblast to the Rhemes New Testament* 180
Fulke, William 174–76, 180, 309
functional equivalents 271, 286–88, 309, 331n5
Fust, Johann 72, 74, 78, 309

Gardiner, Stephen 144
Gaus, Jacob 259
Geneva 146, 148, 233
Geneva Bible 117, 145–60, 162, 172, 184, 187, 309, 325n7(2), 326n2(3)
  in America 188, 250
  and King James Version 190, 202–4
  and Shakespeare 192, 325n6(2)
German, translations into 83, 90, 99, 259
Gilby, Anthony 144, 148, 309
Gill, W. 213
glosses, glossing 40, 62, 309
Goad, Thomas 208
*Golden Legend, The* 79, 80, 81, 155
Goodman, Christopher 144, 148
Goodman, G. 165
*Good News for Modern Man* 269

Good News Translation 271–72, 294
Goodrick, Edward 23, 82, 277
Gosecteste, Robert 321n23
Gothic letters 145, 309
Grafton, Richard 128, 133–34, 137, 179, 309–10
Great Awakening 252
Great Bible 131–39, 149, 162, 165, 168–69, 179, 223
Greek language 57, 92, 95, 97, 227
Greek letters 31
Greek New Testament 92, 225–48, 277–81
Gregory the Great 32, 38
Grey, Jane 144, 322n44
Griesbach, Johann Jakob 241–43, 246, 310
Grindal, E. 164
Guest, E. 164
*Gun Powder Plot* 187, 188
"Gun Wad" Bible 254, 255, 259, 330n9(1)
Gutenberg Bible 70–73, 74–75, 227
Gutenberg, Johann 69, 70–77, 310

Hampton Court conference 186–87, 190, 192, 327n5
Haydock Bibles 180
Haydock, Thomas 180, 310
"He" Bible 193, 196–97, 198, 203, 206, 327n19
Hebraisms 118–19, 126
Hebrew language 26, 95, 97
Henry VII 185, 310
Henry VIII 50, 102, 105, 106, 108, 110, 115, 120, 127–30, 135–37, 172, 310
Herbert, A. S. 204, 325n11(2)
Hereford, Nicholas 52–55, 56, 59, 60, 66, 310
hermeneutics 276
Holbein, Hans 137, 310
Holman Christian Standard Bible 271–72, 274, 275–76, 286–88, 290, 295, 329n9(1), 331n5
Hooker, John 112
Horne, R. 164
Hort, F. J. A. 245–48, 317, 331n4
House of Stuart 185
House of Tudor 185
Howell, John 259
Hudson, Anne 321n27, 322n40
humanism, 323n3(1)
Huss, John 56, 91, 266, 310
Hytchins, Guillaume 166, 323n3(2), 324n14. *See also* Tyndale, William

illuminated manuscripts 32–34, 82, 310
incunabula 76–79, 211, 311

indulgences 88–89, 97
italics 212, 326n20, 328n2

James I 125, 151, 181, 183–88, 311, 326n2(3), 327n3
James, Thomas 60
Jerome 31–32, 53, 91, 113, 297, 311
Jerusalem Bible 331n10
Johann Comma 167, 230, 231, 235, 326n5(1)
Josephus 126
Joye, George 102–3, 311
Juda, Leo 149
"Judas" Bible 211
Jugge, Richard 149, 162, 165, 168, 169, 191, 311
Junius, Franciscus 155, 160, 311

Kethe, William 144, 311
King James Version 106, 125, 149, 155, 160, 169–70, 184, 188–204, 293, 329n9(1)
  in America 250, 260
  and Beza 235
  Hebraisms in 119
  influence of Geneva Bible 150–51
  literary style of 286–89
  modern controversy over 220–24
  readability of 283
  revisions of 205–20, 328n35
Knightley, Richard 311
Knighton, Henry 55, 311
Knox, John 144, 149, 311
Koberger, Anton 78, 311–12
Koberger Bible 78, 80

Lachmann, Caroli 243–44, 246, 248, 312
Langton, Stephen 33
Latimer, Hugh 144
Latin 32, 57–58, 297. *See also* Vulgate
Latin letters 146, 147, 206, 312
Latin Text (Catholic Text) 279
Laud, Archbishop 154
Lawrence, Giles 165
"Leda" Bible 210
Lekprevik, Robert 156–60
Leo X, Pope 88, 228
Lewis, John 60, 64
Lincoln, Abraham 260
Lindberg, Conrad 57
Lindisfarne Gospels 33, 40
literal interpretation 323n1(2)
Lloyd, William 213

Lollards 46, 50, 56, 58, 59, 66, 91, 108, 312, 320n6, 321n27
Lombard, Peter 86
London Polyglot 223
Louvain Bible 173, 181
Lupton, Lewis 151
Lutheranism 111, 116, 324n6(1)
Luther Bible 113, 259, 324n9(1)
Luther, Martin 36, 83–90, 97, 99, 146, 235, 312, 323n2(1)–3(1)

Maccabean revolt 26
Madden, Frederic 57, 59–60, 63
*Mainz Psalter* 72, 77
Manningham, John 330n3(1)
manuscript period 31–34, 76–77, 242
maps, in King James Version 200
Martin, Gregory 172, 175, 312
martyrdom 22, 144
Mary Stuart 156, 177, 184–85, 312
Mary Tudor 122, 128, 130, 143–46, 147, 148, 161, 168–69, 312–13, 322n44, 325n1
Masoretic text 26
Matthew's Bible 126–28, 130–31, 132, 133, 134, 141, 190
Matthew, Thomas 126. *See also* Rogers, John
Mazarin Bible 70, 75
McGrath, Alister E. 327n11
Mead, Joseph 208
meaning 62, 270–72, 274–75, 284
Melanchthon, Philipp 146, 313
Melville, Andrew 327n3
*Message, The* 294, 329n9(1)
metaphor 291
Meteren, Jacobus van 115, 125
Metzger, Bruce 330n17(1)
Middle English 37, 42, 49
Mikesy, Andras 324n9(1)
"Millenary Petition" 327n5
Mill, John 239, 313
miniatures 31, 313
*minium* 31
*Minna* (rebel ship) 262
minuscule 31
missal 322n6
Modern English 37
modern translations 268–77, 283–95
monasteries 85
"More Sea" Bible 211
More, Thomas 47, 60, 96, 102, 110, 113, 115, 313
Mount Sinai 25

moveable type 68, 70–74
Mozley, J. F. 120, 324n7(1)
Munster, Sebastian 134, 149, 165, 313, 325n9(1)
"Murderers" Bible 211

Nag Hammadi 30, 278
Native Americans 250
Nestle-Aland Greek text 277, 279
New American Standard Bible 222, 271, 274, 275, 276, 283, 285, 287, 290, 293. 329n9(1)
New Cambridge Paragraph Bible 218–20
New English Bible 289
New English Translation 295
New International Version 222, 271–72, 274, 294, 329n9(1)
New King James Version 218, 271–72, 274, 275, 276, 285, 287, 290, 294, 329n9(1)
New Living Translation 271–72, 274, 275, 276, 284, 287, 290, 294, 329n9(1)
New Revised Standard Version 294
Nicholas of Lyra 62
Nicholson, James 115, 120, 128, 166–67, 313
ninety-five theses (Luther) 89
nominalism 323n3(1)
nonconformists 162
Normans 41–42
Norton, Bonham 169, 191
Norton, David 213, 219, 328n28
Norton, John 191

octavo 324n18
Ohlhausen, Sidney K. 180
Old English 37–41
Old English letter. *See* black letters
Old Testament manuscripts 25–28
Olivetan, Pierre 149
optimal equivalent 287–88, 313, 331n5
Origen 53, 281
Ory, Matthew 134
Oxford University 215

Packington, Augustine 100, 313
Pagninus, Sanctes 149, 165, 325n2, 329n8
palimpsest 245
papyrus 28–31, 226
parchment 30, 32, 226
Paris, F. S. 211–12, 213, 313
Parker, Matthew 160, 161–66, 313–14
Parkhurst, J. 164
Pearson, A. 164
Pergamum 29–30

**Donald L. Brake's** early academic life was better served by his love for sports. High school in a small Illinois town focused more on athletic achievement than developing love for study and research. Academic success was just a necessary step to be eligible for team sports. Lettering in track, baseball, and basketball seemed a far more important occupation than academia.

Thinking no more of academic achievement, his life took a 180-degree turn when he married his high school sweetheart, Carol. Within a year he was anticipating his first son and commuting to Moody Bible Institute to study for the ministry.

Don's new direction in life gave him a ravenous appetite for books, which was reinforced by Dr. Mercer, theology professor at Moody, who cajoled his students to "sell their shoes" to buy a classic text or a freshly penned theology book. His new love for study was honored when he graduated with his ThM from Dallas Theological Seminary (DTS), receiving the Loraine Chafer Theology Award. Don and Carol, with their children Donnie, Debbie, and Michael, left for Ethiopia to serve as missionaries where Don experienced riots and revolution, as well as assisting in translating biblical and theological subjects into Amharic.

After earning a doctoral degree from DTS, Dr. Brake founded Multnomah Biblical Seminary (at Multnomah Bible College); watched the Gulf War as president of Jerusalem University College in Israel; pastored a fabulous flock in Texas; and, of course, collected rare Bibles.

Dr. Brake's academic and professional peers consider him an authority on the history of the Bible and the various translations and versions in both Greek and English from the sixteenth to the twenty-first centuries.

Dr. Brake has taught and led conferences on the subjects of the biblical canon, history of the English Bible, and New Testament textual criticism. He leads tours and study groups to the Holy Land, Greece and Turkey, and Reformation Europe.

He is currently vice president and dean of Multnomah Biblical Seminary in Portland, Oregon, where he teaches New Testament and theology. Don dreams of the Senior Tour and plays contact sports vicariously through four grandsons, one granddaughter, and the NFL package.

## Contact Information

Multnomah Bible College and Biblical Seminary is committed to biblically based higher education, as well as regionally accredited academic excellence. For more information about the college and seminary, please visit Multnomah's website at www.multnomah.edu.

To correspond with Dr. Don Brake, please send your letter via email to dbrake@multnomah.edu or via mail c/o MBS, 8435 N.E. Glisan Street, Portland, OR 97220.